PARENTS' JOBS AND
CHILDREN'S LIVES

SOCIOLOGY AND ECONOMICS
Controversy and Integration

An Aldine de Gruyter Series of Texts and Monographs

SERIES EDITORS

Paula S. England, *University of Arizona, Tucson*
George Farkas, *University of Texas, Dallas*
Kevin Lang, *Boston University*

Values in the Marketplace
James Burk

Equal Employment Opportunity:
Labor Market Discrimination and Public Policy
Paul Burstein (ed.)

Industries, Firms, and Jobs
Sociological and Economic Approaches
[Expanded Edition]
George Farkas and Paula England (eds.)

Beyond the Marketplace:
Rethinking Economy and Society
Roger Friedland and A. F. Robertson (eds.)

Social Institutions:
Their Emergence, Maintenance and Effects
Michael Hechter, Karl-Dieter Opp and Reinhard Wippler (eds.)

The Origin of Values
Michael Hechter, Lynn Nadel and Richard E. Michod (eds.)

Parents' Jobs and Children's Lives
Toby L. Parcel and Elizabeth G. Menaghan

Power, Norms, and Inflation: A Skeptical Treatment
Michael R. Smith

PARENTS' JOBS AND CHILDREN'S LIVES

Toby L. Parcel and Elizabeth G. Menaghan

ALDINE DE GRUYTER

New York

About the Authors

Toby L. Parcel is Professor of Sociology and Associate Dean, College of Social and Behavioral Sciences at The Ohio State University. She is coauthor (with Charles Mueller) of *Ascription and Labor Markets*, and her research has been published in numerous journals.

Elizabeth G. Menaghan is Professor of Sociology and Director of Graduate Studies in Sociology at The Ohio State University, where she is an adjunct professor at the University's Center for Human Resource Research. She is the author of numerous journal articles.

ALDINE DE GRUYTER
A division of Walter de Gruyter, Inc.
200 Saw Mill River Road
Hawthorne, New York 10532

This publication is printed on acid-free paper

Library of Congress Cataloging-in-Publication Data
Parcel, Toby L.
   Parents' jobs and children's lives / Toby L. Parcel and Elizabeth
G. Menaghan.
     p. cm.—(Sociology and economics)
   Includes bibliographical references and index.
   ISBN 0-202-30483-3.—ISBN 0-202-30484-1 (pbk.)
   1. Work and family—United States—Longitudinal studies.
 2. Children of working mothers—United States—Longitudinal studies.
 3. Dual-career families—United States—Longitudinal studies.
 I. Menaghan, Elizabeth G., 1949- . II. Title. III. Series.
HD4904.25.P37 1994
306.3'6'0973—dc20   94-4084
                                                                CIP

Manufactured in the United States of America

10 9 8 7 6 5 4 3 2 1

To Meredith Lee Gerber and Jacob Martin Gerber

T.L.P.

and

To my parents, William and Grace Galvin Menaghan,
my husband, James Phelan, and our children,
Cathleen Menaghan Phelan and Michael Menaghan Phelan

E.G.M.

Contents

Acknowledgments

We have based this book on a research project to which we have each contributed equally. We think it is stronger for the differing perspectives and bodies of knowledge that we have each brought to the work, as well as for our intellectual similarities and compatibilities. We gratefully acknowledge grant support from the National Institute for Child Health and Human Development (R01 HD23467 and R01 HD26047), without which this volume would not have been possible. We also appreciate support from the Center for Human Resource Research, the College of Social and Behavioral Sciences, and the Department of Sociology, all at The Ohio State University. A number of colleagues were helpful in commenting on portions of this work including Frank Mott, Paula England, Kevin Lang, Randy Olsen, Marta Tienda and Linda Waite. We also appreciate the numerous colleagues who made comments at conferences we attended, and those who served as blind referees. We are particularly grateful to staff at the Center for Human Resource Research for technical assistance and advice regarding the data. In particular we acknowledge Carol Sheets, Rufus Milsted, Paula Baker, David Ball, David Schaffner, Sue Taylor, Mary Wildermuth and Jean Haurin. We are grateful for research assistance from Laura Geschwender, Stacy Rogers, Marta Elliott, Amy Karnehm, Lori Kowaleski-Jones, and Michelle Fondell, and secretarial assistance from Judy Essig and Vicki Back. We also appreciate the encouragement and support we received from Richard Koffler and Arlene Perazzini at Aldine de Grunter. Portions of this work appeared in earlier forms in several journals including *Social Psychology Quarterly, Journal of Marriage and the Family, Journal of Health and Social Behavior*, and *American Journal of Sociology*. Portions of it also appeared in chapters we contributed to *Parent-Child Relations Across the Lifespan* edited by Karl Pillemer and Kathleen McCartney, and *Contemporary Families: Looking Forward, Looking Back* edited by Alan Booth.

Foreword

About a quarter century ago, in his now classic *Class and Conformity* (1969) Melvin Kohn explored the links between class and family life. Using data from the 1950s and 1960s, he showed that when husbands' jobs entailed higher levels of intellectual complexity and self-direction, parents were more likely to socialize their children so as to encourage internalized self-control, and less apt to emphasize blind obedience. In this volume, Parcel and Menaghan provide an updated and broadened consideration of the same basic question that animated Kohn's study—how do jobs affect family life and children?

In today's context—with most mothers employed, more divorces, the recent flowering of gender studies, and better data available—a broader study was appropriate. Today, it is untenable to see the link between class and children's outcomes as hinging exclusively upon fathers' jobs. If there is something about fathers being in more complex jobs that encourages parents to socialize children differently, might this not be true for mothers' jobs as well? This recognition comes in part from the simple fact that more mothers are employed than previously, but it is not only this. The development of gender studies in all the humanities and social sciences has led us to be aware of the frequency with which distortions and omissions in scholarship have resulted from androcentric bias. Past literature on work-family linkages has focused on effects of the quality (in complexity or wages) of fathers' jobs, while ignoring mothers' jobs; or on whether mothers' employment (versus *non*employment, ignoring quality of job held) hurts children, while ignoring the question of whether less time with fathers might also harm children.

Parcel and Menaghan redress these problems. They use a rich longitudinal data set from the National Longitudinal Surveys to explain the cognitive skills and behavioral problems of children. The children were 3 to 6 years old in 1986, and further data were collected on them and their families in 1988. The analyses show how children were affected by a wide range of factors, including parents' education, self-concept, and cognitive skills; extent of employment by each parent; complexity of the job held; earnings; age and number of siblings; family structure; and changes in some of these factors.

Parcel and Menaghan also broaden the theoretical matrix, drawing on literature from both sociology and economics. From economics, they draw upon the "New Home Economics" associated with Gary Becker and others—the application of neoclassical economic theory to the study of the family. From sociology, they draw upon the view of "social structure and personality" associated with Melvin Kohn and colleagues, which posits that adults' occupational experiences affect their skills and values, and this in turn affects socialization of children. They also draw from the notion of social capital introduced by James Coleman as part of his rational choice perspective, which is a bridge between sociological and economic theories.

Their monograph defies a simple summary, in part because of the presence of multiple interaction effects whereby the effects of some factors differ according to levels of others. Both Becker and Coleman have suggested that children—or family efficiency more generally—will suffer when mothers are employed (although I question whether the broader theoretical perspectives out of which they work necessarily imply this). Contrary to these suggestions, and to conservatives' position on the family, Parcel and Menaghan find no across-the-board detrimental effects of women's employment on young children. However, there are some situations in which detrimental effects are found, usually ones in which other family resources have been overextended: for example, when both parents are working overtime. Higher parental education, cognitive skills, self-concept, earnings, and complexity of occupation generally have positive effects on children, either directly or through the kind of home environment they allow the parents to provide.

The importance of this study lies in its having broadened the scope of research on employment-family linkages. In particular, it brings gender into the story—examining how various constellations of employment and family contributions of male and female adults affect boys' and girls' development. Theoretical and empirical pieces of this work will be reconceptualized and replicated for years to come.

Paula England

Chapter 1

How Do Parents' Jobs Affect Children's Lives?

As increasing proportions of mothers with young children enter paid employment, researchers, policymakers, and parents have expressed concern regarding the implications of this trend for children. Parents struggle with the "balancing" of paid work and family obligations, and the frequent need for more time for each set of responsibilities. Policymakers consider the wisdom of alternative actions by governments and firms, each strategy also trying to support some balance between facilitating paid work and family productivity.

At the heart of each of these concerns are often questions concerning how parents' paid work may be affecting children's lives. Is maternal part-time paid work better than full-time paid work when children are young? If having two parents work for pay provides extra income, is this money worth having less parental time with children? How are characteristics of adult paid work environments influencing child cognition, a key foundation for future socioeconomic attainment? How do they influence family life, including parent-child interaction? How do families transmit norms and behavioral patterns across generations? Do children who exhibit behavior problems in early childhood necessarily continue in these patterns into the middle childhood years? Or, does children's social behavior change in response to changing parental occupational conditions and altered family circumstances?

These questions are directly connected to some of the most compelling issues in social science. Sociologists have studied the transmission of inequality across generations, and have highlighted the importance of schooling attained as a key mechanism of intergenerational transmission of status. They have also studied how characteristics of parents and schools impact educational attainment and adult socioeconomic outcomes. Labor economists have stressed the importance of investment in human capital as a critical foundation for economic returns in adulthood. More recently, economists have commented on the role of the family as a critical site for the formation of human capital. Sociologists

1

have become interested in "social capital" in the family as an intervening mechanism between parental characteristics and child outcomes.

These questions also directly bear on social policies implemented at
the federal and state levels, as well as policies implemented by firms.
Recent debates regarding "workfare" versus welfare support inevitably
pose questions regarding the relative importance of maternal care for
young children versus the benefits of paid employment for their families and society at large. They also push to the forefront concerns regarding the quality and availability of nonmaternal care. Families who
depend on public support programs for subsistence may face a series of
difficult choices involving the trade-offs of paid employment and time
spent with children. In stark contrast, a number of private firms have
introduced "family-friendly" worker benefits such as partial reimburse-
ment for day-care expenses, on-site day-care, and cafeteria plans that
allow paid working parents to maximize family benefits by choosing
those they wish to receive. And these are in addition to health, pension,
and vacation benefits. The dichotomy between these public and private
approaches conveys something of the extremes along which families
with paid working parents receive support from key institutions.

Family values became a household term in 1992 when Dan Quayle
reacted to a television show portraying an unmarried Murphy Brown
becoming a single mother. In point of fact, debate regarding family values is not new, but has come to center stage recently as researchers and
policymakers attempt to weigh evidence and struggle with some of the
questions we posed above. For example, Cherlin (1993) and Gill (1993)
debate the relative costs of divorce for women and their children, with
Cherlin arguing against "nostalgia" as a basis for public policy, and Gill
emphasizing the costs to children when parents divorce. Barbara Dafoe
Whitehead has written on both sides of the debate, but recently she has
declared that "Dan Quayle Was Right" (Whitehead 1993), arguing that
single-parent households are harmful to children. Diversity in family
forms, at times seen as a strength to society, may actually weaken it,
with attendant problems such as increased crime, drug use, and ineffective schools. Daniel Patrick Moynihan, initially reviled in the 1960s
because of his thesis that connected black family configuration to poverty, in 1985 argued to more receptive audiences that the problem crosses
racial boundaries now, and that the welfare of the nation's children can
be enhanced by changes in tax policies and welfare schedules (Starr and
Buckley 1985). His original analysis is now cited by some as important
in what it implies both for governmental policy as well as individual
family choices. James Q. Wilson (1993) summarizes both conservative
and liberal perspectives, and argues that while governmental policies
are important, the "culture of the family" needs to be rebuilt.

In this book we provide some new answers to questions regarding how parents' paid work affects children's lives. We develop these answers by studying how variation in parental paid working conditions affects both cognitive and social development among children. Cognitive functioning in childhood is strongly associated with school success in adolescence and educational outcomes in adulthood, and therefore is a critical link in the chains of inequality that span generations. Children's social behavior during childhood concerns both parents and researchers, both because social adjustment is important at any age after infancy, and because poor adjustment may impair well-being in adolescence and adulthood. In addition to both outcomes being important, we need to know whether particular paid working conditions affect cognitive and social outcomes in the same way, or whether their effects are unique.

We take seriously the idea that child development is inherently *longitudinal*. Studying child outcomes at one point in time is useful for showing the association between parental characteristics and child outcomes at that time, but says relatively little about how children change as they mature. In this analysis we study both cognitive growth and change in social behavior. We also study how social capital formation in the home may change over time.

To be sure, there has been considerable research on portions of this most complex problem. Studies published in the 1980s, however, were frequently subject to theoretical and/or empirical limitations. First, there was little agreement in previous work regarding what dimension of maternal employment or maternal paid working conditions should be expected to influence specific child outcomes. While some studies created two or three categories representing maternal employment/nonemployment, or if employed, part-time, full-time, (Schachter 1981; Easterbrooks and Goldberg 1985), others failed to measure this construct (Haskins 1985). When researchers did use similar measures of these constructs, no single theoretical framework was cited as justification. This practice hindered cumulation of findings.

Second, although researchers acknowledged the importance of longitudinal research to address this problem, studies were of relatively short duration (Schachter 1981; Easterbrooks and Goldberg 1985; Farel 1980; studies by Bradley and Caldwell 1980, 1984b; Ramey, Dorval, and Baker-Ward 1981; and Bradley, Caldwell, and Elardo 1979 are exceptions). Third, the studies were almost always conducted on small samples of subjects (Haskins 1985; Easterbrooks and Goldberg 1985; Schachter 1981; Golden et al. 1978 is an exception). This limitation had several implications. First, small sample sizes limited researchers' abilities to apply multivariate techniques of parameter estimation to the data. Instead, they frequently relied solely on tests of statistical significance. These forced choices hinder the development of multivariate modeling in this area of inquiry. Second, the sample sizes in these studies were often too small to permit the assessment of statistical interaction along dimensions the researcher deemed relevant to the problem. Third, the samples themselves were seldom representative of any larger population of interest. They frequently were drawn as "convenience" samples, and while their socioeconomic characteristics were typically reported in some form, they were often homogeneous, with children either from middle-class and relatively well educated homes (Schachter 1981; Easterbrooks and Goldberg 1985) or from disadvantaged environments (Haskins 1985). It is difficult to compare and cumulate findings from several studies of small samples, each with distinctive, but nonrepresentative socioeconomic characteristics.

In part, these deficiencies may have been due to traditions of data production and analysis specific to relevant subfields of psychology. Prediction of cognitive and noncognitive child outcomes has fallen traditionally within the province of psychologists (Eysenck and Kamin 1981; Sternberg 1985; Scarr and Weinberg 1978); studies conducted by psychologists often use small, homogeneous samples and often estimate cross-sectional models. In contrast, while sociologists have not studied child outcomes to as great an extent as psychologists, they have used large samples and longitudinal designs to study socioeconomic processes, and have studied the transmission of adult occupational status across generations; in doing so they have highlighted the importance of schooling and family characteristics as key mechanisms of intergenerational status transmission (Alexander, Fennessey, McDill, and D'Amico 1979; Howell and McBroom 1982). Finally, economists have contributed theory regarding the role of individual choice in these processes, arguing against the often deterministic cast of sociological models and contending that individuals *choose* both paid work arrangements and family configuration to maximize overall utility. As we develop below, the "new home economics" portrays these choices as being made within the context of the family, i.e., jointly with other adult family members.

Most recently, the availability of large data sets and renewed scholarly interest in investigating child outcomes from an interdisciplinary perspective have combined to prompt a number of studies that overcome earlier limitations. One of the earliest was the 1976 National Survey of Children (NSC), in which 2279 children aged 7 to 11 in 1976 were studied. A follow-up designed to examine the effects of marital conflict and marital disruption reinterviewed a subset of these children in 1981 and 1987. Furstenberg, Nord, Peterson, and Zill (1983) use the NSC to trace the life course of children of divorce, and Peterson and Zill (1986) have traced the effects of parental marital disruption on children's behavior problems using these data. The development and distribution of the 1986 Child-Mother data set of the National Longitudinal Surveys of Youth (NLSY), which we use in this book, also generated a great deal of research activity. For example, Moore and Snyder (1991) use these data to study cognitive attainment of firstborn children of adolescent mothers, and McLeod and Shanahan (1993) study NLSY children between ages 4 and 8 and show that early and later poverty affect mothers' parenting practices and children's mental health. Other studies link early maternal employment with young children's verbal skills (Baydar and Brooks-Gunn 1991; Vandell and Ramanan 1992). Finally, the 1988 National Survey of Families and Households (NSFH), a large nationally representative sample of families and households with a follow-up completed in 1993, is now available to researchers (Sweet, Bumpass, and Call 1988). Marks and McLanahan (1993) investigate how the support available to parents raising children varies by gender and family composition, and Thomson, McLanahan, and Curtin (1992) study how family structure affects parental socialization. Thus, our work is part of a new generation of studies that take seriously the social context of children's development and that are able to take advantage of large national samples of parents and children.

As part of this new tradition, our work derives strength from several disciplines. From psychology, we derive a concern for child outcomes and both theoretical and empirical guidance helpful in our own analyses. From sociology, we derive significant inspiration regarding the importance of parental paid working conditions and both family structure and socioeconomic status, two key concepts in the models we develop, as well as appreciation for studies of large heterogenous samples. From economics, we derive the expectation that parental choice may be influenced by overall family utility, and a further appreciation for longitudinal analyses. We now set our discussion of child outcomes within the context of larger-level economic changes that have influenced mothers' labor force participation in the last 20 years. We are particularly interested in economic conditions and maternal labor force participation in the late 1980s since that is when our data were produced, but provide longer-term trend data to set these figures in context.

CHANGES IN PARENTAL PAID WORK, 1960s–1980s

The tremendous increase in women's labor force participation in the 1970s and 1980s has been importantly motivated by changes in the organization and functioning of the U.S. economy. Cyert and Mowery (1987) document changes in both the structure and functioning of the U.S. economy since the 1960s. Median income for men peaked in 1973, when measured in 1988 constant dollars (see England 1992:9). The rate of growth in labor productivity also declined, dropping to less than 1% between 1973 and 1986, the first year the children in our study completed developmental assessments. The character of available employment was also changing. Manufacturing employment accounted for a declining proportion of total private nonagricultural employment during this time period. Most of the new jobs added to the economy were concentrated in four industry groups: wholesale and retail trade; transportation and utilities; finance, insurance, and real estate; and services. While some have argued that many of the jobs created in the 1980s paid less than the manufacturing jobs that were lost and less than those created in earlier decades (Bluestone and Harrison 1982), others argue that this is inconsistent with the substantial growth in professional, technical and managerial positions during the 1970s and early 1980s (see Cyert and Mowery 1987).

Unemployment grew after 1973 relative to levels of the 1950s and 1960s because of the 1974–1975 and 1981–1982 recessions, because of the lack of long-term economic expansions (until the late 1980s), and—until the mid-1970s—because of entrance into the labor force of the huge baby boom cohort. During this time period, men's rates of labor force participation declined while women's increased. Men's declines were steeper for black than white men, with Hispanic men more likely to be in the labor force than white or black men (Blau and Ferber 1986:74). Among white men, declines were importantly due to lower age of retirement, while among minorities, the discouraged worker effect (the unemployed dropping out of the labor force after an unsuccessful period of job search) of prime-working-age males played a greater role. Black and white rates of female participation became more similar as white women's rates increased and black women's rose more slowly; Hispanic women's rates remained still lower.

The large increases in women's labor force participation, from 27.9% in 1940 (Blau and Ferber 1986:69) to 57.8% by 1992 (U.S. Bureau of the Census 1993) reflected a series of changes in the age, marital status, and child care responsibilities of paid working women. Prior to 1940, the typical paid working woman was young and single. Between 1940 and 1960, older married women entered the labor force, while rates of participation for young women did not sharply increase until after 1960. By 1970, employed mothers of school-aged children had become the modal group; the most striking recent change was in the greater employment of mothers of babies and preschoolers (Hoffman 1989). Rates of participation for married women with children under 6 have risen to 54% in 1986 (U.S. Bureau of the Census 1987a), and continued to rise to 59.9%

by 1992 (U.S. Bureau of the Census 1993). Women are now more firmly attached to the labor market, as indicated by reduced turnover and by higher proportions of women working for pay full-time, full-year round, as opposed to part-time and/or part-year. Despite this convergence over time, the temporal patterns of women's employment still differ from the employment of men; somewhat more is part-time and/or part-year, and it is more often interrupted by demands to care for ill, aged, or young family members (U.S. Bureau of the Census 1987a). For these reasons, the percentage of women with some labor force experience is higher than any cross-sectional estimate.

While rates of women's labor force participation increased, the male-female earnings ratio improved only slightly. O'Neill (1985:50) documents that full-time women paid workers earned about 60 to 64% of what male full-time paid workers earned, with only minor fluctuations in this percentage between 1950 and 1980. By 1984 among full-time paid workers 21 to 64 years of age, women earned 70% of what men earned, with that ratio still at 70% in 1991 (U.S. Bureau of the Census 1993). Interestingly, the ratio of female to male earnings varies by occupation; for example, it is 81% for computer programmers and 69% among janitors, but only 55% among sales supervisors, 61% among managers, and 63% among lawyers (U.S. Bureau of the Census 1987b). Data for 1991 also suggest variation, with women in sales earning 56% of what men earn, while women in professional specialties and administrative support (including clerical) earn 72% and women handlers and laborers earn 89% (U.S. Bureau of the Census 1993).

A number of observers suggest that the sluggish rate of change in the aggregate earnings ratio is in part a function of continued occupational sex segregation, or a crowding of women into a relatively small number of jobs. Although researchers have debated the degree to which sex segregation has declined over time (England 1981; Beller 1984; Beller and Han 1984; Bielby and Baron 1984), Reskin and Roos (1990) present considerable evidence that workplace resegregation is very high, even when occupations appear to be desegregating. For example, women comprise an increasing share of medical students, but cluster in a relatively small number of specialties. Jacobs (1989) echoes this more conservative estimate of change with the argument that while increased numbers of women enter male-dominated occupations, they also leave at high rates, thus creating a revolving door through which women pass, with a given group only temporarily occupying positions in male-dominated occupations. Still, it seems likely that some real declines in segregation have occurred, thus moving employed men and women somewhat closer to each other in the paid working conditions they experience. This latter issue is also important as we consider what impact parental paid working conditions have on children, where parental earnings levels are one dimension of a larger number of possible conditions.

These phenomena are interrelated. The transformation from a manufacturing to a service-based economy created large numbers of the types of jobs for which employers have traditionally hired women. At the same time, these jobs were often, although not always, remunerated more modestly than the manufacturing jobs that were disappearing. Many families perceived that in order to maintain or improve standards of living, they needed two earners, where in the fifties and sixties they perceived that the same standard of living could be attained with one male earner. These perceptions were not based in fact, since men's real incomes stopped increasing in 1973, but for only a few years were as low as 1964 levels (see England 1992:9). Families may, however, have increased women's paid employment to compensate for the lack of male earnings increases that they had come to expect. It is also possible that since women's real wages had been rising for most of the century, the opportunity costs for being a homemaker had increased. Changes in ideology likely both reinforced and motivated these changes, thus prompting more women with young children to enter the labor force, but to enter jobs that were more constricted in type than those available to men. As paid working mothers became the norm, questions arose regarding the impact of the shift in allocation of their time for their families, and particularly their children. We now turn to several theoretical perspectives that can help us consider what the implications of these changes might be for children.

CAN CURRENT THEORY SUGGEST HOW PARENTS' JOBS AFFECT CHILDREN'S LIVES?

One of the most significant theoretical developments in the area of work and family in the 1980s comes from economics. Gary Becker's ([1981] 1991) *A Treatise on the Family* extended conventional microeconomic theory to the family, an area of scholarly inquiry previously outside the scope of economics. A significant strength of the theory is its ability to integrate within a single framework the description and analysis of a variety of topics within the realm of family—e.g., fertility, marriage, and the allocation of time, as well as extra-family (but family related) topics such as education, health, bequests, and the distribution of income (Ben-Porath 1982).

Becker's analyses bear on our concern with the effects of parental employment on family life in two ways. First, they help to explain decisions regarding the extent and nature of female labor force participation, a major factor in influencing family economic status, division of household labor, and attendant interactional outcomes. Second, they alert us to concepts and formulations utilized with varying degrees of success in economics, and thus provide foundation for interdisciplinary inquiry regarding employment and family welfare.

Most relevant to our discussion are Becker's hypotheses regarding sex role differentiation within nuclear families, and the relative allocation of husbands' and wives' efforts to market and nonmarket activities (see Blau 1987 for a useful summary). Briefly, Becker argues that households derive utility from commodities that are produced with some combination of market goods and nonmarket time. Since small children are time-intensive commodities, and the substitution of market goods (e.g., day-care centers) may be of questionable quality and difficult to arrange according to a needed schedule, women will reduce labor force participation in order to devote time to this form of production within the home. When two parents are present, this arrangement is most efficient, and provides greater utility for the family as a whole to have mothers rather than fathers make these choices. This conclusion acknowledges existing labor market discrimination that results in women obtaining lower returns to their investments than men. It also recognizes that mothers may invest less in their own human capital than fathers or women without children.

Finally, it is also based on Becker's assumption that women have a biological comparative advantage in breast-feeding and other aspects of child rearing. Knowledge of this biological differential causes women to invest less in themselves than men with the same abilities would invest in themselves. Such knowledge also causes parents to invest less in daughters than in sons. Thus, relatively small initial differences may have major implications based on "efficiency" over the life cycle. For example, these choices do not necessarily maximize a woman's *individual* utility since the choices have long-run negative implications for her accumulation of labor force experience and likely smaller total investments in her human capital useful in market exchange. Although Becker does not treat these issues explicitly, sociological perspectives on power suggest that married women therefore become more dependent on their husbands, with reduced bargaining power in the household. If the marriage does not endure, such choices may have additional negative economic consequences for the mothers and their children. In addition, one can also argue that investment in schooling and labor force experience will produce two opposing effects on market productivity and earnings. On the one hand, such investments increase market productivity and wages in the market, and schooling (as well as experience in some occupations such as teaching and nursing) also increase one's productivity in the household. Such investments render the opportunity costs of staying home higher than they would be in the absence of such investments. On the other hand, they also make the mother a comparatively better child care provider than could typically be hired to substitute for her services. Still, it is important to recognize that even paid working parents spend considerable time with their children, and that investments in schooling, in particular, are important to the children in the time the parents are at home. For these reasons, we consider a comprehensive set of sources of influence on child well-being; our focus on parental paid working conditions is complemented by recognition that the characteristics parents bring to the work force are the same as those they bring to creating the child's socialization environments.

As we have noted, macrolevel economic changes in the 1970s and 1980s have encouraged and required more women to enter the labor force, even when their children are young. Changes in sex role ideology undoubtedly contributed to this change as well. Changes in ideology and paid work arrangements likely prompt rearrangement of traditional sex role responsibilities in the family, contracting out services formerly provided at home, and role overload for mothers and possibly fathers, with the distribution across these alternatives varying by family type and circumstances. To use Becker's terminology, what are the implications for children from the creation of these "inefficient families"? Given that many households with young children contain two adult paid workers, and that in single-parent households that parent is frequently employed, we need to look to variations in parental paid working conditions as explanatory factors in understanding variation in child well-being. Studying the association between variation in parental characteristics and paid work arrangements on the one hand, and child outcomes on the other, should suggest whether there is variation in how children are developing within the increasingly large group of so-called inefficient families.

Economists have found Becker's perspective to be a fertile one for suggesting hypotheses and organizing existing knowledge. Lillard and Willis (1994) study the intergenerational transmission of educational attainment between parents and children in Malaysia, and investigate whether parental levels of schooling influence children's educational attainment, and whether these relationships vary as a function of family economic status, gender composition of the siblings, and the quality of family living environments. Lillard and Brien (1994) model decisions to leave school, marry, and initiate conception as joint decisions, again with data on Malaysia that use Becker's ideas on decisions regarding marriage and childbearing as influenced by economic opportunities out-side the home as well as potential gains from forming households characterized by an efficient division of labor. Thomas (1992) uses Becker's reasoning regarding household resource allocation as a way to predict whether there is differential allocation of household resources to children who differ by gender. These examples illustrate the parsimony of the perspective, in that topics including marriage, educational investments, household transfers of resources, and the timing of first conception can all be addressed within its framework.

More recently, sociologists have used Becker's models to suggest hypotheses regarding the operation of local marriage markets (Lichter, LeClere, and McLaughlin 1991) and the circumstances under which children, a clear example of "marital-specific capital," will contribute to marital stability or instability (Waite and Lillard 1991). A number of sociologists, however, have taken issue with elements of the theory. Berk (1985) responds to the new home economics by arguing that in addition to the household being a "factory" that combines time and resources to produce able paid workers and socialized children, it also produces gendered relations. Gender intervenes directly in the household division of labor via the enactment of gender ideals, gendered patterns of dominance and submission, and norms that regulate the allocation of whole sets of household tasks. These norms influence the allocation of spouses' time to family and market work (Berk 1985:205–6). Household members take into account what *should* be happening when they allocate time and tasks in home production, and thus it is the complex interweaving of these agendas that determines the disproportionate share of household work that women perform, not just notions of efficiency. Change in these arrangements is likely to come from the conflict between the demands for market work and established patterns of home production. Geerken and Gove (1983) combine elements of Becker's utility model of family time allocation with aspects of functionalism from sociology to construct a theory that attempts to explain the labor-leisure-home work choices of contemporary married-couple families, and study the implications of these choices for marital viability. Similar to Berk (1985), they believe that cultural expectations regarding appropriate roles of household members must be treated as one possible determinant of choice, in contrast to pure economic theory, which relegates such notions to the residual category of "tastes."

Bielby and Bielby (1988) challenge Becker's assertion that married women expend less effort in market work than men. According to Becker (1991:74–79), married women will allocate less intense effort to each hour of market work than will employed men, because they expend some energy on household work and child care. He argues that they seek positions that demand less energy than married men. This sex differential in effort might explain why there are sex differences in earnings after controlling for years of experience. Bielby and Bielby (1988), however, using the 1973 and 1977 Quality of Employment Surveys, find that women report slightly greater paid work effort than men—i.e., they score higher on an index where they report having jobs requiring hard work, requiring substantial physical or mental effort, and involving substantial effort beyond job requirements. Women allocate more effort than men with comparable family situations, household responsibilities, market human capital, and job rewards. Women with preschool age children exert effort comparable to men with no preschool children. These findings suggest that women generate the energy they need to combine paid work and family roles.

We have seen that Becker's model of division of labor in the home and allocation of effort between paid work and family directs our attention to the *quantity* of time that mothers allocate to each sphere. Other theoretical perspectives from sociologists provide complementary emphases. Of clear importance are Coleman's (1988 1990) arguments regarding the role of social capital in the socialization process. As he notes, family background consists of (1) financial capital, (2) human capital (parental cognitive skills and educational attainment), and (3) social capital. The first two elements of this trichotomy have long histories of theory and research in economics. Social capital inheres in the structure of relations between and among actors, and includes the time and effort that parents actually spend on children. Stronger bonds between parents and children are a form of social capital that demands both the physical presence of parents and their attention and involvement. Such parental investment is not perfectly related to parents' socioeconomic status, and thus cannot be adequately captured by traditional measures of earnings and parental schooling in models of child outcomes. This notion is echoed by Robert Bradley and Bettye Caldwell, who find far from perfect associations between their measure of children's home environments and indicators of socioeconomic standing. Coleman argues that unless parents use their economic resources and human capital as resources in their parental roles, child socialization may suffer. Parents with more meager resources themselves may still efficiently use them in the child-rearing process, with attendant positive effects on social behavior.

Coleman and others worry, however, that maternal labor force participation will limit the social capital needed to effectively transmit norms and behavior patterns across generations. Part of this may be due to reduced time that mothers will have both to establish bonds with children and to use these bonds in conveying appropriate social behaviors and providing support for cognitive attainment. Part of it may be due to reduced time she spends in the local community, with attendant reductions in contributing to the web of interactions it represents and drawing upon its resources in the interests of her children. Coleman is less clear on whether such employment will weaken the emotional bonds between mothers and children. Some might argue that when mothers invest in the "purposive" structure of the paid work world, parent-child emotional bonds may suffer, independent of the amount of time the two spend together. This may be the case even if the sheer quantity of parent-child time is the major determinant of the intensity of these relationships. Coleman's arguments hint at these issues, without explicit hypotheses. In any case, the reality is that increasing proportions of mothers with young children *are* working outside the home, and there have been steady increases in mothers with infants who return to paid work before their children turn one year old.

We argue that paid work activities of both parents influence the content of child socialization they provide at home, as well as household material base and parental availability. As a mechanism to evaluate the implications of parental paid work, we look to *variations* in the paid working conditions of both mothers and fathers as providing resources relevant to child socialization. We first consider the aspects of children's lives that we think may be affected by parental paid working conditions. These include child cognitive outcomes, child social behavior, and the home environments that parents create for children. We then develop arguments regarding how it is that variations in parental paid working conditions may have implications for child cognition, child social behavior, and the home environments that parents create.

HOW DOES PARENTAL OCCUPATIONAL COMPLEXITY INFLUENCE CHILDREN'S LIVES?

Parental Occupational Complexity and Child Cognition

Several sources argue for connections between parental paid working conditions and child cognitive outcomes. Drawing from social structure and personality frameworks, Kohn and his colleagues have been particularly influential in developing theory linking social class, especially occupational conditions, and psychological functioning (e.g., Kohn 1977; Kohn and Schooler 1982, 1983). Kohn argues that the actual paid working conditions parents face in their jobs are important determinants of parental child-rearing values. White-collar work more often involves manipulation of ideas or symbols, or involves interpersonal dealings; it may be complex and be performed under conditions of indirect supervision, permitting greater autonomy and self-direction. Blue-collar work more often requires manipulation of things, is more standardized, and is more closely supervised. Kohn argues that job incumbents come to value the characteristics demanded on the job more generally, for themselves and for their children, and he demonstrates the expected linkage between occupational conditions and parental values. Specifically, white-collar parents place more emphasis on self-direction and internalization of norms, while blue-collar parents stress conformity to externally imposed standards (Kohn 1977). The conditions of work that are more common in less well paid jobs—routinization, low autonomy, heavy supervision, and little demand or opportunity for substantively complex work—also erode intellectual flexibility, an important component of cognitive skills (Kohn and Schooler 1973, 1978) and exacerbate psychological distress (Kohn and Schooler 1982, 1983; Miller, Schooler, Kohn, and Miller 1979; Lennon 1987; Miller 1988). The distress aroused by low occupational standing has expectable intergenerational consequences in that parents with higher distress display less attentive, responsive, and stimulating parental behavior and provide less optimal child-rearing environments (Menaghan 1983a, 1983b; Belsky 1984a). Schooler (1987) has summarized a number of findings suggesting that exposure to complex environments in childhood impacts both childhood and adult psychological functioning. Consistent with this claim, Miller, Kohn, and Schooler (1985) demonstrate that the substantive complexity of schoolwork promotes cognitive functioning for both high school and college students, even with parental abilities and socioeconomic status controlled. Gecas (1979) provides compatible theoretical arguments. Another way to view these ideas is to suggest that they constitute a specific theory regarding how parental human capital affects children. Specifically, having a parent in a complex job can be a resource for children in that it sets a high level of expectation regarding self-direction and intellectual flexibility, qualities that should increase children's socioeconomic well-being as they mature.

Parental Occupation Complexity and Child Behavior Problems

Behavior problems in the early years of childhood are important in their own right, as well as having negative consequences for adult well-being and success. Undercontrolled, or acting out, behavior has been a particular concern. Among children initially studied at ages 2–6, those with severe undercontrol problems were almost three times as likely as others to be categorized as having severe problems at follow-up 7 years later (Fischer, Rolf, Hasazi, and Cummings 1984). Other researchers have also documented continuity between antisocial, aggressive, or undercontrolled actions in childhood and similar difficulties in adulthood (Caspi, Elder, and Bem 1987; Forgatch, Patterson, and Skinner 1988; Kohlberg, LaCrosse, and Ricks 1972; Mechanic 1980; Robins 1966, 1979). While short-term gains from aggressive, destructive behavior encourage its persistence (Caspi and Elder 1988; Patterson et al. 1989), in the long run such behavior can lead to peer rejection, labeling by teachers as a problematic child, and academic failure (Forgatch, Patterson, and Skinner 1988; Patterson and Bank 1989). Antisocial children are often rejected by members of their normal peer group, which deprives them of *positive* socialization influences. As a result, these children are not only behaviorally impaired, but also socially unskilled (Patterson, DeBaryshe and Ramsey 1989). Patterson et al. (1989) find that rejected, antisocial children frequently lack skills such as perception of peer group norms, peer group entry, and interpretation of prosocial interactions.

The aggressive and destructive quality of undercontrolled behavior problems makes children with such problems more visible; but excessively inhibited and fearful—sometimes labeled overcontrolled—behavior has also been inversely related to later social competence (Fischer et al. 1984). Overcontrolled behavior is associated with later learning difficulties (Kohn 1977), and Caspi, Elder, and Bem (1988) argue that extremely shy, inhibited boys have difficulty initiating action, and are likely to delay marriage, parenthood, and paid work careers. They are underrepresented among occupational high achievers, and are overrepresented among those whose marriages end in divorce. Caspi, Elder, and Bem (1987, 1988) conclude that both under- and overcontrolled behavior propels individuals into trajectories of life events that perpetuate ineffective coping styles and maladaptive behaviors.

We argue that parents with high levels of occupational complexity will encourage children to internalize behavioral norms, thus resulting in lower levels of behavior problems. Parents with lower levels of occupational complexity may rely more heavily on external controls as socialization devices, and these controls should be associated with higher levels of behavior problems. Thus, occupational complexity forms a link between the forms of social control parents experience on the job and the mechanisms of control they use in socializing their children. We develop these arguments more completely in Chapter 5, where we analyze data to inform these issues.

Parental Occupational Complexity and
Children's Home Environments

Children's immediate family environments are a potent source of both cognitive stimulation and affective experience, and studies have demonstrated that family environments have important consequences both for children's later cognitive performance and academic achievement (Bradley 1985; Bradley and Caldwell 1987; Bradley, Caldwell, and Rock 1988; Ketterlinus, Henderson, and Lamb 1991; Parcel and Menaghan 1990) and for children's emotional well-being and behavior problems (Rogers, Parcel, and Menaghan 1991). Children's home environments also influence their emotional and behavioral development. Home environments that provide appropriate levels of physical safety, cognitive stimulation, and warmth are related to fewer behavior problems as well as better cognitive performance (Bradley 1985; Gottfried, Gottfried, and Bathurst 1988; Parcel and Menaghan 1990). The quality of the home environment may also mediate the effects of maternal workplace conditions on children's behavior problems (Menaghan and Parcel 1991). Indeed, the quality of parent-child relations and the quality of the home environment that parents provide are important pathways by which parents' social experiences and position affect their children's life chances, and they may function as critical factors conditioning the intergenerational transmission of socioeconomic inequality (Ketterlinus et al. 1991; Parcel and Menaghan 1990; Rogers et al. 1991).

Katsillis and Rubinson (1990) argue that as societies become more democratic and demands for equality of opportunity and meritocratic selection increase, there are fewer direct mechanisms such as inheritance, transfer of property rights, and so on, by which family advantage can be passed on to children. Indirect mechanisms emerge, particularly those that work through education. These indirect mechanisms have more uncertain outcomes. In such a process, children's own effort and engagement are demanded, and levels of parental investment and involvement may mediate and moderate the influences of parental background. Parental success in motivating child effort and performance becomes critical in affecting eventual child cognitive and social outcomes. This argument suggests that the transmission of parental status may depend on parental efforts to provide stimulation and to develop warm and supportive relationships to their children; factors that disrupt such activity and involvements will have negative effects on eventual child outcomes, while factors that increase such activity will produce better outcomes than a simple transmission of family background model would predict.

Coleman and others point to the extent of parental, particularly maternal, investment in the labor force as one factor affecting family social capital. Such arguments view the fact of maternal employment as a potential social problem. We argue, however, that the actual working demands that parents encounter on the job are at least as important as number of paid work hours in affecting parental values and parent well-being and in shaping the quality of children's home environments. We develop these arguments more completely below.

Underlying these arguments regarding the connections between parental paid working conditions and child cognitive and social outcomes is the implicit assumption that these effects operate within the context of the child's home environment. We argue that the conditions parents face on the job affect the home environments they create for their children, and that these home environments in turn have significant impacts on the causally subsequent child outcomes we investigate. Thus far we have identified occupational complexity as a critical dimension of parental paid working conditions that can influence child outcomes. We now turn to ideas regarding parental paid work hours and parental wage levels as important influences in children's lives.

PARENTAL WAGES AND CHILDREN'S LIVES

Low wages hamper parental efforts to provide adequate material resources for their children, and produce feelings of distress that affect parent-child interaction (Siegal 1984). Fathers' earning capacity is particularly likely to affect their sense of self-worth and adequacy as the primary family breadwinner (Elder, van Nguyen, and Caspi 1985; Kessler, Turner, and House 1988; McLoyd 1989, 1990). Relatively poor father earnings may also make maternal employment essential to ensure family economic well-being; when such employment is undesired by either husband or wife, low father earnings may be a source of marital dissatisfaction and conflict, contributing to a less optimal family environment (McLanahan and Glass 1985; Ross, Mirowsky, and Huber 1983; Menaghan 1990b, 1991). The greater compression of paid working women into a more limited number of occupations and a limited range of wage levels, as well as the normative definition of wives' earnings as secondary, makes it likely that variations in mothers' wages will be less consequential to family economic status and family environments than fathers' earnings, at least among married mothers. Nevertheless, higher maternal wage levels should exert some positive impact.

More generally, although several studies have shown a positive relationship between complexity and wages (Parcel and Mueller 1983a, 1983b; Parcel 1989), we expect there may be independent effects of wages and complexity on several aspects of children's lives.

PARENTAL PAID WORK HOURS
INFLUENCE CHILDREN'S LIVES

An important part of Coleman's arguments regarding the importance of social capital in the socialization process concerns the *quantity* of time parents spend with children. As noted above, long parental paid work hours may hinder the creation of needed relationships among parents and community members outside the household. These relationships contain social capital in the form of well-developed social norms with effective sanctions that help promote appropriate internalization of norms governing child social behaviors, supporting cognitive development, and generally constructing suitable home environments.

Parental paid work hours vary, either because of parental choice or normative constraints. Part-time paid work is more positively sanctioned for employed mothers than for fathers, for whom such schedules would be perceived as underemployment (Thompson and Walker 1989). Some argue that maternal part-time paid work maximizes maternal well-being while still permitting adequate time to shoulder parental and household responsibilities (Moen 1989; Moen and Dempster-McClain 1987; Miller et al. 1979); such arrangements may facilitate appropriate self-controls among school age children. Turning to overtime paid work, given the finite number of hours in the day, very long paid work hours for either parent may be detrimental to "quality" parental time. If both parents work long hours, the duration of marital and parent-child interaction may become limited, and the quality of social capital may suffer (Kingston and Nock 1987; Nock and Kingston 1988). This may be especially true in families where mothers work for pay *and* fathers take on overtime hours. Long paid work hours may heighten work/family conflict and strain among both men and women (Piotrkowski, Rapoport, and Rapoport 1987; Voydanoff 1987). Women may feel such effects more keenly, given greater responsibility for household tasks in addition to their paid work outside the home (Lennon 1987; Voydanoff 1987). Such role overload may negatively affect the mother's parenting style, her ability to provide a supportive home environment, and her ability to both help children internalize appropriate standards of social control and make optimal progress cognitively. Of course, some of these relationships would shift if fathers took on more child-rearing responsibilities. If mothers worked long hours for pay, and fathers worked more moderate hours and simultaneously devoted additional effort to child socialization, would child socialization proceed normally? This hypothesis is difficult to evaluate given the low frequency with which this pattern is currently represented in our society.

HOW DOES FAMILY STRUCTURE AFFECT CHILDREN'S LIVES?

Thus far our discussion has highlighted the role of parents' paid work in influencing children's lives. We also know that characteristics of families and of the parents and children themselves will play an important role. Coleman (1988) argues that current American families, containing relatively few adults who often spend extensive time outside the family household in paid work, may be structurally deficient in family social capital overall; the situation of a single-parent family where the parent works long hours for pay may be particularly problematic. Earlier work has shown that more difficult family circumstances, including higher number of children, constrain parental nurturance and stimulation, with negative effects on the quality of children's home environments and on child intellectual and behavior outcomes (Blake 1989; Bradley and Caldwell 1984b; Haveman, Wolfe, and Spaulding 1991; Menaghan and Parcel 1991; Parcel and Menaghan 1990; Rogers et al. 1991; Steelman and Powell 1991; Zuravin 1988). Such effects may be particularly substantial for dual-earner families with greater competing occupational demands. While most studies have treated family size as a stable characteristic of families, obviously family size is likely to change during a child's early years. The birth of additional siblings presents additional demands on parents and is expected to have a negative effect on the quality of stimulation and nurturance the older child experiences. In addition, number of children has been inversely linked to measured intelligence of offspring in many studies (see Heer 1985); Blake (1989) finds family size effects are particularly strong for measures of verbal facility, and persist even after adjusting for major family background characteristics. She argues that verbal facility is strongly affected by the amount of parent-child interaction, which is higher when there are fewer children in the family.

A variety of studies have found that the presence of a spouse has a positive effect on the quality of the home environment (Conger, McCarty, Yang, Lahey, and Kropp 1984; Crouter, Belsky, and Spanier 1984;

MacKinnon, Brody, and Stoneman 1982, 1986) and on child outcomes (McLanahan and Booth 1989; Haurin 1992; Wojtkiewicz 1993). As with family size, presence/absence of a spouse is a dynamic characteristic of families likely to undergo change over time; we expect that departure of a spouse will have a negative impact. Although parental separation may reduce family conflict, it also begins a long period of adjustment to altered family circumstances and to poorer economic conditions (Wallerstein 1984). The emotional and economic difficulties surrounding marital termination tend to compromise parents' abilities to behave in ways that facilitate children's adjustment (Hetherington, Cox, and Cox 1978; Patterson and Bank 1989; Patterson et al. 1989; Rickel and Langner 1985). We therefore consider these expected family influences in assessing the effects of parental occupational conditions on children's family environments, with attendant effect on child outcomes themselves.

HOW DO CHARACTERISTICS OF PARENTS AND THE CHILDREN THEMSELVES AFFECT CHILDREN'S LIVES?

We think it is useful to view parental characteristics as *resources* that parents can use in the socialization process. Some parents have higher levels of these resources than other parents, with associations among a set of parental resources likely to be positive but far from perfect. In addition, some parents are more effective in using the resources they possess in providing appropriate socialization for their children. These resources include such characteristics as parental education and mental ability, characteristics of parents' own families of origin, and parental psychological states. We can also view these characteristics as the level of human capital parents need to produce children. We now describe why we expect several types of parental resources to influence their children's lives.

Parental Schooling and Mental Ability

We expect that parental levels of schooling and mental ability will have positive effects on children's lives. Given extensive literature suggesting that child verbal facility is predictable from measures of parental mental ability, we expect a positive influence of maternal mental ability on child verbal facility. Even with these controls, there may still be a positive effect of maternal level of schooling on child verbal facility, again a function of the greater resources more educated mothers will have to facilitate child development. Higher educational attainment has also been repeatedly linked to both parental values encouraging self-direction, which may promote appropriate internalization of behavioral norms (Wright and Wright 1976: Kohn and Schooler 1983; Luster, Rhoades, and Haas 1989), and the provision of more stimulating home environments (Bradley 1985).

Race

Several studies suggest that maternal ethnic background will influence maternal values and assumptions regarding appropriate mother-child interaction (Laosa 1981) and be associated with child home environments (Elardo and Bradley 1981). Everyday stressors associated with minority group status may also affect mother-child interaction independent of values. In addition, extensive research indicates an association between racial minority status and measures of mental ability, particularly the Peabody Picture Vocabulary Test—Revised (PPVT-R), a measure of receptive vocabulary (Zigler, Abelson, and Seitz 1973; Cargile and Woods 1988). We also expect maternal ethnicity to be related to family home environments even when individual resources are controlled. Other studies suggest that maternal ethnicity influences maternal values and assumptions regarding appropriate mother-child interaction (Laosa 1981), and ethnicity has been shown to be associated with scores on one measure of children's home environments (Bradley and Caldwell 1984a; Elardo and Bradley 1981) as well as with scores on the NLSY home environment measures (Baker and Mott 1989; Menaghan and Parcel 1991), with American black and Chicano families scoring lower than nonblack, non-Chicano families.

Parents' Socioeconomic Background

The extensive tradition of research in status attainment traces the association between parental background and socioeconomic attainment. Although findings typically suggest that much of the association between parental and child status is due to levels of schooling that children can obtain, there are clearly indirect effects of parental background on children's achievement as well as smaller direct effects that are important to model.

Parental Age

We expect that in our sample of 21- to 28-year-old mothers, older mothers will have children with higher measured ability scores, since, particularly compared to mothers in their early twenties, they likely have greater personal resources to facilitate child development. Within the restricted age range of mothers with whom we will be concerned, we expect that the greater maturity and experience of older mothers will contribute to more positive home environments.

Maternal Self-Concept

Independent of the form of control mothers experience on the job, maternal beliefs about mastery may have important effects on children's lives. A positive self-regard and an optimistic expectation that one's own efforts can yield positive effects are both social products of previous experiences and psychological resources on which individuals can draw in adulthood (Rosenberg and Pearlin 1978; Menaghan 1990a; Rosenberg, Schooler, and Schoenbach 1989). Some individuals perceive themselves to be in substantial control of life events, while others tend to view events as beyond their control (Gecas 1989). Adults who feel a greater sense of control over their lives engage in more planning and problem-solving efforts (Wheaton 1983), use more effective coping efforts such as optimistic comparison and negotiation (Menaghan 1983b), are less mistrusting of others (Mirowsky and Ross 1983, 1984; Rotter 1980), and are less emotionally distressed (Pearlin and Schooler 1978; Pearlin, Lieberman, Menaghan, and Mullan 1981; Rosenfield 1989; Turner and Noh 1983). Accordingly, initial beliefs about the possibility of mastery tend to be confirmed, making individual beliefs about mastery relatively stable over time (Gecas 1989).

Researchers have paid less attention to implications of adult mastery for children. We would expect, however, that mothers who feel a greater sense of control would be more active in attempting to influence their children's behavior. Appropriate parenting behaviors and strategies are also necessary if children are to internalize appropriate standards of social control. Research on parental socialization efforts indicates that coercive control and harsh physical punishments, while effective in the short term, are likely to generate resentment and defiance in the long run (Patterson 1984). Inductive approaches aimed at internalization of norms and values are associated with higher social competence, fewer behavior problems, and higher feelings of self-esteem and mastery (Langman 1987; Peterson and Rollins 1987). Mondell and Tyler (1981) concluded that parents with a greater belief in mastery are more likely to adopt such positive parenting styles, and encourage independence and active problem solving in their children.

In addition, maternal self-concept is expected to have direct effects on children's home environments. That is, greater self-esteem and a greater sense of control over one's environment should increase a mother's perceptions that she can make a positive difference in her children's development and increase her efforts to enhance children's environments (Gecas 1989; Mirowsky and Ross 1986; Menaghan and Parcel 1991).

We also expect a positive association between internal locus of control and child verbal facility. Mothers who expect that they can influence their own lives are likely to take greater initiative with reference to their children, which may be reflected in measures of child mental ability and behavior.

Child Health

We also allow for the possibility that children with health limitations that hinder full participation in play and school will have lower verbal facility and more behavior problems. Child health problems may constrain parental, particularly maternal, employment as well as prompt parents to attempt to compensate for children's limitations by providing a stimulating and supportive environment. However, mothers with less healthy children (as indicated by problems in the first year of life or currently) may make a conscious effort to compensate for child health problems by providing a stimulating and warm home environment.

Child Gender

Given repeated findings of gender differences in verbal facility (Maccoby and Jacklin 1974; Stevenson and Newman 1986; Blake 1989), we expect that boys will score lower on measured verbal facility. Mothers may also vary their interaction with daughters and sons (Bronfenbrenner, Alvarez, and Henderson 1984; but see Bradley and Caldwell 1979, 1987; Bradley, Caldwell, Rock, Hamrick, and Harris 1988). Following Johnson and Kaplan (1988), we expect that greater behavior problems may be reported among young boys than young girls, in response to greater aggressive behavior exhibited by boys. Parents may also treat sons and daughters differently (see Bronfenbrenner et al. 1984), although Bradley and his colleagues generally find no gender differences on the full Home Observation for Measurement of the Environment (HOME) measures (Bradley and Caldwell 1984a, 1987; Bradley, Caldwell, Rock, Hamrick, and Harris 1988).

Child Age

We expect older children to evidence stronger cognitive outcomes given the longer period they have had for exposure to cognitively stimulating activity and general developmental maturity. The rationale for predicting a unidirectional effect of child age on social outcomes is less clear, since it is more likely that the nature as opposed to frequency of child behavior problems will change as a child grows older. For models predicting social outcomes, we therefore include it in a more exploratory context.

Child Shyness

Performance on standardized cognitive assessments involves an oral response to an interviewer who may not be familiar to the child. For children who are by temperament shy, such a testing situation may artificially deflate their scores. Controlling for the interviewer's assessment of child shyness at the beginning of the interview helps to eliminate this possibility.

DO MOTHERS' JOBS AFFECT CHILDREN
MORE THAN FATHERS' JOBS?

Thus far our arguments have frequently been phrased in terms of the effects of *parents'* paid working conditions and characteristics on child outcomes, without systematic attention as to whether the effects of mothers' and fathers' characteristics differ. Much conventional wisdom, as well as theory, explicitly or implicitly assumes that it is the *mothers'* characteristics that primarily affect children's lives. Psychologists concerned with child development argue that mothers' interactions with their children in early childhood provide an important foundation for future child welfare. Belsky (1984a) and others following attachment theory as developed by Bowlby (1969) and Ainsworth (1973) argue that maternal absence, including daily absence for employment outside the home, may weaken maternal-child attachment. Weaker levels of attachment imply greater levels of child insecurity, with attendant social mis-

behavior as children mature; a few studies also document negative associations between child insecurity and child cognitive outcomes. Becker
assumes that efficient families will allocate homemaking and child care
to women, and thus reductions in women's time allocated to these activities will negatively affect both home environments and child welfare.
Ignored by each of these approaches is the role that currently employed
fathers play in contributing to home environments (other than obvious
financial contributions), as well as the role that fathers are likely to play
when the children's mothers are employed outside the home. When
mothers do not work for pay, then the fathers' occupational statuses
likely set the tone for socialization of the young. When both parents are
employed, fathers are likely to contribute somewhat more to production
of work in the home, although several sources argue that the mothers'
work at home actually decreases little relative to when she was not
employed (Thompson and Walker 1989). We take as problematic, however, the relative impact of maternal and paternal characteristics on
child outcomes. Only by empirical investigation can we evaluate
whether traditionally held assumptions regarding the relative effects of
maternal and paternal characteristics are true.

While such aspects of employment as opportunities for self-direction
and freedom from direct supervision have effects on both men's and
women's cognitive and psychological states (Miller et al. 1979; Schooler
1987), the implications of occupational experiences for parent-child
interaction may vary for fathers and mothers. Given greater female involvement with young children even when both parents are employed,
aspects of mothers' own occupations may have stronger implications for
children's home environments than fathers' occupational conditions.
Consistent with this argument, Simons, Whitbeck, Conger, and Melby
(1990) argue that mothers' values and attitudes may set the climate of
family interaction. They found that mothers' values had direct effects on
how fathers interact with their school age children; in contrast, fathers'
values did not directly affect mothers' behavior. In contrast, Kohn and
his colleagues showed that occupational position, and socioeconomic
status more generally, affected both mothers' and fathers' values; and
both parents' values had consequences for the values of their children
(Kohn, Slomczynski, and Schoenbach 1986). Part of the differences in
findings may reflect the increasing salience of fathers as children grow
older (Lamb 1981; Rossi 1985) since Simons et al.'s study focused on sev-
enth-graders and Kohn studied older adolescents and young adults. If
fathers are less central when children are younger, the influence of their
characteristics on preschool and early school age children's home environments will be weaker than the influence of mothers' characteristics;
these influences may become more equal as children grow older (Lamb

1981; Rossi 1985; Kohn et al. 1986). In addition, we expect that the resources that both parents bring to their current situations will affect parent-child interaction. Prior research has emphasized mothers' *cognitive* resources, both educational attainment and measures of IQ, but father's cognitive resources also contribute to the overall cognitive stimulation for children in the family (Wright and Wright 1976). Parents' *psychological* resources have not been considered in previous empirical research, but social psychological theory suggests positive direct and indirect effects.

HOW MIGHT CHANGES IN PARENTAL PAID WORK AND FAMILY STRUCTURE AFFECT CHILD DEVELOPMENT?

Inherent in the concept of development is the notion that since children change over time, behaviors and cognitive capabilities that we observe at one point in time may only be suggestive for future outcomes. Because outcomes at one point in time are only imperfect predictors of future behaviors, we explicitly consider the factors that may introduce variation in outcomes over time. We also argue that the factors that produce change in child outcomes are likely similar to those that influence change in children's home environments. We now specifically consider how change in parental circumstances may influence future cognitive achievement, behavior problems, and the home environments that parents create for children.

When we study *change* in social behavior, we look to *change* in parental circumstances as causative factors. Particularly in families with young parents, children may experience multiple changes both in their parents' paid work lives and in their family composition. Since early adulthood constitutes the "floundering phase of the life course" (Namboodiri 1987), young parents may change employers and paid working conditions during this time and experience periods of unemployment or underemployment (see also Rindfuss, Swicegood, and Rosenfeld 1987). Such changes in employment status and employers may reduce parental attention to young children as well as produce short-term family economic strain (Downey and Moen 1987). Even welcome changes in paid working conditions, such as promotions, pose challenges that divert attention and energy that might otherwise be devoted to family needs, thus placing the socialization burden more heavily on other family members. Such processes may be compounded in dual-earner households as changes for one partner may prompt renegotiation and rearrangement of responsibilities, and as reduced time together threatens marital satisfaction (Kingston and Nock 1987).

The early adult years are also a time of frequent family change, including marital dissolution. The open conflict between unhappy spouses that may precede separation is unlikely to set positive examples for children regarding appropriate self-controls; such socialization efforts may be hampered after separation given the reduced resources of the single-parent households (Astone and McLanahan 1991; Baydar 1988; Furstenberg and Seltzer 1986; Zill 1988; Wallerstein 1984). Another common change in family situation is the birth of additional children. Additional children also increase the total burden on parents, and there may be less time to encourage and support appropriate internal standards among older children in the family. Since pregnancy, childbirth, and early infant care often interrupt paid employment among young women, the family's economic status may suffer temporarily. Under any of these circumstances or in combination, children are more likely to exhibit acting out or withdrawn, excessively dependent behaviors.

Furthermore, such studies have treated characteristics such as father presence and family size as stable properties of families; as we develop below, such characteristics are highly dynamic, particularly when children are young, and changes in these characteristics may have implications for children's social behavior. In addition, we know relatively little about the *stability* of early differences among families in their ability to provide optimal home environments, or about potential alterations over time in children's home environments as a function of their parents' changing occupational and family circumstances. Studies in the psychological and educational literatures have emphasized the effects of stable attributes of the mother, particularly educational attainment, IQ, and ethnicity, as well as family composition, particularly father presence and family size (Bradley 1985; Bradley et al. 1988a). These studies suggest that the quality of home environments will be relatively stable over time, with relatively disadvantaged families persisting in providing suboptimal home environments and vice versa. But support for this assumption of stability is mixed; although Bradley and Caldwell (1987) characterize the quality of home environments as "moderately stable" through the first few years, they also report that stability varied across the race-gender groups they studied and was lower for nonwhites and for boys.

While individual attributes may be stable then, these arguments suggest that expectable changes in occupational and family lives may significantly alter the home environments that young children experience; such factors have seldom been considered in prior research on children's family environments. They also suggest that prior emphasis on father presence or absence, although important, may be incomplete because even when present, fathers vary in their social characteristics and in the paid working conditions they experience; and their presence is not a necessarily a permanent characteristic of children's lives.

DO THESE PROCESSES HOLD UNIFORMLY
ACROSS SOCIAL GROUPS AND CONDITIONS?

As noted above, one of the limitations of much psychological research regarding employment effects on children is its inability to investigate whether empirical relationships observed in a general group of cases also hold for specific subgroups of children, where the subgroups may be defined by race and ethnicity, or child gender. Such a limitation is frustrating, because both general sociological theory as well as theories specific to particular family processes and child outcomes suggest that these statistical interactions may exist. If they do, then sole reliance on strictly additive models may lead to misleading conclusions. As noted above, sociologists and child development researchers have frequently argued that the processes through which children attain various levels of cognitive skills or come to exhibit levels of behavior problems may vary by child characteristics. Our strategy will be to estimate standard models for these outcomes across values of these characteristics, and report findings where differences in the processes are substantial and theoretically interpretable. Several general and specific expectations guide our analyses. Researchers have documented racial differences in social outcomes and life processes across a wide variety of studies. Regarding cognition, several studies have documented racial differences in mean levels of test scores, which suggests that the processes responsible for these differences may vary as well. Given extensive documentation regarding racial differences in returns to variables predicting earnings among adults, there may be analogous differences in returns to children's cognition and home environments, as well as in the processes that lead to variation in levels of behavior problems.

Gender is a fundamental basis for biological and social differentiation, and there are numerous studies documenting sex differences in outcomes and behaviors in early childhood (Rutter 1983; Ehrhardt 1985). Such differences prompt additional questions regarding whether the processes responsible for these outcomes differ as well. For example, Desai, Chase-Lansdale, and Michael (1989) find that boys are more susceptible to cognitive delay owing to early maternal paid work than are girls. Additional literature suggests that boys are more prone than girls to be identified as undercontrolled, while girls may be more likely to exhibit overcontrol. We suggest that gender is an important basis around which we need to assess interaction in processes governing the determination of children's cognitive outcomes, their levels of behavior problems, and the nature of their home environments.

In addition, we test a number of additional interactions suggested by theory. We are particularly concerned with whether parental paid working conditions have stronger or weaker effects depending upon family structure. For example, stress-amplifying arguments suggest that demanding jobs with higher levels of complexity and longer paid work hours may have more negative effects on children if there are family transitions such as marital dissolution or the birth of additional children. Stress-buffering arguments suggest that stronger home environments and intact marriages protect children from the potential stresses of longer parental paid work hours and lower parental earnings. We evaluate these ideas selectively in our study of the effects of parental paid working conditions on children's lives.

PLAN OF THE BOOK

This chapter has laid the theoretical foundations for our analysis of parents' jobs and children's lives. In Chapter 2 we describe more fully the data we will use to study this question and the measures of the central variables in the analysis. In Chapter 3 we consider the ways in which parents' jobs affect the home environments that they create for their children. We study both the determinants of home environments in 1986, as well as the extent to which these same factors influence changes in these home environments by 1988. These findings set the stage for our considering the extent to which children's home environments influence their cognitive and social outcomes directly, as well as short-term changes in these outcomes. In Chapter 4 we present data regarding how parental paid working conditions and key controls influence child cognition. We study both verbal facility among 3–6 year olds, as well as reading and mathematics achievement when these children are 5–8 years old. In Chapter 5 we consider how these same factors influence child social adjustment. We study the effects of these variables on levels of behavior problems among 4–6 year olds in 1986, as well as how these factors influence change in behavior problems among these same children in the ensuing 2 years. Chapter 6 allows us to consider whether the timing of maternal paid work has discernible effects on child outcomes measured later. In particular, we investigate whether maternal paid work early in the child's life affects both cognitive and social child outcomes measured when the child is 3–6 years old. Chapter 7 reorients our thinking from the consideration of direct to indirect effects on child outcomes. Although the models estimated in Chapters 3–6 portray only the direct effects of parental paid working conditions on children's home environments and child outcomes, the findings suggest that it is fruitful to discuss how parental background characteristics in particular may have important indirect effects on their children's lives. Chapter 7 presents a modified path model that describes these findings more fully than is possible in the chapters devoted to describing direct effects. Finally, Chapter 8 provides a summary of our key findings and comments more broadly on their implications. We revisit the notions of family efficiency and family social capital, and link our findings to the hypotheses derived from these traditions. We also speculate on the likely implications of alternative paid work and family policies that are currently under discussion.

Chapter 2

Data, Samples, and Variables

DATA

The data for our study come from periodic surveys of a cohort of mothers along with developmental assessments of their children. The cohort of mothers was derived from the National Longitudinal Surveys of Youth (NLSY) cohort, a panel study of a national sample of youths who were 14–21 years old in 1979. The initial sample was derived from two sampling frames. The first was a cross section of youth in the population at that time and the second oversampled black, Hispanic, and economically disadvantaged nonblack, non-Hispanic youths so as to provide additional cases for analyses of the economically disadvantaged. The NLSY has had a 91.8% retention rate for all respondents over the duration of the panel; this rate is slightly higher (92.7%) for the female NLSY cohort (Baker and Mott 1989).

Of the 4,918 young women in the youth cohort, over 50% ($N = 2,918$) had become mothers by 1986, when they were 21–28 years old. With funding from the National Institute of Child Health and Human Development (NICHD), in 1986 the Center for Human Resource Research (CHRR) at Ohio State University in cooperation with NORC (formerly the National Opinion Research Center) at the University of Chicago completed interviews and assessments for 4,971 children of the youth cohort mothers. Given the age of the cohort in 1979, the sampling frames from which it was derived, and the year of the child survey, these children represent early and on-time births from a cohort of disproportionately lower socioeconomic status mothers. Specifically, over a third of the assessed children were born when their mothers were in their teens, and about half were born when their mothers were aged 20–24.

NICHD convened a national panel of child development experts to guide the assessments of the children. Both cognitive and socioemotional measures were included, with specific measures varying by children's age. In all cases, interviews were conducted face to face with trained field interviewers under the direction of NORC. In many cases, the

31

interviewers were the same people who had interviewed the mothers for several years prior to 1986, and thus had potentially developed rapport with the mother and with the children. All measures and procedures are described in Baker and Mott (1989).

Our study uses a series of related and overlapping samples derived from this data resource. Given our central interest in the effects of maternal paid working conditions on child outcomes, one key sample focuses on the subset of currently employed mothers who had a child aged 3–6 years old in 1986, the year of the first developmental assessment. We focused on children aged 3–6 for several reasons. First, children younger than 3 cannot be reliably assessed on social and developmental outcomes of interest to our study. Second, given that this survey in 1986 and 1988 by necessity studied the children already born, the oldest children are necessarily born to very young mothers. This fact makes them atypical of a cohort of children of that age, thus hampering inferences to that more general population. Studying children under 7, although still representing early and on-time births, does not introduce this problem in an extreme way. Where more than one child in this age group was present in a family, we selected the younger child as our target child. Selecting a single child per mother provides the advantage of not overrepresenting mothers with high fertility and data regarding child care arrangements were more complete for the youngest children. The few children who did not live with their mothers were excluded from the analysis. In addition, mothers whose children had extremely low birth weights (below 1500 grams) indicating high risk for compromised development were excluded from the analyses. These criteria yielded a subsample of 781 employed mothers of young children aged 3–6 who had completed age-appropriate cognitive assessment. We selected 4- to 6-year-old children from this group for analyses of social development, since social outcomes were not assessed in children younger than four years; this resulted in a sample of 536 children. We conducted a descriptive analysis suggesting what differences we might have found in our samples had we chosen the target child at random, instead of selecting the younger or youngest child (data not shown). These differences are few and unsystematic.

We follow this sample both forward in time to 1988, the year of the second NLSY Child Assessment, and backward to the child's first 3 years of life. By following the sample forward to 1988 we can investigate the extent to which the child's academic achievement is understandable from earlier measures of verbal facility, parental paid working conditions, and parental and child background conditions. We can also study the extent to which levels of behavior problems and the nature of children's home environments have changed during this interval, and assess how changes in parental paid working conditions and family configuration may have contributed to these changes. The 1988 sample used to study child cognition and children's home environments contains 721 children, which reflects sample attrition and a very small number of residential changes between 1986 and 1988. The 1988 sample used to study behavior problems contains 493 children. We follow the children backward in time to the first 3 years of their lives to study whether family configuration and parental paid working conditions early in the child's life have a discernible effect on key outcomes later in the child's life. This changed sample contains 768 children which reflects the omission of the few children who did not live with their mothers in the first three years of life. We studied behavior problems on 528 of these children. Because of the longitudinal nature of our study, some of the measures we describe below are tapped at more than one point in time; when appropriate, we construct additional measures to capture changes during the child's life that we think are causally related to the child outcomes we study.

MEASURES

We now describe the measures we have used to conduct our analyses, beginning with the key cognitive and social child outcomes we are interested in explaining. We then turn attention to the measure of children's home environments, both a key dependent and key independent variable in our analyses. We then describe measures of our independent variables, beginning with parental paid working conditions, followed by measures of parental and child characteristics and family structure.

Child Cognitive Outcomes

We use two types of measures of child cognition. For younger children we focus on verbal facility, a concept that we interpret as the child's proclivity to recognize spoken Standard American English. We use as our indicator of verbal facility the Peabody Picture Vocabulary Test-Revised (PPVT-R), which is among the best established indicators of verbal intelligence and scholastic aptitude across childhood (Dunn and Dunn 1981). The PPVT-R measures a child's receptive or hearing vocabulary of Standard American English. The interviewer says a word and the child points to one of four pictures that best portrays the meaning of the word. The difficulty level of the words increases as the child goes through the test.

The PPVT-R was standardized on a nationally representative sample of 4200 children in 1979, and numerous studies have replicated the high split-half and test-retest reliability estimates reported for the standardization sample (see Dunn and Dunn 1981). Although the PPVT-R does not tap the full range of cognitive dimensions covered in the Stanford-Binet or Wechsler Intelligence Scale for Children (WISC) measures, it has high concurrent validity with these broader measures (Sattler 1974), significant concurrent associations with standardized measures of mathematics knowledge and reading comprehension, and high predictive power in explaining early and later school achievement (Baker and Mott 1989).

Minority and disadvantaged children score lower on the PPVT-R than they do on more broadly based measures, suggesting that the test may underestimate abilities for such children. Black children's scores are generally lower than nonblacks', even among Head Start populations with similar family background characteristics (Lee, Brooks-Gunn, and Schnur 1988). Some argue that minority children are more likely to approach the interviewing situation with wariness and fear, and try to terminate the situation as quickly as possible by using stereotyped response sets that produce extremely low scores. Such children may show significant improvement in scores in a second administration, even in the same week, or when a period of nonthreatening interaction or play with the interviewer precedes the testing (Zigler et al. 1973). To reduce such effects in the NLSY, the PPVT-R was scheduled near the end of the Child Assessment. In addition, raw scores equal to age-standardized scores more than 4 our standard deviations below the mean were considered invalid; such scores were treated as missing (see Baker and Mott 1989 regarding test administration and scoring). We further used the interviewer's report of the child's initial shyness and anxiety in the interview as an additional control in multivariate analyses.

Our second set of cognitive outcomes measures children's intellectual achievement in both reading recognition and mathematics. The Peabody Individual Achievement Test (PIAT) Reading Recognition Assessment measures word recognition and pronunciation ability (Baker and Mott 1989:87). Skills measured include matching letters, naming names, and reading individual words aloud. The test begins with preschool-level items and progresses in difficulty to the high school level; the children establish a "basal" by answering 5 consecutive items correctly; when they answer 5 out of 7 items incorrectly, they reach a "ceiling" and the assessment is stopped. The test was normed in the 1960s to have a mean of 100 and a standard deviation of 15. However, the appropriately weighted NLSY sample mean is higher than expected at 105, with relatively fewer low scores than would be expected on the basis of the norming sample (Baker and Mott 1989:89). Baker and Mott (1989:89) speculate that societal changes including widespread use of preschools and educational television for children may have raised the floor of children's reading performance without affecting the ceiling. Correlations between PIAT math and reading recognition are in the .48 to .63 range, the higher correlations being found among older children (Baker and Mott 1989:90). Correlations with PPVT-R are between .30 and .56, again with the higher correlations among the oldest age groups.

The PIAT Mathematics Assessment measures mathematics achievement for children aged 5 and over. The test begins with basic skills such as numeral recognition and progresses to tap concepts from geometry and trigonometry. This test was administered to children with a "PPVT age" of 5 and older. They enter the test at an age-appropriate item and establish a basal by answering 5 consecutive questions correctly. Again, a ceiling is reached, and the test terminated, when the child answers 5 out of 7 questions incorrectly. The one month test-retest reliability is .74 with lower levels reported at lower grades (Dunn and Markwardt 1970, Table 9, as noted in Baker and Mott 1989). PIAT math correlates between .47 and .57 with PPVT for specific age groups in the NLSY child sample (Baker and Mott:86). Again as with PIAT reading, the test was normed in the late 1960s on a national sample of children to have a mean of 100 and a standard deviation of 15 (Baker and Mott 1989:85). Since we are studying a sample of children who are early and on-time births, we would expect the mean score of our sample to be lower than the national average. Unexpectedly, the mean is 99.8, with fewer children scoring in the top 20% and bottom 20% of the distribution than in the norming sample (Baker and Mott 1989:86). Again, widespread viewing of children's television (e.g., "Sesame Street") may have lowered the frequency of the lowest scorers, while having no impact on learning of more advanced concepts. It may also be that in this sample the frequency of high scorers is reduced since there is an association between PIAT math scores and maternal age.

Measures of Behavior Problems

The NLSY Child Assessment included 28 items tapping parents' reports of child behavior problems that had been selected by Zill and Peterson for inclusion in the 1982 Child Health Supplement to the

National Health Interview Survey (Zill 1988). These items were primarily drawn from the larger Child Behavior Checklist (CBCL) developed by Thomas Achenbach and Craig Edelbrock (1981, 1983), which has been in development and use since the mid-1960s for measuring and assessing child behavior problems, but they drew as well from Rutter (1970), Graham and Rutter (1968), and Kellam, Branch, Agrawal, and Ensminger (1975). Items were chosen to represent relatively common behavior syndromes in children, e.g., acting-out, depressed-withdrawn behavior, and anxious-distractible behavior, rather than rare behaviors indicative of serious pathology. The items have good test-retest reliability and discriminant validity (Nicholas Zill and James Peterson, private communication).

The information on the frequency of behavior problems of the children is reported by the child's mother. Although the well-being of the mother may influence her reports of the child's behavior, the mother's perceptions, whether or not they are accurate, determine her actions toward the child and thus her influence on the child's behavior. Achenbach, McConaughy, and Howell (1987) conducted a meta-analysis of research on emotional and behavior problems in children, and concluded that parent reports were consistent with the reports of other informants, including teachers and mental health professionals. Their findings permit confidence that the results obtained using maternal reports of behavior problems are not likely to deviate widely from evaluations of mental health professionals.

The measure used here is based on a series of factor analyses performed on the 1986 data by Parcel and Menaghan (1988) and on subsequent confirmatory factor analyses conducted with the 1988 data set. Twenty-six items were asked of all children, while two items were applicable only to children attending school. The items include difficulties in interaction with other children and at home, difficulties in concentration, having a strong temper, and being argumentative; these are considered indicators of undercontrol of behavior. Other items such as being withdrawn, demanding attention, being too dependent/clingy, and feeling worthless/inferior tap overcontrol. Because many children aged 4–6 were not yet in school, the 1986 measure is constructed by combining the 26 items asked of all children. By 1988, virtually all children are in school, and the summary behavior problems measure sums all 28 items. Items are standardized to zero means and unit variance in 1986, and 1986 means and variances are used to standardize 1988 items before summing. At each time point, these measures have high internal consistency (alpha = .88 in 1986 and .90 in 1988), reflecting the substantial correlation between under- and overcontrolled behavior problems in nonclinical samples.

Children's Home Environments

Both the 1986 and the 1988 panels included age-appropriate sets of items derived from the Home Observation for Measurement of the Environment (HOME) scales (Bradley and Caldwell 1984a, 1984b). These scales tap three dimensions of children's home environments: the degree of appropriate cognitive stimulation; the degree of maternal warmth toward the child; and the extent to which the home is safe and reasonably clean. The HOME scales were devised to identify and describe homes of infants and young children who were at significant developmental risk (Bradley, Caldwell, Rock, Hamrick, and Harris 1988; Elardo and Bradley 1981); they have proved useful in identifying home environments associated with impaired mental development, clinical malnutrition, abnormal growth, and poor school performance (Bradley 1985). They have been used in several countries outside the United States and with a variety of ethnic groups in the United States, including blacks, whites, Mexican-Americans, and other Spanish-speaking Americans (Bradley et al. 1988b). The full HOME scales are derived both from asking mothers questions and from interviewer observation. The scales tap cognitive variables, including language stimulation, provision of a variety of stimulating experiences and materials, and encouragement of child achievement; social variables, including responsiveness, warmth, and encouragement of maturity; and physical environmental variables, including amount of sensory input and organization of the physical environment. Early measurement efforts focused on developing appropriate instruments for young infants and toddlers (Bradley and Caldwell 1977), followed by scale development for preschoolers (Bradley and Caldwell 1979) and elementary-school-age children (Bradley et al. 1988b).

In consultation with Bradley, CHRR selected items from each of these age-appropriate measures for inclusion in the 1986 assessments. Each measure included both maternal report items and interviewer observations. We subjected these items to factor analysis for each of two age groups: preschool children from age 3 to 5 years 11 months, and elementary school children 6 years of age and older. For each age group, 5 factor-based scales were constructed. Three scales, tapping cognitive stimulation, quality of physical environment, and warmth of maternal response to child were common to each age group. Factor-based scales were constructed for the two age groups using the items loading at .35 or greater for the cognitive stimulation, physical environment, and warm response factors. Alpha reliability for both scales was .71. These scales were standardized within age groups and then combined across the two age groups to create the measure of home environment used in this analysis. Mean substitution was used in the analysis to reduce the number of missing cases.

The Cognitive Stimulation scale for the preschool age group consisted of 8 items, including questions about number of children's books and the provision of help with learning numbers, shapes, and letters; the Enrichment Opportunities scale for the elementary age group consisted of 7 items including number of child's own books and frequency of attending performances or visiting museums. The Warm Response scale for the preschool age group consisted of 4 items including mother's conversing pleasantly with child and verbal response to child's requests; the Warm Response scale for the elementary age group was constructed of the same items, with encouragement of child's verbal contributions replacing one item from the preschool scale. The Good Physical Environment scale for the preschool age group was comprised of 4 items including whether the home was clean and safe; for the elementary age group the scale was comprised of the same items. Additional detail regarding this measure is available in Parcel and Menaghan (1989).

We used confirmatory factor analysis to affirm the stability of the factor structure over time. Rather than standardizing items using time-point-specific means and variances, we used 1986 means and standard deviations to standardize items at both time points. This procedure preserves any changes in level or variability that may have occurred between 1986 and 1988.

Parental Paid Working Conditions

We focus on occupational complexity, wage levels, and hours of paid work as the central parental paid working conditions affecting child outcomes. We measure these characteristics for both parents if both are employed at the key time points we study: 1986, 1988, and in the child's first year or first 3 years of life.

Occupational Complexity

Our measure of occupational complexity is derived from the fourth edition of the *Dictionary of Occupational Titles* (DOT) data matched to 1980 detailed census occupational codes (see Parcel 1989 for additional discussion of these procedures). The original 42 items include involvement with data, people, and things, temperaments needed to perform paid work activities, physical demands of jobs, and environmental paid working conditions. In order to allow for data reduction, Parcel (1989) performed factor analyses of these data using principal components analysis and oblique rotation; these procedures suggested that occupational variation in DOT measures could be captured by 5 job content measures, the first of which, substantive complexity, is used in this analysis. Based on these findings we constructed a factor-based scale (Kim and Mueller 1978) for each parent for substantive complexity that includes 19 items tapping direction, control, and planning; talking; influencing people; intelligence; preference for abstract versus routine activities; complexity of paid work with data and people; communication of data versus activities with things; preference for scientific and technical vs. business activities; numerical and verbal aptitudes required; General Educational Development (GED), a measure of educational level required for job activities; Specific Vocational Preparation (SVP), extent of on the job training required; form, clerical, and spatial perceptions; reaching, handling, fingering, feeling; repetitive or continuous processes; sensory or judgmental criteria. Cronbach's alpha for this scale is .94. High levels of complexity are found in jobs such as elementary and secondary school teaching, management, marketing and public relations, and computer programming. Jobs involving low levels of complexity include food preparation, maids, truck drivers, longshoremen, and pressing machine operators.

Parental Earnings

We also measure the earnings rate of the mother's job, as measured by her hourly wage. We estimate wage levels for fathers by dividing mother-reported total annual spouse earnings in the preceding calendar year by the product of mother-reported usual spouse paid work hours per week and mother-reported total spouse weeks worked in that year.

Parental Paid Work Hours

We measure the extent of employment in terms of usual hours worked per week for both mothers and fathers in 1986 and 1988. Variables were constructed to detect nonlinearities in effects of parental paid work hours. Dummy variables contrasted male part-time (less than 35 hours) and male overtime (greater than 40 hours) with male full-time (35–40 hours) paid work; unemployed fathers are included in the part-time category. Given the greater heterogeneity among mothers' hours, low part-time (less than 20 hours) and moderate part-time (20–34 hours) were distinguished in addition to overtime (more than 40 hours) paid work weeks; these three patterns were contrasted with full-time paid work schedules.

When we tap paid working conditions in the child's first year of life or over the child's first 3 years of life, measures of hours rely on averages of respective parents' reported usual hours during those years. Mothers with no employment during year 1 or the first 3 years received missing values for all paid work hours dummies for that period. Similarly, absent fathers received missing values for all paid work hours dummies for any period they were absent. Thus, paid work hours variables capture variations in paid work hours among employed parents.

We adopt analogous strategies in measuring occupational requirements and wage levels for the early time periods. We also express all wages in 1986 constant dollars so that wage levels can be meaningfully compared across time. We assess changes in maternal employment status over time by constructing dummy variables to identify the subsets of mothers who were not paid working in 1988, those who did not work in the child's first year of life, and those who did not work throughout the child's first 3 years of life.

Family Composition and Change in Family Composition

We measure both marital status of the mother and number of children as key aspects of family composition. For the initial analyses of 1986 outcomes we represent mothers' marital status with a dummy variable (married and living with the spouse = 1). For studying children's behavior problems, mother's marital history is measured with a set of three dummy variables distinguishing four groups: mothers who had married or remarried within the last year; mothers who had separated or divorced within the same time period; mothers who have been stably unmarried for at least a year; and stably married mothers. For analyses of 1988 outcomes, 1986 marital status and 1988 marital status are dummied and combined to distinguish four groups: mothers who were unmarried at both time points; those who were married at both time points; those who were unmarried in 1986 and married in 1988 (marriage started); and those who were married in 1986 but no longer married in 1988 (marriage ended). We assess initial family size by the number of the mother's children living in the household in 1986. For 1988 outcomes, we also include a dummy variable capturing whether additional children were born during the period between the two interviews.

Additional measures of family composition and structure are needed when we assess the role of early parental paid working conditions on child outcomes. For the first year of life we constructed a dummy coded 1 if the mother was married, the reference category being unmarried during the child's first year of life. A continuous variable taps the child's number of older siblings during the first year of life. Regarding family configuration early in the child's life, dummy variables represent whether the mother was stably married in the child's first 3 years of life, and whether she was unstably married for part of the time period, the reference category being mothers who were unmarried throughout the first 3 years of the child's life. A continuous variable taps the number of the target child's older siblings; a dummy variable taps whether additional children were born to the mother in the child's first 3 years of life. For models including first-year characteristics, a continuous variable measures the number of the target child's younger siblings in 1986 (born after the first year of life). For models including the first 3 years of the child's life, a dummy variable taps whether additional children were born between the time the child turned 3 and 1986, when the child outcomes were assessed.

Parental Background Characteristics

Maternal Background Characteristics

Ethnicity of the mother is coded as a set of dummy variables to distinguish four groups: Mexican-American; other Hispanic; black; and non-Hispanic, nonblack (which we will refer to as white). The codes are taken from mother's initial interview in 1979. We measured the *age* of the mother in years as of 1986. We measured maternal *years of schooling* by the highest grade completed by the mother. We measured mother's *intellectual ability* by her score on the Armed Forces Qualification Test taken by all NLSY participants in 1980. The AFQT consists of the sum of scores on four subtests of the Armed Services Vocational Aptitude Battery, including word knowledge, paragraph comprehension, numeric operations, and arithmetic reasoning; it measures developed abilities rather than aptitude (Baker and Mott 1989), and correlates positively with age, family socioeconomic status (SES), being white, and residence outside the South (*Profiles of American Youth* 1982).

We assess the *socioeconomic status of the mother's own family of origin* by using child's maternal grandmother's level of schooling. Given marital homogamy, we expect strong associations between socioeconomic characteristics of our sample mothers' parents. Because data on the mothers' fathers (children's maternal grandfathers) were more likely to be missing than were data on maternal grandmothers, we chose maternal grandmother's educational attainment to reflect SES; it is measured by the highest grade she completed as of 1979. Since socioeconomic level also varies with family composition, we also distinguished mothers living with a father or stepfather at age 14 from other family structures.

We measured *maternal schooling* at several time points depending on the model being estimated. For 1986 and 1988 outcomes, we measured schooling in years at those respective time points. In our investigation of early effects, we measured educational attainment as of the child's first and third years of life.

We measured *maternal self-concept* as a composite of maternal mastery and maternal self-esteem. Maternal mastery is measured with a scale constructed from 4 items taken from Rotter's (1966) locus of control measure included in the initial 1979 interview. These items assess the degree to which the women feel that they have control over the direction of their lives; are able to follow through with the plans they make; are able to get what they want without relying on luck; and have influence over the things that happen to them. This scale has a reliability of .38 (Cronbach's alpha) suggesting the measure is a composite of several dimensions of control, although all of the items used tap personal control rather than control ideology (see Gecas 1989). Similarly low internal consistency has been reported for the complete Rotter scale as well, but it is possible that a larger pool of items would have enabled us to construct a more internally consistent measure from a subset of items. We explored the construct validity of our measure by calculating correlations between the NLSY measure and constructs such as economic well-being and education (data not shown) and found that the pattern and approximate strength of correlations were similar to those reported using more psychometrically adequate measures of mastery (see Mirowsky and Ross 1989), permitting some confidence in the measure.

Self-esteem was measured in 1980 with the 10-item Rosenberg self-esteem scale. As with mastery, we standardized the individual items to zero means and unit variances for all NLSY mothers, and summed the standardized individual items for a summary score. The self-esteem scale is highly consistent (alpha = .85).

To construct our measure of maternal self-concept, we constructed a composite of the respective Z-scores of the mastery and self-esteem measures. Use of the 1979 mastery and 1980 self-esteem measures provides information about mastery and maternal self-concept before or about the time these women gave birth to the target child we study. Thus in this research, maternal self-concept represents initial personal control resources. While Andrisani (1978) provides evidence for the impact of labor market experience on locus of control, thus suggesting mastery's temporal instability, other research suggests that beliefs about self and society may be more stable over time than his findings would imply. Downey and Moen (1987:331) report a .53 correlation between mastery measures in 1972 and 1975–1976 for women heading their own house-

holds, Mortimer, Lorence, and Kumka (1986) report a stability coefficient of .73 over 10 years for young men, and Gurin and Brim (1984:297)
report a stability coefficient of .78 over 2 years. Gecas (1989) notes that
sense of mastery seems to operate as a self-fulfilling prophecy, leading
to behavior that makes positive outcomes more likely and so confirms
initial beliefs. Although there has been no reassessment of mastery in
the NLSY, longitudinal data on self-esteem find relatively high stability
(*r* corrected for attenuation = .52) for the NLSY mothers over 7 years
(Menaghan 1990a). We treat our measure as indicating the mothers'
early but relatively enduring sense of mastery over life circumstances
and positive view of their own self-worth.

Paternal Characteristics

Because the children's fathers are not NLSY respondents who have
been followed since 1979, we have less background information on
them. As with maternal age and levels of schooling, paternal ages and
levels of schooling are measured in years. Variables are constructed to
tap these constructs during the child's first year of life, at the child's
third year of life, in 1986, and in 1988.

Child Characteristics

Sex of the child is coded 1 if male. *Child health* is measured as a
dummy variable coded 1 if mother reports child having a chronic health
condition that limits school attendance or play or sports activities, and
coded 0 otherwise. *Low birth weight* is a dummy variable coded 1 if the
child's birth weight was below 5.5 lb, thus suggesting increased risk for
compromised development. *Child shyness/anxiety* is based on the interviewer's evaluation of child demeanor at the start of the Child Assessment. The scale runs from 1 to 5, with 1 representing not at all shy/anx-
ious and 5 representing extremely shy/anxious.

WEIGHTING, MISSING DATA,
AND ANALYTICAL STRATEGY

Because the original NLSY sample oversampled minority and economically disadvantaged white youth, NORC has constructed sample
weights to equate the sample with a nationally representative sample of
adolescents and adults aged 14–21 years on January 1, 1978.[1] All analyses reported here use weighted samples. The fact that the NLSY contains

a disproportionate number of women from lower SES households therefore does *not* bias the analyses since these cases have been weighted down to reflect their relative frequency in the larger population. Their presence in the sample does help to increase the precision of the estimates derived using the data, particularly if one is interested in estimates for such subgroups. Without such weights, the estimates of means would be severely biased. We also used these weights in all bivariate and multivariate analyses. Throughout all analyses, we used mean substitution to reduce problems with missing data.

Our analytic strategy involves multiple regression with dummy variables. Our models are estimated by entering sets of variables in sequences guided by our theoretical arguments. We typically enter parental and child background characteristics first, followed by work and family conditions, followed by children's home environments, where relevant.[2] Final models enter these sets simultaneously, with intermediate models specified to show how changes in work and/or family conditions over time may be affecting child outcomes.

TESTING FOR STATISTICAL INTERACTION

As we indicated in Chapter 1, we take seriously the likelihood that the processes we study may vary for children with differing social characteristics. To investigate these possibilities, we used Chow tests (Cohen 1983) to assess whether given models differed by such factors as child gender and maternal race. Where indicated, we tested whether specific coefficients were significantly different between the two groups by adding specific interaction terms representing the product of the independent variables and group characteristics to the pooled equation. We have also argued that adequate examination of the causal chains linking parental social background and children's outcomes must include attention to likely interactive effects among our explanatory variables. We examine three major kinds of interactions. First, we evaluate whether the effects of more difficult paid work and family conditions may be buffered by parental cognitive and psychosocial resources. Second, we examine whether the effects of paid work conditions vary depending on the family responsibilities parents are simultaneously shouldering. Third, we examine whether effects of one parent's paid working conditions vary depending on the paid working conditions of the other parent. We report the results of these estimations in conjunction with the additive findings in respective chapters.

NOTES

1. Individual case weights are constructed for each survey year to conform the sample to independently derived population totals for individuals aged 14–21 on January 1, 1979; they take into account the probability of selection at the baseline (1979) interview, differential nonresponse at the initial screening and baseline interview phases, and random variation associated with sampling. The weights assigned by NORC produce group population estimates when used in tabulations; thus, the sum of weighted cases is quite large. For these analyses, the NORC weights are divided by a constant so that the sum of weighted cases equals the unweighted number of cases.

Because the sample is a multistage stratified random sample rather than a simple random sample, actual standard errors are somewhat larger than the standard errors computed by conventional statistical routines, thus potentially increasing the risk of Type 1 error. The ratio of the correct standard error to the computed standard error is termed the *design effect*. Design effects vary for the different strata in the sample, and no single design effect can be constructed that can be broadly applied to regression analyses. Illustrative computations of design effects for specific problems suggest that design effects for the full NLSY sample ranged around 1.5 in 1979 and around 1.25 to 1.35 in 1986; they have been decreasing over time as geographic mobility occurs for many members (Center for Human Resource Research 1988). Rather than apply an arbitrary adjustment, we report probability at the .05, .01, and .001 levels so that the reader can distinguish marginally significant effects and interpret them accordingly.

2. Because of the sample restrictions we impose regarding child age, it varies within narrow limits in all our analyses. In addition, given the constricted age range of our mothers and the fact that our sample does not include women who do not yet have children or who have children younger than those we study, there is a correlation between child and maternal age. Therefore, these variables are not included in models simultaneously. Although in most models we prefer to study the effects of maternal age on child outcomes in order to assess how this maternal resource affects children's lives, when studying child social behavior we substitute child age in order to more directly assess whether levels of behavior problems vary by this child characteristic.

Chapter 3

Parents Jobs' and Children's Home Environments

In this chapter we consider the effects of parental paid working conditions on children's home environments. In Chapter 1 we argued that children's home environments may be an important pathway through which parents transmit the norms and values they hold to their children. If this is the case, then we should see predictable empirical relationships between parental background, paid work, family structure, and home environments; in subsequent analyses of child outcomes, we should also see that home environments are important predictors of these outcomes, and that inclusion of home environments in these models weakens the predictive powers of background, paid work, and family structure characteristics. Alternatively, we might see that despite clear predictability to children's home environments from background, paid work, and family factors, and despite a clear impact of home environments on several child outcomes, home environments may not weaken the effects of other background variables. Rather, the home environment may act as one of several important pathways through which children absorb the norms and values they need to develop both cognitively and socially. This chapter lays the foundation for this analysis by portraying the extent to which we can explain variation in children's home environments by variation in parental paid working conditions, family composition, and parental and child background characteristics.

In Chapter 1 we argued that the mechanisms through which parents can pass on family and social class advantage to children vary across societies (see Katsillis and Rubinson 1990). Direct mechanisms such as inheritance and transfer of property rights may be particularly important in preindustrial societies. In meritocratic societies these remain important among the wealthy. However, for the vast majority of society, educational achievement becomes an intervening institution between parental background and offspring socioeconomic attainment, and indirect mechanisms become more important. Parental effort, involvement, and investment therefore may facilitate the children's effort that translates into eventual educational attainment and adult socioeconomic attainment. Thus transmission of status across generations may be importantly affected by the extent to which parents maintain warm and supportive relationships with their children, and also demonstrate parental support for cognitive activity, provide appropriate cognitive stimulation for their children, and create an emotionally supportive context for socialization.

In addition, our models that predict children's home environments as a partial function of parental paid working conditions bring important evidence to bear on Coleman's concerns regarding family social capital. If family social capital is affected by the amount of time that parents spend with their children, we should see clear relationships between parental paid work hours and the quality of children's home environments. Although Coleman's concerns about the weakening of family social capital are tied to *maternal* paid employment, our models will also enable us to understand the relationship between paternal paid work hours and the quality of children's home environments. Similarly, parental occupational complexity influences the norms and values around which parents create their children's home environments. Therefore, our investigation of the effects of maternal and paternal occupational complexity on home environments suggests how parental paid working conditions influence the *nature* of family social capital. Parental wages could affect both the *quantity* and *nature* of family social capital. Families with higher incomes may purchase more educational materials, and provide children with more lessons and outings than families with lower wages. The nature of these experiences may also vary with parental income because higher-income parents can afford private lessons and more exclusive social opportunities, while lower-income parents may rely largely on community-sponsored activities and participation in formal religion. Thus, the impact of parental wages may reflect both dimensions of family social capital.

Finally, it is also important to consider how capacities to provide optimal home environments may shift over time, i.e., to evaluate temporal alterations in children's home environments as a function of parents' changing occupational and family circumstances. We have argued that for many families, children's early years are characterized by change in parents' paid work lives and in family composition. Changes in job or in employers, or the interspersing of paid work and schooling with unemployment or underemployment are frequent in young families. Young women's employment is also likely to be interrupted by pregnancy, childbirth, and early infant care. These changes in employment status and employers may deflect parental attention from young children and may also bring at least short-term fluctuations in the family's economic circumstances. Even welcome changes, such as promotions at paid work that improve the family economic resources, may divert attention and energy that might otherwise be devoted to family needs, thus increasing the burden on other family members and carrying costs for the overall family environment.

The early adult years are also a time of frequent family change. They are a time of high risk for marital dissolution. Both the conflict preceding separation and the efforts following separation to establish new family organization and routines as single parental families, as well as the emotional highs and lows parents experience in resuming dating and moving toward new partnerships, may undermine family environments for children (Astone and McLanahan 1991; Baydar 1988; Furstenberg and Seltzer 1986; Zill 1988; Wallerstein 1984). The birth of additional children also changes families. Such births vary in the extent to which they are expected or desired. In either case, the birth of additional children increases the total burden on parents, and may compromise the quality of stimulation and warmth available to other children in the family. We therefore consider the importance of changes in paid work and family circumstances as predictors of change in family home environments, as well as the role of enduring parental background characteristics.

As noted in Chapter 2, our strategy involves multivariate analysis of children's home environments as a function of parental and child background, parental paid work characteristics, and family structure. We first describe the characteristics of the sample we use to study both children's home environments in this chapter and child cognitive outcomes in Chapter 4. We then estimate models predicting 1986 children's home environments. With these data as foundation, we then estimate models of short-term change in children's home environments.

FINDINGS

Descriptive Findings for a Key Sample

Table 3.1 presents some basic descriptive data from the sample we will use to study both children's home environments and their cognitive outcomes. Our sample of children aged 3–6 years old is 50% male, with only 6% of children having low birth weights and only 5% having health problems that interfere with schooling or play. Mothers average over 25 years of age, and slightly over 12 years of schooling. The sample is 18%

Table 3.1.   1986 Home Sample: 1986 Variable Means, Standard Deviations, and Correlations with Home 1986 ($N = 781$)

Variable	Mean	Std. dev.	Correlation with Home 1986
Home 1986	.21	.89	
Child characteristics 1986			
Health problems	.05	.22	.06
Low birth weight	.06	.23	.02
Male	.50	.50	.03
Parental characteristics			
Mother			
Ethnicity			
Black	.18	.39	-.16*
White	.74	.44	.21*
Mexican Hispanic	.04	.21	-.12*
Other Hispanic	.03	.18	-.02
Age 1986	25.57	2.05	.21*
Education 1986	12.11	1.54	.21*
AFQT 1980	67.60	19.02	.25*
Positive self-concept	-.03	.82	.25*
Family of origin			
Two parents at age 14	.79	.40	.15*
Grandmother education	10.86	2.59	.13*
Spouse			
Age 1986	28.78	3.63	.11*
Education 1986	12.20	1.71	.27*
Maternal work characteristics 1986			
Occupational complexity	-5.68	11.20	.19*
Hourly wage	5.67	2.95	.12*
Work hours			
1–20	.15	.36	.03
21–34	.19	.39	.04
35–40	.56	.50	-.04
Over 40	.11	.31	-.03
Spouse work characteristics 1986			
Occupational complexity	-5.43	10.05	.12*
Hourly wage	9.31	5.20	.14*
Work hours			
Under 35	.04	.21	-.13*
35–40	.57	.50	.05
Over 40	.38	.49	.01
Family characteristics 1986			
Married	.70	.46	.09*
Number of children	1.84	.77	-.12*

*Significant at $p < .05$, two-tailed test.

black, 7% Hispanic, and 74% white. Mothers' average AFQT is 67.60, which is above the average of 50 normed on the 1980 NLSY sample. Close to 80% of the mothers came from two-parent families, and the average woman had a mother who had attained close to 11 years of schooling. When married, the mothers' spouses average close to 29 years of age and have achieved an average of just over 12 years of schooling.

Turning to parental paid work characteristics, both mothers and fathers have levels of occupational complexity that are below zero. These findings reflect the fact that these workers hold occupations with lower levels of complexity than the average for a sample of occupations where every occupation receives equal weight, as compared to a distribution that is weighted by the occupations actually held by this distribution of paid workers. Mothers earn an average of $5.67 per hour while fathers' earnings average $9.31. Fifty-six percent of mothers work for pay full-time, while 11% average greater than full-time hours. Close to 20% work for pay 21–34 hours per week, with an additional 15% working for pay 1–20 hours per week. Interestingly, the percentage of fathers reporting full-time paid work is similar to that of mothers. However, part-time employment is less typical for fathers, with only 4% reporting less than 35 hours of paid work per week. Overtime hours, however, are quite typical for fathers, with 38% reporting that they typically work for pay more than 40 hours per week. We also consider characteristics of the children's families. Seventy percent of the mothers in this sample are married, and they have an average of 1.84 children. This lower than average level of fertility likely reflects that these 21- to 28-year-old mothers have not yet completed their fertility.[1]

The data on correlations suggest that children's home environments are positively associated with maternal AFQT and self-concept, intact family of origin, grandmother education, and white maternal ethnicity; maternal and paternal education, ages, occupational complexity, and wages; and mother being married. The quality of home environments is negatively correlated with black and Mexican Hispanic ethnicities, with paternal part-time paid work, and with greater numbers of children in the family.

Table 3.2 provides some additional descriptive data for the sample with which we study variations in 1988 children's home environments. Children's home environments in 1988 are positively associated with maternal and paternal levels of schooling, parental occupational complexity, mother's age and wage levels, and mothers being stably married between 1986 and 1988. Home environments are negatively associated with mothers' having stopped paid work between 1986 and 1988, full-time maternal paid work in 1988, maternal separation or divorce between 1986 and 1988, and mothers being stably single during this same interval.

Table 3.2.   1988 Home Sample: 1988 Variable Means, Standard Deviations, and Correlations with Home 1988 ($N = 721$)

Variable	Mean	Std. dev.	Correlation with Home 1988
Home 1988	.51	.76	
Child characteristics 1988			
Health problems	.03	.16	.02
Parental characteristics 1988			
Mother			
Age 1988	27.57	2.04	.12*
Education 1988	12.18	1.55	.25*
Spouse			
Age 1988	31.19	4.65	−.09
Education 1988	12.20	2.19	.24*
Maternal work characteristics 1988			
Occupational complexity	−3.76	10.46	.12*
Hourly wage	7.08	3.63	.13*
Stopped working (since 1986)	.21	.41	−.10*
Work hours			
1–20	.12	.33	.06
21–34	.14	.35	.07
35–40	.62	.49	−.10*
Over 40	.12	.33	.01
Spouse work characteristics 1988			
Occupational complexity	−3.69	10.22	.12*
Hourly wage	10.85	6.84	.04
Work hours			
Under 35	.05	.23	−.08
35–40	.59	.49	.07
Over 40	.36	.48	−.04
Family characteristics 1988			
Number of children	2.06	.84	−.16*
Family changes 1986–1988			
Marriage patterns			
Stably married	.61	.49	.10*
Marriage ended	.09	.29	−.09*
Marriage started	.07	.25	.03
Stably single	.24	.43	−.08*
Additional children born	.22	.42	−.06

*Significant at $p < .05$, two-tailed test.

Multivariate Findings

Table 3.3 helps us understand how parental and child background, and parental paid work and family characteristics influence variations in the strength of 1986 children's home environments. Panel 1 displays the effects of parents' and children's characteristics on children's home environments. Panel 2 retains controls for child background characteristics only, and displays the effects of parental paid work and family characteristics in 1986. Panel 3 includes both child and parental background characteristics, as well as parental paid work and family characteristics in 1986. In this and all subsequent multivariate tables, we show all coefficients that are statistically significant. We also show the coefficients if they were significant in one panel, but dropped below significance in a subsequent model. If a variable was not significant in any model in the table, the fact that it was controlled is noted in the relevant table footnote. Sets of dummy variables are statistically significant unless otherwise indicated.

Panel 1 suggests that only one child characteristic affects 1986 home environments: the positive effect of child health problems on 1986 levels of home environments suggests that paid working parents of children with health problems improve their home environments, possibly as a means of coping with these challenges and/or compensating for them. However, parental background characteristics are particularly important influences on children's home environments. We observe significant effects of ethnicity, in that children of black and Mexican Hispanic mothers experience less optimal home environments than do white children. Children of older mothers, those with higher levels of schooling and those with more positive early self-concepts experience better home environments, as do children of more educated fathers and those whose mothers' households contained two parents when they were 14.

Panel 2 suggests that parental paid work and family characteristics also influence the quality of children's home environments. Children of mothers whose jobs are high in occupational complexity experience better home environments, as do children whose fathers earn higher wages. Paternal part-time employment is associated with poorer home environments. Children with married mothers experience stronger home environments, and the negative effect of number of siblings suggests that the quality of home environments becomes diluted across increased numbers of children. Panel 3 allows us to investigate whether each of these effects is maintained when these two sets of characteristics—background and paid work/family conditions—are controlled simultaneously. The child and parental characteristic effects noted above are all maintained, with the exception of the maternal education effect, which drops

Table 3.3.   1986 Home: The Impact of Child, Background, and 1986 Work and Family ($N = 781$)

Variable	Child & background (1) B	Beta	Child, work, & family 1986 (2) B	Beta	Child, background, work, & family 1986 (3) B	Beta
Child characteristics 1986						
Health problems	.29c	.07	.23	.06	.31c	.08
Parental characteristics						
Mother						
Ethnicity						
Black	-.38a	-.17			-.33a	-.14
White*	—	—			—	—
Mexican Hispanic	-.44b	-.10			-.46b	-.11
Other Hispanic	-.16	-.03			-.23	-.05
Age 1986	.05b	.10			.07a	.15
Education 1986	.05c	.09			.01	.02
Positive self-concept	.16a	.14			.16a	.14
Family of origin						
Two parents at age 14	.14d	.06			.13d	.06
Spouse						
Education 1986	.09a	.14			.09a	.14
Maternal work characteristics 1986						
Occupational complexity			.01a	.15	.01b	.10
Spouse work characteristics 1986						
Hourly wage			.02c	.09	-.00	-.01
Work hours						
0–35			-.53b	-.10	-.33d	-.06e
35–40*			—	—	—	—
Over 40			.01	.01	-.04	-.02
Family characteristics 1986						
Married			.24a	.12	.07	.04
Number of children			-.18a	-.16	-.23a	-.20
Constant	-2.97a		.15		-2.72a	
R^2	.17		.10		.21	
Adjusted R^2	.15		.08		.19	

a: $p < .001$; b: $p < .01$; c: $p < .05$; d: $p < .10$; two-tailed test.

a: $p < .0005$; b: $p < .005$; c: $p < .025$; d: $p < .05$; one-tailed test.

e: Set of dummy variables is not significant.

*: Reference category for categorical variable.

Note: Variables that are not significant in any panel are not displayed. All panels also control for the child characteristics Low Birth Weight and Male. Panels 1 and 3 also control for the background characteristics Maternal AFQT 1980, Grandmother education, and Spouse age 1986. Panels 2 and 3 also control for the work variables Maternal hourly wage, Maternal work hours 1986, and Spouse occupational complexity 1986.

below significance. The maternal occupational complexity effect is maintained, while the paternal paid working conditions and marital status effects become nonsignificant. The model continues to show a strong negative effect of number of siblings. These findings suggest that there are strong, direct effects of maternal background on children's 1986 home environments, and a general lack of evidence that these effects are mediated by current parental paid work or family structure.[2,3,4]

Interactions among Major Explanatory Variables

As noted in Chapter 2, we examine three types of interactions to more adequately assess the effects of parental work on children's lives. First, we consider the interactive effects of paid work and family conditions and parental cognitive and psychosocial resources. Second, we examine whether paid work interacts with family responsibilities. Third, we examine whether effects of one parent's paid working conditions interact with those of the other parent.

Regarding the first set of interactions, resources by conditions, we find an interaction between maternal psychosocial resources and spouse occupational complexity; variations in maternal resources are more critical when fathers' occupational complexity is low, and conversely, variations in fathers' occupational complexity are more critical when maternal resources are low. Echoing this pattern, the presence of a spouse is more positive when mothers' education is low.

We also find evidence of the second sort of interaction, between paid work and family conditions. The effects of mothers' wages, nonsignificant in the additive model, vary depending on family size; positive effects are more powerful when family size is low and blunted as family size increases.

Finally, we also find that effects of one parent's paid work conditions vary depending on the other's. The negative effects observed for fathers' low paid work hours vary depending on how much employed mothers are working. It is when mothers are also working less than full-time schedules that effects are most negative. This suggests that one parent's paid working conditions can offset the effects of the other's, with either partner's full-time paid work moderating any negative impact of part-time employment.

Interactions by Race and Gender

Chow tests for race and gender differences were not significant for race but were significant for gender. Significantly different effects were found for mother being married and for fathers' low part-time paid work hours. Marriage has a positive effect for both boys and girls but is more beneficial for boys; marriage is also more positive the lower the mother's education. Fathers' low paid work hours, adverse when mothers also work part-time, are more negative for boys than for girls.

Explaining 1988 Home Environments

Table 3.4 allows us to investigate whether these same factors influence levels of children's home environments in 1988, and whether we can also understand short-term changes in children's home environments within the same framework. As in Table 3.3, Panel 1 assesses the effects of parental and child background characteristics on home environments, in this case home environments in 1988. Panel 2 parallels the third panel of Table 3.3 and includes both parental and child characteristics and changes in both paid work and family variables in 1988. Panel 3 taps changes in children's home environments by including the 1986 levels of home environments as an explanatory variable in an equation that has 1988 level of home as a dependent variable. It also includes measures of both 1986 and 1988 parental paid working conditions, as well as direct measures of changes in family structure over the interval. Coefficients associated with the 1986 levels of independent variables in Panel 3 can therefore be interpreted as the direct lagged effects of 1986 levels on changes in home environments from 1986 to 1988. These coefficients underestimate the *total* lagged effect of 1986 levels since the indirect effects that operate through later levels of occupational conditions are statistically controlled. With these initial levels also in the equation, the coefficients for 1988 paid work variables represent the effects of recent changes in occupational conditions on changes in home environments (Kessler and Greenberg 1981). Where Panels 1 and 2 develop estimates of the cross-sectional effects of current (1988) parental employment status and family size, the change equations estimate the effects of changes in employment status and in family size over time by including dummy variables identifying patterns of employment status over time and the birth of additional children over the last 2 years.

The cross-sectional and change models provide complementary insights into the social processes producing and maintaining children's home environments. As several authors have noted, any cross-sectional regression models, no matter how well guided by theory, may still contain findings that are a function of specification error due to omitted variables (Rao and Miller 1971). A stricter test of the effects of such variables on any outcome is to estimate a change model that, by virtue of including the prior level of the dependent variable, includes the effects of omitted variables, thus eliminating this form of bias. Since the change equation controls for omitted variables, findings that appear in Panel 3 are less likely to have been produced through specification error than findings that appear in Panels 1 and 2. Nevertheless, the change model also has an important limitation. Because it controls for earlier levels of home environments, it will underestimate effects of variables with longer lags than the interval between the two time points. Thus, the nonchange models may contain additional findings that suggest hypotheses worthy of future investigation, particularly investigations that vary the lag between time points. We take these respective strengths into account when interpreting our findings.

The findings in Panel 1 parallel those in Table 3.3 in that maternal black and Mexican Hispanic ethnicities are negatively associated with home, while parental schooling and maternal self-concept have positive effects. In addition, we find slightly poorer home environments when children have older fathers, an effect not found in 1986. Also as in 1986, these effects are maintained when we add paid work and family characteristics to the model in Panel 2; in addition, maternal age has a weak positive effect. Family variables also have effects on 1988 levels: the anticipated positive effect of mother being married is significant, as is the anticipated negative effect of numbers of children in the household. However, 1988 occupational conditions do not have significant effects on the quality of 1988 home environments.

The data in Panel 3 suggest that it is useful to understand changes in children's home environments within the framework of changes in parental paid working conditions and family structure. Clearly, a strong predictor of the quality of children's home environments in 1988 is the quality of these environments 2 years earlier. Even with this stringent control, however, a number of background, parental paid working conditions, and family structure variables have significant effects. Boys experience weaker improvements in home environments over the interval than do girls, as do black children compared with whites. Higher levels of maternal education and more positive maternal self-concept are associated with improvements in home environments over the interval, while greater spouse age is associated with worsening of home environments over the same period. Higher levels of 1986 maternal occupational complexity and higher levels of 1986 maternal hourly wage are associated with improved home scores, as are 1988 low maternal part-time hours, relative to 1988 maternal full-time paid work. Higher 1986 paternal wages are associated with short-term improvements in children's home environments. However, 1986 paternal part-time paid work is associated with deterioration of home environments. Finally, family size strongly affects 1988 levels of children's home environments. Home environments in 1988 are negatively affected by number of children in

Table 3.4. 1988 Home: The Impact of Child, Background, 1986 Work, 1988 Work, 1988 Family, Family Changes 1986–1988, and 1986 Home (*N* = 721)

Variable	Child & background (1)		Child, background, work, & family 1986 (2)		Child, background, work 1986 & 1988, family changes, & home 1986 (3)	
	B	Beta	B	Beta	B	Beta
Child characteristics 1986						
Male	−.06	−.04	−.08	−.05	−.10c	−.07
Parental characteristics						
Mother						
Ethnicity						
Black	−.43a	−.22	−.39a	−.20	−.31a	−.16
White*	—	—	—	—	—	—
Mexican Hispanic	−.25d	−.07	−.24d	−.07	−.15	−.04
Other Hispanic	−.23	−.05	−.20	−.05	−.17	−.04
Age 1988	.01	.03	.03d	.07	.01	.03
Education 1988	.08a	.17	.07a	.14	.05c	.09
Positive self-concept	.20a	.21	.20a	.21	.14a	.15
Spouse						
Age 1988	−.02b	−.11	−.02b	−.10	−.02b	−.09
Education 1988	.04b	.10	.03c	.08	.01	.03
Maternal work characteristics 1986						
Occupational complexity					.01c	.09
Hourly wage					.02d	.07
Spouse work characteristics 1986						
Hourly wage					.01d	.06
Work hours						
0–35					−.62a	−.14
35–40*					—	—
Over 40					−.05	−.03
Maternal work characteristics 1988						
Work hours						
1–20			.20c	.08e	.22c	.09
21–34			.03	.01	−.00	−.00
35–40*			—	—	—	—
Over 40			.11	.04	.10	.04
Family characteristics 1988						
Married			.13c	.08		
Number of children			−.17a	−.19		
Family changes 1986–1988						
Number of children 1986					−.15a	−.15
Additional children born					−.24a	−.13

Table 3.4. (continued)

Variable	Child & background (1)		Child, background, work, & family 1986 (2)		Child, background, work 1986 & 1988, family changes, & home 1986 (3)	
	B	Beta	B	Beta	B	Beta
Home 1986					.22[a]	.26
Constant	−.47		−.32		.60	
R²	.18		.22		.33	
Adjusted R²	.16		.19		.29	

a, $p < .001$; b, $p < .01$; c, $p < .05$; d, $p < .10$; two-tailed test.

a, $p < .0005$; b, $p < .005$; c, $p < .025$; d, $p < .05$; one-tailed test.

e, set of dummy variables is not significant. *, reference category for categorical variable.

Note: Variables that are not significant in any panel are not displayed. All panels also control for Child health problems 1988, Low birth weight, and Maternal AFQT 1980. Panels 2 and 3 also control for Maternal occupational complexity 1988, Maternal hourly wage 1988, Mother stopped working 1986–1988, Spouse occupational complexity 1988, Spouse hourly wage 1988, and Spouse work hours 1988. Panel 3 also controls for Maternal work hours 1986, Spouse occupational complexity 1986, and Marriage patterns 1986–1988.

the family in 1986, as well as by the number of additional children born between 1986 and 1988. These findings provide important support for resource dilution effects within households.

Interactions among Major Explanatory Variables in Predicting Change

Again, we find that maternal resources are more critical under difficult conditions, with maternal self-concept more important when family size is large and the spouse has only part-time paid work in 1988. Similarly, maternal education is more important when spouses' 1988 wages are low. These interactions can also be expressed conversely in that the adverse effects of low spouse paid work hours, low spouse wages, and large family size are moderated when maternal resources are greater. Paid work and family changes also interact in their impact: neither stopping paid work nor ending one's marriage was significant alone, but the combination of both of these events is associated with declining home environment scores.

Race and Gender Differences

Chow tests for race and gender differences in the final 1988 home equation were not significant. Thus, we do not find support for the argument that short-term changes in home environments are generated by differing processes for boys than for girls or for black children than for other children.

SUMMARY AND DISCUSSION

We constructed this analysis of children's home environments around three issues. First, we were interested in providing one piece of evidence regarding the place of home environments in the causal chain of parental social background and child outcomes. We argued that the data in this chapter would inform the issue of whether parental paid working conditions and family structure influenced children's home environments, a necessary but not sufficient condition to establish whether children's home environments intervene between parental status and child outcomes. Second, to inform theory, we were interested in whether we could detect relationships between the quantity and nature of parental paid work demands and children's home environments as a means to infer whether parental paid work affected the quantity and nature of family social capital. Third, we considered whether the static models we had developed to predict variation in children's home environments in 1986 were also useful in understanding short-term changes in children's home environments.

The findings proved informative on each of these questions. First, the data clearly show that parental paid working conditions, family composition, and parental background are important predictors of both 1986 and 1988 children's home environments. Children's home environments are less positive when mothers are lower in self-concept, or when they are black or Mexican Hispanic as compared with white, and they are more positive when mothers are more educated. They are also less positive when family size is larger.

We also find that parental paid working conditions have discernible effects on children's home environments. That 1986 maternal complexity is associated with stronger home environments in 1986 and with improvements in home environments between 1986 and 1988 provides consistent support for the notion that the nature of parental paid work activities will influence children's home environments. The findings are clearly consistent with theory developed by Kohn and his colleagues suggesting that parental experience on the job influences parental values and behaviors relevant to parenting. In this case, mothers who work in occupations with more substantively complex activities create home environments that are more cognitively enriched and more affectively and physically appropriate than those created by mothers who work in occupations with less complex activities. Taking the effects of parental background and parental paid working conditions on home environments together, we have begun to trace one facet of the causal chain that links parental background with child outcomes.

The model also proves useful in studying short-term changes in children's home environments. Boys and blacks experience less improvement in home environments over the interval than girls and whites, while more positive maternal self-concept and higher levels of maternal schooling promote greater improvements in home environments. The birth of additional children is associated with less improvement in home environments. This finding provides important support for resource dilution effects, an inference that is reinforced in that the effect is present in both the 1986 and the 1988 models, as well as the change model. Parental paid work also influences changes in children's home environments. Higher levels of 1986 wages for both parents and high levels of 1986 maternal complexity are associated with short-term home improvements, as is low part-time maternal paid work in 1988. However, part-time paternal paid work in 1986 is associated with deteriorating home environments, and there is no significant relationship between maternal paid work hours in 1986 and short-term changes in children's home environments. These findings suggest that mothers and fathers do not substitute for one another in terms of their time inputs into family home environments. This is an important direction for future research, and one that may have practical implications for the strategies parents use to construct children's home environments. We return to this theme in our concluding chapter.

We also find that combinations of parental characteristics, family structure, and parental paid working conditions have nonadditive effects on the home environments that parents create for their children. For example, in understanding variation in 1986 children's home environments, we found that maternal self-concept was a more critical resource when fathers had jobs low in complexity. Mother's wages were not significant in the additive model, but showed positive effects when family size was low and reduced effects when family size was higher. Similarly, fathers' low work hours were more negative when mothers were also working part-time hours, and the presence of a spouse was more positive when mother's education was low. We found similar patterns in our study of short-term changes in children's home environments in that maternal self-concept took on greater importance when fathers were working only part-time in 1988, and when family size was large. The combination of divorce and stopping paid work was associated with decrements in home environments, and maternal education was more helpful when paternal wages were low. These findings strongly reinforce our inclination to simultaneously consider the roles of parental resources, parental paid work, and family structure on children's lives. We return to this theme in subsequent chapters as we continue to consider the idea that parental paid work may be more or less helpful to children, depending on other resources on which parents may draw as well as other responsibilities they must shoulder.

How much evidence do we have that parental paid working conditions influence the quantity and nature of family social capital, as evidenced by children's home environments? As noted above, the change equation indicates that parental paid work hours have differential effects on home depending on which parent is working, with low maternal hours in 1988 strengthening home environments but low paternal hours at the earlier time point weakening them when mothers were also working part-time. These findings provide evidence that the number of hours parents spend working will have an impact on family social capital. Lower maternal paid work hours may enable mothers to create stronger home environments by spending more time with their children, although mothers' stopping paid work entirely did not have a similar effect and moderate part-time paid work hours also conveyed no significant advantage. We also note that low paternal paid work hours at an earlier time point may, when combined with low maternal paid work hours, weaken the family's material base to the point where there are discernible effects on the nature of children's home experiences; note that these effects hold independent of parental wage levels. These findings also imply either that paternal low paid work hours do not result in fathers spending increased time to promote the home environment, or that such efforts do not result in a stronger cognitive or social atmosphere. It may also be that the psychological effect of low paternal paid work hours, clearly nonnormative in current society, may have deleterious effects on home environments that we cannot directly detect. On the other hand, very low maternal paid work effort appears to have positive effects on changes in the home over a 2-year interval. It appears as though the effects of parental paid work hours on home environments vary by parental gender, alerting us to potentially different roles that the parents in these families may be playing as they create environments to support children.

In contrast, although weak, the positive effects of both maternal and paternal 1986 wages suggest that earnings of both parents have positive effects on children's home environments, thus suggesting that this resource operates similarly regardless of parental gender. Finally, the positive effect of maternal complexity on short-term changes in children's home environments suggests that the complexity of parental paid work activities can be a resource for children as it contributes to strengthening the home environment that children experience. That paternal complexity has no effect for any of the home models we have considered suggests the possibility that, as with parental paid work hours, maternal and paternal occupational complexity may have differing effects on children's home environments. It is clearly appropriate to consider both maternal and paternal paid working conditions' effects on children's lives, since we cannot assume that their influences are the same.

Overall, these findings provide mixed support for Coleman's worries that maternal paid work is damaging to family social capital. Consistent with his concerns are the findings regarding 1988 low maternal paid work hours on changes in children's home environments, although there are no effects of maternal hours in 1986 or 1988 in cross-sectional analyses. Inconsistent are the positive effects of maternal complexity and wage levels. However, these findings are merely one piece of the puzzle. They may not be duplicated when we turn our attention to directly studying the child outcomes themselves or, alternatively, those findings may provide corroborating and compatible evidence on some or all of the issues we have considered here. We continue to consider these alternative possibilities as we turn directly to studying child cognitive and social outcomes themselves.

NOTES

1.   Two variables are reported in the form of Z scores: maternal self-concept, and Home 1986. In the general NLSY population of children they average zero and have a standard deviation of one. The self-concept measure averages close to zero for this sample, while 1986 children's home environments for this sample of children with employed mothers are a bit stronger than the zero average for all NLSY children.

2.   Our models consider mothers' and fathers' earnings from employment, but do not include controls for nonwage income, such as income from interest or dividends or income from local, state, or federal assistance programs. We evaluated the implications of this omission by examining amounts of other income and including nonwage income in final additive models predicting the 1986 levels of children's home environments that we study here, as well as the measures of child cognition (PPVT-R) and social adjustment (behavior problems) we study in Chapters 4 and 5.

Calculating nonwage family income as net family income minus income of self and spouse from wages, farm earnings, or military pay, we find that the median amount of nonwage income is $250 in 1986. Three-quarters of the mothers have less than $3,000 in nonwage income. Calculating this as a proportion of each mother's family income, we find that such income is less than 2% of income for half the sample, and less than 20% of total family income for 75% of the sample. We conclude that such income is limited in this group of young employed mothers.

Bivariate associations of nonwage income and 1986 outcome measures are all small and statistically nonsignificant; no correlation is greater than .07. When we add nonwage income as an additional predictor of 1986 outcomes to additive models that also include each parent's hourly wages, we find that nonwage income has weak ($p < .10$) positive effects on the quality of children's home environments and on children's PPVT-R scores, but no significant effect on their behavior problems. Controlling for variation in nonwage income does not significantly alter other findings.

3. We also compared the findings we obtained using dollar wage amounts and categorical paid work hours with models using the natural logs of parental wages and the natural logs of the hours worked for pay in the early years (see Chapter 6), in 1986, and in 1988. Substituting a logged form of wages should strengthen the effects of wages if the actual form of the relationship between wages and outcomes is characterized by diminishing returns at higher levels of wages. However, we do not find that effects are consistently affected in a single direction. Of the 12 final equations we reestimated, findings were unchanged in 7. Three effects that were significant at $p < .05$ became nonsignificant and in two cases a wage effect became significant at the $p < .10$ level where it had been nonsignificant. We conclude that we cannot reject the simpler linear form of the relationship between wages and outcomes.

Given the numerous nonlinearities in effects of paid work hours found in our models, especially of low-paid work hours for fathers, it is not surprising that models using logs of the continuous paid work hours variables generally explained somewhat lower proportions of variance overall than did the dummy forms of paid work hours. In several cases, the logged linear form of paid work hours was nonsignificant where we had found a strong nonlinear effect; in others, the sign and significance of the linear hours variables matched our findings, but without providing as much information. Overall, we conclude that effects of paid work hours are better captured by the set of dummy variables we use here.

4. Our models divide family economic resources into those contributed by mothers and those contributed by fathers. In families where two parents are present and the wage levels of mothers and fathers are correlated, it is possible that our strategy leads us to understate the direct contributions of total family income on children's home environments and cognitive and social outcomes. We also separate hours worked for pay and wages per hour; but the same wage rate yields far higher total earnings when the worker works longer paid work weeks than when he is employed less than full-time. For this reason also, our models may understate the contributions of total earnings.

To check this possibility, we examined the correlations between total family income and our outcome variables, and reestimated our final additive models substituting total family income for the two individual wage variables. Correlations between total family income and 1986 outcomes were similar to those for the individual parents' wages variables. For example, correlations with home environments were .12 for mothers' wages, .14 of spouse wages, and .13 for total family income; corresponding correlations with PPVT-R were .16, .13, and .18; and corresponding correlations with behavior problems were −.11, −.06 (ns), and −.12.

Substituting total family income for the two parents' wage variables in additive multivariate models, we find that total family income has no significant direct effects on home environments, PPVT-R, or behavior problems when background variables are controlled. For home environments, we had found no significant direct effects of either parents' wage; similarly, there is no direct effect of family income, and substituting this measure does not alter other findings. For PPVT-R, we had found a significant positive effect of mothers' wages, but not for fathers, on children's scores. When both parents' earnings are combined into a single overall family income measure, this pattern produces a weaker effect that falls below statistical significance ($p < .13$); other findings are unchanged. For children's 1986 behavior problems, we had found no significant direct effects of parents' wages once background was controlled. We reach the same conclusion using total family income; other findings remain unchanged except that the protective effects of mother being married, significant at $p < .10$ in our models, becomes nonsignificant net of total family income. Thus, it does not appear that our emphasis on wage income and on each spouse's hourly wage levels has caused us to underestimate effects of total economic resources in the family on children's outcomes. To the contrary: considering mothers' wages separately from fathers' permitted us to observe an effect of mothers' wages on children's receptive vocabulary that was obscured by the overall income measure.

Chapter 4

Parents' Jobs and Children's Cognition

We have argued that parents' jobs will affect children's cognitive outcomes. In this chapter we study the extent to which this is true, and specify the conditions under which the relationships we hypothesize to exist hold. We study both verbal facility, a measure of verbal aptitude, as well as cognitive achievement, as measured by both a reading and mathematics achievement test.

PREDICTING VERBAL FACILITY

Descriptive Findings

Table 4.1 displays the basic descriptive data and the zero-order correlations between PPVT-R, our measure of verbal facility, and our independent variables. Notice that the children's average PPVT-R (94.57) is below the normed average of 100, which likely reflects the disproportionate representation of children born to young mothers. Negative predictors of PPVT-R include being shy at the interview, nonwhite maternal ethnicity, and higher number of mothers' children. PPVT-R is positively associated with maternal age and schooling, maternal AFQT and self-concept, intact family of origin, grandmother's schooling, maternal wage and complexity levels, paternal wages, being married and children's home environments. These associations are consistent with our expectations. In addition, both sets of parental paid work hours are significantly associated with PPVT-R. Maternal full-time paid work hours are negatively related to PPVT-R, while maternal high part-time hours show a positive association. Paternal full-time paid work hours show a positive relationship, while part-time and over-time hours show negative associations. Our analyses allow for the possibility that there are nonlinear relationships between parental paid work hours and child outcomes.

Table 4.1.   1986 PPVT-R Sample: 1986 Variable Means, Standard Deviations, and Correlations with PPVT-R (*N* = 781)

Variable	Mean	Std. dev.	Correlation with PPVT-R 1986
PPVT-R 1986	94.57	17.28	
Child characteristics 1986			
Health problems	.05	.22	−.03
Shy in interview	−.02	1.02	−.10*
Low birth weight	.06	.23	−.05
Male	.50	.50	−.06
Parental characteristics			
Mother			
Ethnicity			
Black	.18	.39	−.41*
Mexican Hispanic	.04	.21	−.13*
White	.74	.44	.46*
Other Hispanic	.03	.18	−.08*
Age 1986	25.57	2.05	.18*
Education 1986	12.11	1.54	.14*
AFQT 1980	67.60	19.02	.41*
Positive self-concept	−.03	.82	.14*
Family of origin			
Two parents at age 14	.79	.40	.19*
Grandmother education	10.86	2.59	.26*
Spouse			
Age 1986	28.78	3.63	.03
Education 1986	12.20	1.71	.18*
Maternal work characteristics 1986			
Occupational complexity	−5.68	11.20	.15*
Hourly wage	5.67	2.95	.16*
Work hours			
1–20	.15	.36	.05
21–34	.19	.39	.11*
35–40	.56	.50	−.09*
Over 40	.11	.31	−.05
Spouse work characteristics 1986			
Occupational complexity	−5.43	10.05	.04
Hourly wage	9.31	5.20	.13*
Work hours			
Under 35	.04	.21	−.08
35–40	.57	.50	.10*
Over 40	.38	.49	−.07
Family characteristics 1986			
Married	.70	.46	.13*
Number of children	1.84	.77	−.14*
Home 1986	.21	.89	.34*

*Significant at *p* < .05, two-tailed test.

Multivariate Models Predicting PPVT-R

Table 4.2 displays the regression of child PPVT-R standardized scores on maternal employment variables under varying controls. Following our assumptions regarding temporal ordering of variables, we first control for both child and maternal characteristics (Panel 1). We then assess the effects of 1986 parental paid working conditions and family characteristics while controlling only for child background (Panel 2), and then include both maternal/paternal and child background as well as 1986 paid work and family characteristics (Panel 3). We subsequently include home environments (Panel 4). Panel 1 suggests that parental characteristics have strong effects on children's levels of verbal facility when aged 3–6. Maternal ethnicity is strongly related to child PPVT scores, with children of Hispanic and black mothers scoring lower than those of whites. Maternal age and measured mental ability positively affect child verbal facility, as does grandmother's schooling. In addition, higher levels of paternal schooling are associated with higher levels of child verbal facility. Only one child characteristic is associated with verbal facility. That is, being rated as shy/anxious by the interviewer is negatively associated with test performance.

Panel 2 demonstrates that all the maternal paid working conditions effects are statistically significant and appropriately signed when the maternal background characteristics are left uncontrolled. In particular, occupational complexity and hourly pay positively impact PPVT-R, and the functional form of the paid work hours dummies suggests benefits to child verbal facility for part-time paid work. Children's verbal facility also benefits from higher paternal hourly wages, and shows a weak negative relationship with paternal low work hours. Current family characteristics also have significant effects because mother being married and having fewer children are associated with higher child verbal facility. We note, however, that current paid work, family circumstances, and child background explain a much smaller proportion of variance in child PPVT-R than does the first model, i.e., .11 versus .28.

Panel 3 shows that the hours worked and earnings effects are maintained when the maternal background factors are reintroduced; for the first time we see that the coefficient differentiating overtime from full-time maternal paid work is negatively associated with PPVT-R, net of controls. We also see that this same relationship holds for fathers, thus suggesting that contemporaneous overtime paid work for both mothers and fathers may hinder child verbal facility. Occupational complexity is no longer significant net of maternal background, since jobs with complex work activities are held by those with higher levels of schooling and AFQT. Among the family characteristics, only number of children

Table 4.2. 1986 PPVT: The Impact of Child, Background, and Work, Family, and Home (N = 781)

Variable	Child & background 1		Child, work, & family 1986 2		Child, background, work, & family 1986 3		Child background, work, family, & home 1986 4	
	B	Beta	B	Beta	B	Beta	B	Beta
Child characteristics 1986								
Shy in interview	-1.43b	-.09	-1.33c	-.08	-1.28c	-.08	-1.15c	-.07
Male	-1.50	-.05	-1.95d	-.06	-1.54	-.05	-1.65d	-.05
Parental characteristics								
Mother								
Ethnicity								
Black	-15.05a	-.36			-14.78a	-.35	-13.85a	-.33
White*	—	—			—	—	—	—
Mexican Hispanic	-8.54a	-.11			-9.09a	-.12	-7.81b	-.10
Other Hispanic	-8.00b	-.09			-9.04b	-.10	-8.39b	-.09
Age 1986	.64c	.08			1.08a	.14	.90b	.11
AFQT 1980	.11b	.12			.10b	.12	.10b	.12
Family of origin								
Grandmother education	.79a	.12			.78a	.12	.78a	.12
Spouse								
Education 1986	.97c	.08			1.00c	.09	.75d	.07
Maternal work characteristics 1986								
Occupational complexity			.12c	.08	.04	.03	.02	.01
Hourly wage			.73a	.13	.40c	.07	.40c	.07

	Panel 1		Panel 2		Panel 3		Panel 4	
Work hours								
1–20			4.04[c]	.09	1.82	.04	1.56	.03
21–34			4.67[b]	.11	3.64[b]	.09	3.43[c]	.08
35–40*			—	—	—	—	—	—
Over 40			-1.26	-.02	-3.43[c]	-.07	-3.05[d]	-.06
Spouse work characteristics 1986								
Hourly wage			.31[c]	.08	-.05	-.01	-.05	-.01
Work hours								
0–35			-5.95[d]	-.06[e]	-3.89	-.04	-3.04	-.03
35–40*			—	—	—	—	—	—
Over 40			-1.63	-.04	-3.25[c]	-.08	-3.13[c]	-.08
Family characteristics 1986								
Married			5.34[a]	.15	-.54	-.02	-.73	-.02
Number of children			-3.37[a]	-.16	-3.31[a]	-.16	-2.71[a]	-.13
Home 1986							2.74[a]	.15
Constant	58.76[a]		91.51[a]		58.03[a]		65.26[a]	
R^2	.28		.11		.33		.34	
Adjusted R^2	.26		.10		.30		.32	

[a] $p < .001$; [b] $p < .01$; [c] $p < .05$; [d] $p < .10$; two-tailed test.
[a] $p < .0005$; [b] $p < .005$; [c] $p < .025$; [d] $p < .05$; one-tailed test.
[e] Set of dummy variables is not significant.
*Reference category for categorical variable.

Note: Variables that are not significant in any panel are not displayed. All panels also control for the following child characteristics: Child health problems 1986 and Low birth weight. Panels 1, 3, and 4 also control for the following background characteristics: Maternal education 1986. Maternal positive self-concept, Two parents at age 14, and Spouse age 1986. Panels 2, 3, and 4 also control for the work variable Spouse occupational complexity 1986.

retains significance, owing to selection processes favoring intact marriages and higher spousal earnings among mothers with more favored
background characteristics. The parental and child background characteristics we noted in Panel 1 all retain statistical significance, and the
inclusion of current paid work and family conditions increases
explained variance by about 14% over Panel 1 (.33 versus .28).

Panel 4 presents the final equation that incorporates measures of
child's home environments. Regarding child and maternal background,
the persistent racial effects remain and the weak gender effect reappears.
Even with home environments controlled, children continue to derive
advantage from greater maternal age, maternal AFQT, and grandmother's schooling. They also benefit from higher maternal hourly pay, and
while the lower category of part-time paid work is not statistically different from full-time paid work, the form of the relationship is nonlinear
as expected and the set of variables is statistically significant. Children's
home environment is a strong predictor of verbal facility, and additional analysis (not presented here) reveals that all subdimensions of home
environment contribute to this effect. Family size maintains its substantial negative effect. These findings suggest substantial support for the
effects of both parental background characteristics and home and family
variables on child verbal facility, with evidence that, in the presence of
stringent controls, parental paid working conditions are also relevant.[1]

Assessing Statistical Interactions Suggested by Theory

We now evaluate a number of interactive hypotheses to further our
understanding of the determinants of child verbal facility (data not
shown). Maternal AFQT score, a significant positive predictor of child
PPVT in the additive model, interacts with the occupational complexity
of fathers' occupation. Consistent with the argument that maternal
resources are particularly important when conditions are more difficult,
variations in maternal cognitive skills have a greater impact when
fathers are employed in occupations that provide little complexity, and
are less important when fathers' occupational complexity is greater.
Conversely, fathers' occupational complexity is more critical for children
whose mothers are lower in cognitive skills. There is also evidence for a
stress-amplifying process such that the combination of poor paid working conditions and difficult family circumstances has multiplicative
effects. Specifically, larger family size, negative overall, is particularly
adverse when fathers' wages are low.

When two parents are present, effects of each parents' paid working
conditions may be amplified or buffered by the other's conditions. We
find that the strength of the effects of mothers' wages, significant and

positive overall, varies depending on the extent of fathers' paid work hours, with wages particularly crucial when fathers are working less than full-time. Conversely, adverse effects of fathers' low paid work hours are offset by higher maternal wages.

Assessing Statistical Interaction by Race and Gender

Chow tests for race and gender differences in the final equation were nonsignificant for child gender but significant for race. Race differences in effects were minor, however, with a trend ($p < .10$) for benefits of high maternal wages to be weaker for black children than for others.[2]

PREDICTING LATER READING AND ARITHMETIC SKILLS

We now consider whether the models we have developed to investigate parental paid working conditions' effects on children's early verbal facility are also useful in studying children's later cognitive achievement. To address this, we follow our sample of children forward 2 years to 1988 when they were aged 5–8. By this time, at least some formal schooling has taken place for most children. As we noted in Chapter 2, the NLSY administered both PIAT reading and PIAT mathematics Achievement tests to all children at least 5 years old in 1988. Thus, we can assess the extent to which data on PPVT-R form a useful basis for predictability to later achievement, and whether the parental background and paid working conditions effects important in understanding PPVT-R have similar important effects on early achievement.

Descriptive Findings

Table 4.3 presents the means and standard deviations of the sample we use to study PIAT math and PIAT reading. Because these outcomes are measured in 1988, we use 1988 measures of parental background conditions where possible. However, since the sample is close to coincident with the sample we used to study PPVT-R, and because characteristics such as parental schooling change minimally over the 2-year period, the basic descriptive characteristics of the sample are similar to those described in Chapter 3. Wages of both parents have risen, as have average levels of occupational complexity, although they remain below average. The distribution of paternal paid work effort is similar to that in 1986, but 21% of the mothers are no longer employed. Among the employed mothers, a higher proportion of mothers work for pay full-time as opposed to either of the part-time categories.

There have been additional changes in family configuration during the 2-year interval. Although 61% of the sample were married at both time points and 22% were unmarried at both points, 9% were divorced and 7% began a marriage. More than 1 in 5 bore additional children in this interval. Children's home environments are stronger in 1988 than in 1986.

The final columns of Table 4.3 show how these independent variables are related at the zero-order level to math and reading achievement. The two outcome measures are themselves correlated at .52. A few variables are significantly associated with both of these outcomes. Maternal schooling, wages, occupational complexity, paternal wages, and children's home environments are positively associated with children's measured levels of achievement, while increased numbers of children are associated with lower levels of measured achievement. PIAT math is also positively associated with maternal age, and being stably married, but negatively associated with divorcing and being stably single. In addition, there is a negative relationship between maternal full-time paid work and PIAT-Math, but a positive relationship with maternal high part-time hours. Fathers' occupational complexity is a positive predictor of children's reading achievement while paternal low work hours is negatively associated with reading achievement.

Multivariate Models Predicting PIAT reading

Table 4.4 presents models predicting PIAT reading as a function of several sets of background, family, and paid working conditions variables. Panel 1 shows the effects of maternal and child background on PIAT reading among 5- to 8-year-olds. In Panel 2 we add the effects of current 1988 paid work and family conditions to these background controls. Panel 3 adds 1988 children's home environments to the variables included in Panel 2. Panel 4 allows us to investigate the effects of changes in parental paid work and family conditions on children's early reading achievement. We assess the effects of these changes by including measures of both 1986 and 1988 parental paid work and family conditions in the model. We also control for PPVT-R, thus providing control for the effects of early verbal facility on early reading achievement. Finally, Panel 5 maintains these controls and, in addition, controls for both 1986 and 1988 children's home environments. Thus, this panel assesses the effects of change in children's home environments on early reading achievement, net of the effects of change in parental paid working conditions and family structure.

Table 4.3.   1988 PIAT Samples: 1988 Variable Means, Standard Deviations, and Correlations with 1988 Dependent Variables ($N = 721$)

Variable	Mean	Std. dev.	Correlation with Math 1988	Correlation with Read 1988
PIAT Math 1988	101.81	11.72		.52*
PIAT Reading 1988	105.22	11.50		
Child characteristics 1988				
Health problems	.03	.16	.01	−.02
Parental characteristics				
Mother				
Age 1988	27.57	2.04	.14*	.04
Education 1988	12.18	1.55	.19*	.26*
Spouse				
Age 1988	31.19	4.65	.02	.01
Education 1988	12.20	2.19	.07	.20*
Maternal work characteristics 1988				
Occupational complexity	−3.76	10.46	.10*	.09*
Hourly wage	7.08	3.63	.18*	.20*
Stopped working (since 1986)	.21	.41	−.07	−.01
Work hours				
1–20	.12	.33	−.08	−.05
21–34	.14	.35	.14*	.08
35–40	.62	.49	−.10*	.01
Over 40	.12	.33	.08	−.04
Spouse work characteristics 1988				
Occupational complexity	−3.69	10.22	.08	.12*
Hourly wage	10.85	6.84	.10*	.16*
Work hours				
Under 35	.05	.23	−.05	−.11*
35-40	.59	.49	.00	.07
Over 40	.36	.48	.02	−.02
Family changes 1986–1988				
Marriage patterns				
Stably married	.61	.49	.13*	.01
Marriage ended	.09	.29	−.11*	−.04
Marriage started	.07	.25	.00	−.03
Stably single	.24	.43	−.07*	.03
Additional children born	.22	.42	.02	.04
Family characteristics 1988				
Number of children	2.06	.84	−.06	−.10*
Home 1988	.51	.76	.29*	.27*

*Significant at $p < .05$, two-tailed test.

Table 4.4. 1988 PIAT Reading: The Impact of Child, Background, Work 1986, Work 1988, Family 1988, Family Changes 1986–1988, Home 1986, Home 1988, and PPVT 1986 (N = 721)

Variable	Child, background (1) B	Beta	Child, background, work, & family 1988 (2) B	Beta	Child, background, work, family & home 1988 (3) B	Beta	Child, background work 1986 & 1988, family changes, & PPVT (4) B	Beta	Child, background work 1986 & 1988, family changes, home 1986 & 1988, & PPVT (5) B	Beta
Child characteristics 1988										
Low birth weight	-4.70^b	-.09	-4.34^c	-.08	-4.43^c	-.09	-4.31^c	-.08	-4.71^b	-.09
Male	-2.09^b	-.09	-1.79^c	-.08	-1.60^c	-.07	-1.71^c	-.08	-1.53^d	-.07
Parental characteristics										
Mother										
Age 1988	-.42^c	-.08	-.26	-.05	-.32	-.06	-.36	-.07	-.46^c	-.08
Education 1988	.72^c	.10	.65^c	.09	.49	.07	.45	.06	.32	.04
AFQT 1980	.17^a	.28	.18^a	.29	.18^a	.30	.17^a	.28	.17^a	.29
Positive self-concept	.93^d	.07	1.04^d	.08	.57	.04	.99^d	.07	.48	.03
Spouse										
Education 1988	.51^c	.08	.29	.05	.20	.03	.11	.02	.09	.01
Maternal work characteristics 1988										
Occupational complexity			-.08^d	-.07	-.09^d	-.07	-.10^c	-.08	-.10^c	-.08
Stopped working (since 1986)			1.50	.05	1.64^d	.06	1.43	.05	1.43	.05
Spouse work characteristics 1988										
Hourly wage			.24^b	.11	.25^b	.11	.17^d	.08	.19^c	.09

	Panel 1		Panel 2		Panel 3		Panel 4		Panel 5	
Work hours										
0–35			-6.67^b	−.11	-6.21^b	−.10	-4.85^c	−.08[e]	-4.64^d	−.08[e]
35–40*			—	—	—	—	—	—	—	—
Over 40			−.77	−.03	−.57	−.02	−.16	−.01	−.10	−.00
Family characteristics 1988										
Number of children			-1.17^c	−.09	−.77	−.06				
Family changes 1986–1988										
Number of children 1986							-1.24^c	−.08	−.69	−.05
Home 1986									1.24^c	.10
Home 1988					2.36^a	.16			1.66^b	.11
PPVT 1986							$.12^a$	.17	$.10^a$	.15
Constant	91.00^a		89.77^a		90.52^a		84.88^a		87.48^a	
R^2	.17		.21		.23		.24		.26	
Adjusted R^2	.16		.18		.20		.20		.22	

[a] $p < .001$; [b] $p < .01$; [c] $p < .05$; [d] $p < .10$; two-tailed test.
[a] $p < .0005$; [b] $p < .005$; [c] $p < .025$; [d] $p < .05$; one-tailed test.
[e] Set of dummy variables is not significant.
*Reference category for categorical variable.

Note: Variables that are not significant in any panel are not displayed. All panels also control for Child health problems 1988, Maternal ethnicity, and Spouse age 1988. Panels 2–5 also control for the following 1988 work and family variables: Maternal hourly wage 1988, Maternal work hours 1988, Spouse occupational complexity 1988, and Married 1988. Panels 4–5 also control for the following 1986 work variables and family changes: Maternal occupational complexity 1986, Maternal hourly wage 1986, Maternal work hours 1986, Spouse occupational complexity 1986, Spouse hourly wage 1986, Spouse work hours 1986, Marriage patterns 1986–1988, and Additional children born 1986–1988.

Panel 1 suggests that both child and parental background characteristics have important effects on early reading achievement. Boys and children with low birth weights are at a disadvantage in early reading achievement. Children with more educated mothers and fathers, and with mothers who have higher levels of measured mental ability and stronger self-concepts, are more advantaged in early reading skills. With these factors controlled, older mothers have children with lower levels of reading achievement. This may reflect selectivity effects not captured by variables included in the models; with other background variables controlled, older mothers, who necessarily bore these target children sooner, may fail to use the resources we commonly associate with age to their children's advantage. Panel 2 adds measures of 1988 parental paid working conditions and family configuration; the findings suggest that these effects are relatively sparse. Greater numbers of children in the family hinder reading achievement, as does paternal low work hours. Children are advantaged by higher levels of paternal wages, but unexpectedly hindered by higher levels of maternal complexity ($p < .10$). Addition of these paid work and family conditions does result in some "washing-out" of maternal age and paternal education effects, although maternal AFQT, schooling, and self-concept retain significance.

Panel 3 incorporates the measure of children's 1988 home environments. We find that children's home environments in 1988 are important determinants of their early reading achievement. We also note that controlling for home environments "explains" the findings involving number of children, as well as the positive effects of maternal schooling and self-concept. That is, the effects of number of children, maternal schooling, and maternal self-concept operate through children's home environments. Panel 4 adds PPVT-R, our measure of verbal facility, to the model predicting reading achievement and also controls for earlier (1986) paid work and family conditions. We see that PPVT-R is a strong predictor of early reading achievement, although not as strong as maternal measured mental ability. Addition of PPVT-R and earlier paid work and family conditions leaves most of the findings from Panel 3 unchanged, with the exception that the negative effect of paternal underemployment becomes nonsignificant with PPVT-R controlled. As found in Panel 2, we find some support for resource diffusion effects associated with greater numbers of children, and positive effects of maternal resources implied in maternal self-concept; these effects become nonsignificant when home environments are controlled. We note that both 1986 and 1988 home environments exert positive and substantial effects on early reading achievement. As in Panel 3, the family size and self-concept effects disappear, and as in Panel 1, the effect of maternal age is negative.

Assessing Statistical Interactions Suggested by Theory

The additive model had suggested that increases in mothers' occupational complexity had an adverse impact on children's reading scores, which was inconsistent with our theoretical expectations. Interactive tests modified this conclusion since increases in mothers' complexity had a significant negative impact only for the subset of mothers who had also had an additional child between 1986 and 1988. We have argued that a higher level of substantive complexity in one's occupation should benefit children. This interaction suggests, however, that the combination of a mother's taking on increasing challenges on the job at the same time that family size is increasing as well may hinder the development of children's reading skills.

Although maternal work hours were not significant overall, there is an interactive effect of work hours. Specifically, very low paid work hours were more negative than full-time schedules for mothers who had an additional child but not for other mothers. We have argued earlier that when mothers' paid work hours are very low, regular child care arrangements and a more equitable division of household labor that would support mothers' employment may be less likely to occur. Mothers who cut back drastically on their paid work schedules in part to accommodate the recent birth of a child may end up with less supportive arrangements than they enjoyed formerly, resulting in lower than expected cognitive gains for their children. Thus, while increased job complexity may take a toll when mothers have had additional children, reductions in paid work hours also appear problematic.

Assessing Statistical Interaction by Race and Gender

Chow tests for race and gender effects proved nonsignificant for race but significant for gender. Two variables that had not been significant in the combined models had significantly differing effects for boys and girls. *Mother's new marriage* had significant adverse effects for girls but had no effect for boys. Interestingly, *children's health problems* were associated with lower reading skills for boys but with higher reading skills for girls, producing the overall near-zero coefficient in the combined models.

These findings suggest that the process that determines early reading achievement is somewhat different from the process that determines verbal facility as measured 2 years earlier. Parental wages and hours exert a stronger effect on verbal facility than on reading achievement, although parental wages are significant for both outcomes. Parental personal and family resources figure prominently in both models, although the specific resources vary somewhat. Maternal AFQT and children's home environments are important in both models, but maternal race is important only in predicting verbal facility, not in actual early reading skills.

Multivariate Models Predicting PIAT-Math

Table 4.5 uses the same analytic strategy to assess the effects of key independent constructs on early mathematics achievement. Panel 1 suggests that maternal and child background characteristics are important in predicting this outcome. Boys lag slightly behind girls, and children are noticeably handicapped by low birth weight. Blacks and Mexican Hispanics score lower than whites, and children of more highly educated mothers and those with higher levels of measured mental ability score better. Panel 2 suggests that these effects are maintained with the addition of controls for paid work and family characteristics at the time of assessment; in addition, a weak positive effect of maternal age appears. Surprisingly, relative to children of mothers who work full-time, children of mothers who work high part-time and over-time hours are advantaged, while children of mothers who work low part-time hours are disadvantaged. Children with married mothers do slightly better than children with unmarried mothers, and children in families with greater numbers of children do somewhat worse than children in smaller families.

Panel 3 suggests that the family characteristic effects just noted are due to their effects on current home environments. In addition, maternal age, maternal schooling, and child gender effects work through home environments as well. Panels 4 and 5 allow us to assess the effects of change on early mathematics achievement. Panel 4 taps changes in parental paid work and family configuration over the 2-year interval; it also controls for PPVT-R. Panel 5 assesses the effects of these changes as well as changes in children's home environments during the same period. Panel 4 suggests that controlling for PPVT-R explains the association between race and mathematics achievement. In addition, with PPVT-R controlled, paternal low work hours and paternal overtime paid work in 1986 appears to have lagged negative effects on mathematics achievement, relative to paternal full-time paid work at that time. In addition, a negative effect of paternal education appears. Panel 5 suggests that for math achievement, both 1986 home and improvements in home have positive effects. The remaining effects from Panel 4 are maintained and a weak negative maternal self-esteem effect appears, except for paternal low work hours.

Assessing Statistical Interactions Suggested by Theory

Our puzzling additive findings regarding mothers' paid work hours are explained by patterns of statistical interaction. That is, mothers' 1988 paid work hours interact with the birth of additional children; we find that mothers' 1988 paid work hours have significant effects *only* for mothers who have had an additional child. For them, very low paid work hours are associated with worse math skills, consistent with the pattern observed for reading outcomes. However, moderate part-time hours tend to be better than full-time schedules for those who are also new mothers, while overtime schedules are not significantly different from full-time schedules for any group of mothers.

Effects of parents' increases in occupational complexity varied depending on family size, with 1988 complexity scores of both parents more positive when family size was low than when there were higher family demands. This pattern recalls the finding for reading skills that increased occupational complexity for mothers who had recently increased their family size had adverse effects. Again, it appears that occupational complexity, which we have argued should have generally good effects for children, is also a challenge that absorbs the time and emotional energy of adult workers in a way that may not be fully compatible with larger numbers of children or with recent additions to family size.

Changes in mothers' employment status from 1986 to 1988 had differing effects depending on mothers' 1986 paid working conditions. Withdrawal from the labor force had a strong *positive* effect on children's scores when mothers had been working overtime schedules but no effect for other mothers.

Effects of parents' 1988 wage levels also vary, with low wages particularly negative when other resources are also low. In particular, mothers' wages have more powerful effects for less well educated mothers, and fathers' wages have more powerful effects when home environments are less strong. Conversely, these interactions suggest that family resources are particularly critical when paid work rewards are low.

Assessing Statistical Interactions by Race and Gender

As found for PIAT reading equations, Chow tests for race and gender differences in models of arithmetic skills were nonsignificant for race but significant for gender. Both very low 1986 maternal paid work hours and low 1986 paternal paid work hours had significant negative effects on boys' later arithmetic skills but no significant effects for girls.

SUMMARY AND DISCUSSION

In this chapter we have been concerned with the effects of parental paid working conditions, family structure, and parental and child back-

Table 4.5. 1988 PIAT Math: The Impact of Child, Background, Work 1986, Work 1988, Family 1988, Family Changes 1986–1988, Home 1986, Home 1988, and PPVT 1986 (N = 721)

Variable	Child, background (1) B	Beta	Child, background, work, and family 1988 (2) B	Beta	Child, background, work, family, and home 1988 (3) B	Beta	Child, background work 1986 & 1988, family changes, & PPVT (4) B	Beta	Child, background work 1986 & 1988, family changes, home 1986 & 1988, & PPVT (5) B	Beta
Child characteristics 1988										
Low birth weight	-5.66^b	$-.11$	-5.35^b	$-.10$	-5.46^b	$-.10$	-5.37^b	$-.10$	-5.86^a	$-.11$
Male	-1.39^d	$-.06$	-1.33^d	$-.06$	-1.10	$-.05$	-1.24	$-.05$	-1.05	$-.05$
Parental characteristics										
Mother										
Ethnicity										
Black	-4.68^a	$-.16$	-4.00^b	$-.14$	-2.92^c	$-.10$	-2.06	$-.07$ [e]	-1.05	$-.04$ [e]
White*	—	—	—	—	—	—	—	—	—	—
Mexican Hispanic	-4.41^c	$-.08$	-4.25^c	$-.08$	-3.58^d	$-.07$	-2.80	$-.05$	-1.76	$-.03$
Other Hispanic	-1.92	$-.03$	-1.41	$-.02$	$-.84$	$-.01$	$.50$	$.01$	$.83$	$.01$
Age 1988	$.30$	$.05$	$.40^d$	$.07$	$.32$	$.06$	$.24$	$.04$	$.11$	$.02$
Education 1988	$.70^c$	$.09$	$.49^d$	$.07$	$.29$	$.04$	$.28$	$.04$	$.13$	$.02$
AFQT 1980	$.15^a$	$.24$	$.14^a$	$.23$	$.15^a$	$.24$	$.13^a$	$.21$	$.14^a$	$.23$
Positive self-concept	$-.20$	$-.01$	$-.21$	$-.01$	$-.78$	$-.05$	$-.32$	$-.02$	$-.95^d$	$-.07$
Spouse										
Education 1988	$-.10$	$-.02$	$-.32$	$-.05$	$-.41$	$-.06$	$-.54^c$	$-.08$	$-.56^c$	$-.09$
Spouse work characteristics 1986										
Work hours										
0–35							-4.30^d	$-.06$	-2.46	$-.04$

	b	β	b	β	b	β	b	β	b	β
35–40*							—		—	
Over 40							−2.86[b]	−.10	−2.82[b]	−.10
Maternal work characteristics 1988										
Work hours										
1–20			−2.47[d]	−.06	−3.04[c]	−.08	−2.71[d]	−.07	−3.11[c]	−.08
21–34			2.76[c]	.07	2.67[c]	.07	2.30[d]	.06	2.09	.06
35–40*			—		—		—		—	
Over 40			2.64[d]	.07	2.32[d]	.06	2.74[c]	.07	2.37[d]	.06
Family characteristics 1988										
Married			1.58[d]	.06	1.22	.05				
Number of children			−1.25[c]	−.09	−.77	−.06				
Home 1986					2.81[a]	.19			1.81[a]	.14
Home 1988									1.79[b]	.12
PPVT 1986							.15[a]	.22	.13[a]	.18
Constant	79.83[a]		81.19[a]		82.08[a]		75.62[a]		79.48[a]	
R^2	.17		.20		.23		.27		.30	
Adjusted R^2	.16		.18		.20		.23		.26	

a, $p < .001$; b, $p < .01$; c, $p < .05$; d, $p < .10$; two-tailed test.

a, $p < .0005$; b, $p < .005$; c, $p < .025$; d, $p < .05$; one-tailed test.

e, set of dummy variables is not significant. *, reference category for categorical variable.

Note: Variables that are not significant in any panel are not displayed. All panels also control for Child health problems 1988 and Spouse age 1988. Panels 2–5 also control for the following 1988 work variables: Maternal occupational complexity 1988, Maternal hourly wage 1988, Spouse occupational complexity 1988, Spouse hourly wage 1988, and Spouse work hours 1988. Panels 4 and 5 also control for the following 1986 work variables and family changes: Maternal occupational complexity 1986, Maternal hourly wage 1986, Maternal work hours 1986, Spouse occupational complexity 1986, Spouse hourly wage 1986, Marriage patterns 1986–1988, Number of children 1986, and Additional children born 1986–1988.

ground on child cognition. Theoretically, we are interested in whether variations in the quantities and forms of family social capital, as a function of paid work, family, and/or background, are having discernible effects on child cognition. Findings from the analysis of PPVT-R suggest that while parental paid working conditions influence levels of PPVT-R among 3–6 year olds, the strongest influences come from maternal background characteristics and current family structure and home environments. Higher levels of maternal AFQT, stronger home environments, greater maternal age, higher levels of spouse education, and higher levels of maternal grandmothers' schooling are all associated with greater verbal facility, while nonwhite maternal race, being male, being shy, and the family having greater numbers of children are associated with lower levels of verbal facility. Two types of parental paid working conditions also influence verbal facility. Higher levels of maternal wages are associated with higher levels of PPVT-R, and overtime hours by either parent are negatively associated with PPVT-R.

Several of these findings provide evidence regarding how the forms and amounts of family social capital may be influencing child cognition. The resources that parents bring to the family in terms of their cognitive capabilities, their educational levels or those of other family members, their financial contribution to the family, and the home environments that they create suggest variation in the forms and nature of social capital on which parents can draw during the socialization process. Findings regarding the negative effects of higher numbers of children and overtime parental paid work hours, as well as salutary effects of high part-time maternal paid work hours, speak to the importance of the quantity of family social capital devoted to children. The interactive effects are consistent with these interpretations since forms of social capital as represented by maternal AFQT and wages are more important under adverse conditions involving paternal low work hours and fathers occupying low-complexity jobs. Similarly, resource dilution effects indicated by greater family size are more detrimental when family wages are low.

The racial effects are more troublesome to interpret. They clearly persist across specifications, and do not diminish noticeably with the addition of parental paid working conditions, family structure, and children's home environments. They may capture forms of test bias untapped by controlling for children's initial levels of shyness, and/or they may reflect cultural differences in the nature/amounts of family social capital devoted to children also untapped by other controls. They may also tap everyday stressors inherent in minority group status. Below we consider the strength of these findings relative to the nonsignificance of race in the models of reading and mathematics achievement.

Given our analyses of verbal facility as well as both reading and mathematics achievement in early childhood, we are able to identify continuities in prediction from verbal facility to reading achievement, and similarities in the determinants of the two forms of cognitive achievement. The findings suggest that there are relatively few common predictors across these sets of equations. As with PPVT-R, children's reading achievement benefits from maternal AFQT and stronger home environments, and is lower for boys than for girls (see Panel 3 in Table 4.4). However, we fail to observe the effects of race, number of children, parental paid work hours, and family educational levels that were present for PPVT-R. Instead, the findings regarding the effects of changes in parental paid working conditions and in family structure/home environments suggest that in addition to the AFQT and sex effects noted above, improvements in children's home environments between 1986 and 1988 promote reading achievement. In addition, higher spouse wages in 1988 and higher PPVT-R in 1986 promote reading achievement, while low birth weight has a negative effect.

Unexpectedly maternal age has a negative effect on PIAT reading. So there are fewer direct sources of influence on reading achievement than on verbal facility, with the strongest effects attributable to AFQT, changes in home environments, and PPVT-R. In Chapter 7 we consider the roles that background characteristics that work through PPVT-R are playing in indirectly affecting reading achievement. The interactive findings provide additional support for the resource dilution hypothesis in that increases in maternal complexity and low maternal paid work hours are detrimental only if the number of children increases during the 2-year interval. Again, the quantity of family social capital, i.e., the amount of parental time investment in children, appears relevant for children's reading achievement.

The findings regarding PIAT math bear similarity to both those regarding PPVT-R and PIAT reading. Findings involving the positive effects of AFQT and 1986 home environments suggest that the nature of family social capital can promote or hinder children's mathematics achievement, while findings regarding parental paid work hours point to concerns regarding the quantity of time parents may have to promote their children's cognitive skills. But hasty conclusions suggesting that more parental time at home is better would be unwarranted. Low paid work hours are detrimental to math skills of children whose mothers have borne an additional child during the interval, while moderate part-time paid work hours are better than full-time schedules in cases of additional children. Also, increases in parental complexity are helpful when family sizes are smaller, and maternal labor force withdrawal helps if mothers had been working overtime. Thus, particular combinations of paid work and family circumstances may be more or less helpful to promoting child achievement. Other interactions point to combinations of paid work and family conditions that may alter the forms of family social capital used in socialization; maternal financial resources matter more when mothers are less educated, while paternal wages matter more when home environments are weaker. These findings suggest the possibility of some trade-off between paid work and family in constructing appropriate social capital for children. It may be that if one set of resources is weaker, stronger resources in the other sphere may partially compensate in providing a socialization environment that facilitates cognitive achievement. We return to this theme in our concluding chapter.

NOTES

1.   As indicated by our discussion in Chapter 1, it is also possible that the characteristics of the child care environment will influence either child cognition or child social behavior, or both. Although this might be a major alternative explanation of child outcomes, we find that, for our sample, these effects are not evident for either dependent variable. We therefore do not display these analyses in this or subsequent chapters, but instead address this issue in detail in the Appendix. We return to the implications of these findings in our concluding chapter.

2.   We also estimated equations distinguishing unmarried mothers who had a male partner living in the household (19% of the unmarried mothers) and identifying the presence of the mother's mother in the household (10% of all mothers, and 23% of unmarried mothers). These aspects of family composition had no significant effect. Because the effects might vary with mothers' marital status, these variables were also entered into separate equations for the unmarried mothers only; again, even in this subgroup, neither the presence of grandmother nor of boyfriends had a significant direct effect. We also tested the possibility that the effect of grandmother's education would be greater when grandmother was present in the household; however, this interaction was not statistically significant in the full sample or in the separate equation for unmarried mothers.

Chapter 5

Parents' Jobs and Children's Behavior Problems

How do families transmit norms and behavioral patterns across generations? Do children who exhibit behavior problems in early childhood necessarily continue in these patterns into the middle childhood years? Or does children's social behavior change in response to changing parental occupational conditions and altered family circumstances? In this analysis we investigate the impact of parental personal resources, family composition, and parental paid working conditions on both levels of behavior problems in the early school age years and on the changes in these problems that have occurred over a 2-year period.

As we noted in Chapter 1, children's social behavior during childhood concerns both parents and researchers, both because social adjustment is important at any age after infancy, and because poor adjustment may impair well-being in adolescence and adulthood. Children who are aggressive, or undercontrolled, during early childhood often persist in this pattern (Fischer et al. 1984; Caspi et al. 1987, 1988; Kohlberg et al. 1972; Patterson et al. 1989), with long-term implications including negative labels from teachers, academic difficulties, and peer rejection. These consequences disrupt opportunities to develop better social skills, thus encouraging the persistence of aggression (Patterson and Bank 1989; Patterson et al. 1989). The anxiety, fearfulness, and social withdrawal that characterize overcontrolled behavior also tend to persist, since such behaviors impede normal assertiveness in social situations (Caspi et al. 1987).

In this chapter we argue that the forms of workplace control parents experience on the job will influence their parenting styles at home, as will family composition and parental personal resources. Both parenting styles and parental personal resources influence the transmission of appropriate social controls across generations. As these resources change, they have implications for changes in children's social adjustment.

Coleman's (1988, 1990) claims regarding the role of social capital in the socialization process provide theoretical guidance for the analysis.

87

We have noted that social capital clearly includes the time and effort that parents actually spend on children. It refers both to the quantity and quality of interaction and the bonds that develop among family members. However, Coleman also argues that norms are a critical form of social capital. Can recent increases in maternal labor force participation limit the social capital needed to effectively transmit appropriate norms and behavior patterns across generations?

Coleman argues that at the individual level, mothers employed outside the home may have reduced time available both to establish bonds with children and to use these bonds to encourage appropriate social behaviors. These arguments point to concern regarding the *duration* of parental-child contact. Collectively, there may be reductions in the time mothers spend in the local community contributing to the web of interactions it represents and drawing upon its resources in the interests of their children. Such arguments assume no change in fathers' time with children or in the local community.

Given the reality that increasing proportions of mothers with infants and young children *are* working for pay outside the home, however, we have argued that paid work activities of both parents now influence the social capital available to children and the forms of social control they experience at home, as well as influencing the household material base and parental availability. Moreover, we must consider more than paid work hours and the *amount* of parent time available for children. Parents vary widely in the paid working conditions they encounter, and we expect these variations to have theoretically expectable consequences for the quality of parental interaction with children and the *nature* of social capital relevant to child socialization. In addition, the social capital embedded in family structure, as well as parental personal characteristics, should affect child socialization. Therefore, we also study how variations in parental personal resources and in family composition may influence internalization of behavioral norms.

We also argue that studying *change* in behavior problems provides a more demanding test of the effects of parental paid working conditions and family composition on this social outcome than does estimating nonchange models of behavior problems. Changes in parental employment status and employers may reduce parental attention to young children as well as produce short-term family economic strain (Downey and Moen 1987). Changes in family composition may also alter the amount or quality of parental attention given to young children, and thus influence later levels of behavior problems.

As noted above, an alternative to each of these explanations is that relatively stable parental personal characteristics will be critical to influencing children's social behavior in middle childhood. Parents who believe that their own actions and initiative substantially influence their own life outcomes are likely to adopt an active as opposed to passive model in parenting. Such an active model likely includes parental efforts at encouraging children to adopt internal models of personal behavior. We argue that these internal models should result in children exhibiting fewer behavior problems than parenting models that either fail to stress internal standards or frequently feature external contingencies such as physical punishment.

We now develop arguments regarding why (1) parents' occupational conditions and (2) family composition should influence children's behavior problems. We then review more established literature suggesting the impact of parental social characteristics on children's behavior problems, in preparation for testing models that synthesize these explanations to investigate levels of behavior problems and short-term changes in this aspect of child social behavior.

THEORETICAL BACKGROUND

Why Should Occupational Conditions Matter?

Jobs vary in the form of control that employers exercise, and we argue that the form of workplace control that parents experience will influence their parenting styles. Edwards (1979) distinguishes among (1) simple hierarchy, exemplified by the personalistic boss-worker relationship found in small shops and informal work settings; (2) technical control, e.g., the pace of the assembly line dictates the pace of paid work and the degree of division of labor; and (3) bureaucratic control, where management controls workers by promoting a rules orientation, consistency in work habits, and internalization of loyalty to the firm. Under conditions of bureaucratic control, supervision is less direct and less continuous, occupational demands are more complex, and the worker has greater opportunity to exercise judgment, participate in problem-solving, and develop innovative solutions to paid work dilemmas. Workers subject to bureaucratic control may perceive greater autonomy and self-supervision than workers subject to simple and technical controls.

In Chapter 1 we noted that occupational complexity forms a critical link between forms of social control parents experience on the job and parenting styles that transmit norms of social control to children. Kohn and his colleagues have demonstrated that the substantive complexity and opportunities for self-direction and autonomy that occupations offer affect parental child-rearing values and the kinds of behavior they encourage in their children, since they encourage the styles of behavior most conducive to success in their own type of paid work (Kohn 1977; Kohn and Schooler 1982, 1983; Kohn et al. 1986; Miller et al. 1979; Schooler 1987). Parents in high-complexity occupations put less emphasis on *direct* parental control and instead promote children's internalization of parental norms, thus reducing the frequency of acting-out behavior problems via more effective internal controls within children themselves. Two mechanisms appear to be at work. First, these parents appear less restrictive toward their children, display greater warmth and involvement, and report reduced use of physical punishments (Luster et al. 1989). Second, their child-rearing style stresses general principles of behavior that the child can use to guide behavior in specific instances, including during parental absence. Thus, we argue that parental occupational complexity is associated with variation in interactional styles and norms relevant to child socialization.

Variation in parental paid work hours may also affect children's behavior problems. An important part of Coleman's arguments regarding the importance of social capital in the socialization process concerns the *quantity* of time parents spend with children. As noted above, long parental paid work hours may also hinder the creation of needed relationships among parents and community members outside the household, thus affecting the quality of social capital available to children in the community. These relationships contain social capital in the form of well-developed social norms with effective sanctions that help promote appropriate internalization of norms governing child social behaviors. If such social capital is weakened or ill formed, increases in behavior problems become more likely. Although Coleman views mothers' paid work hours as particularly problematic, we argue that both parents' paid work involvements are likely to impact child socialization.

We also need to consider the possibility, however, that low parental paid work hours may also be detrimental to child internalization of appropriate behavioral norms. Low parental paid work hours are likely associated with lower household earnings, often accompanied by feelings of parental distress that may interfere with effective parenting. Following previous analyses demonstrating nonlinear relationships between parental paid work hours and child outcomes (Parcel and Menaghan 1990, 1994), we allow for the possibility that there are nonlinear relationships between parental paid work hours and child social behavior.

Parental earnings levels also impact parenting (Piotrkowski et al. 1987; Voydanoff 1987). Low earnings reduce the household material base from which children's economic environments are derived, and also cause parental distress that threatens constructive parent-child interaction (Siegal 1984; Elder et al. 1985; Kessler et al. 1988; McLoyd 1989, 1990; Mirowsky and Ross 1986; Whitbeck et al. 1991), with implications for children's social behaviors.

Changes in these same factors are likely to influence changes in children's behavior problems. Above we have noted that young adults are especially likely to experience periods of unemployment and underemployment, possibly followed by additional employment in a different job. These circumstances inevitably produce changes in paid work hours, earnings levels, and paid working conditions that may influence parental socialization efforts with children. Even welcome changes in paid working conditions, such as promotions, pose challenges that can place the socialization burden more heavily on other family members.

Effects of Family Composition and Characteristics

Earlier work has shown that more difficult family circumstances, including higher numbers of children, constrain parental nurturance and stimulation, with negative effects on child outcomes (Blake 1989; Bradley and Caldwell 1984b; Haveman, Wolfe, and Spaulding 1991; Menaghan and Parcel 1991; Parcel and Menaghan 1990; Steelman and Powell 1991; Zuravin 1988). Families that contain relatively few adults have difficulties in creating and sustaining sufficient social capital to effectively transmit norms of social control across generations; some research shows that two-parent families have stronger home environments, (Conger et al. 1984; Crouter et al. 1984; MacKinnon et al. 1982, 1986), a predictor of lower levels of behavior problems. Research shows that stronger home environments produce fewer behavior problems (Bradley 1985; Gottfried et al. 1988; Moore and Snyder 1991; Rogers et al. 1991). The quality of the home environment may also mediate the effects of workplace conditions on children's behavior problems (Menaghan and Parcel 1991). We therefore think it critical to consider the family social capital as indicated by variations in children's home environments that may influence social behaviors in middle childhood.

We also argue that changes in family composition may influence short-term changes in behavior problems. We expect that departure of a spouse will have a negative impact on child social behavior. Socialization efforts also may be hampered after separation, given the reduced resources of single-parent households (Astone and McLanahan 1991; Baydar 1988; Furstenberg and Seltzer 1986; Wallerstein 1984) and the tendency of single parents to reduce the generational boundaries that bolster their authority (Nock 1988). Although parental separation may reduce family conflict, it also begins a long period of adjustment to altered family circumstances and to poorer economic conditions (Waller-stein 1984), either of which could hinder children's adjustment (Hether-ington et al. 1978; Patterson and Bank 1989; Patterson et al. 1989; Rickel and Langner 1985).

Although most studies have treated family size as a stable character-istic of families, the birth of additional children may limit the time par-ents can spend in helping children internalize appropriate self-controls. Since pregnancy, child birth, and early infant care often interrupt paid employment among young women, the family's economic status may suffer temporarily. Under any of these circumstances or in combination, children are more likely to exhibit acting-out or withdrawn, excessively dependent behaviors.

Effects of Parental Resources and Child Characteristics

As noted above, we also consider the likelihood that parental person-al resources will influence their children's social behaviors, likely through such mechanisms as parenting styles. Parents with more posi-tive self-concepts are expected to be more effective in child socialization. Appropriate parenting behaviors and strategies are also necessary if children are to internalize appropriate standards of social control. Research suggests that coercive parenting and physical punishments generate resentment and defiance (Patterson 1984), while inductive approaches aimed at internalization of norms and values produce high-er social competence, fewer behavior problems, and higher feelings of self-esteem and mastery (Langman 1987; Peterson and Rollins 1987). Parents higher in mastery and self-esteem adopt more positive parent-ing styles, and encourage independence and active problem solving in their children (Gecas 1989; Menaghan and Parcel 1991; Mondell and Tyler 1981). Greater cognitive resources and self-confidence promote social competence, and more competent adolescents and young adults may make choices that lead to more stable marital bonds and greater work satisfaction (Clausen 1991). In addition, parents with higher levels of schooling may show greater skill in managing children's behavior (Gecas 1989).

We can view these human capital and background characteristics as additional indicators of family social capital that likely contribute to child socialization. Mothers who have a positive view of themselves and who perceive that they are in substantial control of life events may have higher expectations for self-control on the part of their children, and thus transmit this norm to them during the socialization process. The mother-child interactions during which she conveys these expectations thus constitute a specific form of norm transmission, with norms being a key form of social capital. Similarly, mothers with greater cognitive ability and higher levels of educational attainment likely hold norms favoring the use of these talents/characteristics, norms that they also transmit in the socialization of children. We view such maternal resources as relatively stable assets.[1]

In addition, we control for maternal ethnicity since other studies suggest that maternal ethnicity influences maternal values and assumptions regarding appropriate mother-child interaction (Laosa 1981). We also control for child characteristics that may affect reported problems. We control for age, although given the limited age range of our sample, the effects of age may be weak. Following Johnson and Kaplan (1988), we also control for gender, given the greater propensity of boys to exhibit aggression. Finally, we control for low birth weight and current child health problems, since children with health conditions that limit their normal play and school activities may exhibit higher levels of behavior problems than children without these limitations.

In summary, in considering initial levels of behavior problems, we hypothesize that maternal reports of children's behavior problems will be affected by parental paid working conditions, maternal personal resources, and family circumstances. Regarding paid working conditions, we hypothesize that longer paid working hours, lower wages, and restriction to occupations low in complexity hinder the development of appropriate social norms. We expect that more positive maternal self-concept will increase maternal involvement and thus decrease reported problems. Finally, we hypothesize that the absence of a spouse or partner, as well as recent maternal marital transitions and weaker home environments, will increase reported behavior problems. We control for maternal and child background characteristics in evaluating these hypotheses.

SAMPLE AND METHODS

This analysis uses the subsample of NLSY employed mothers' children who were 4–6 years old in 1986, and follows them up in 1988; the time between the 1986 and 1988 child assessments was approximately $2\frac{1}{2}$ years, making the study sample children approximately $6\frac{1}{2}$ through $8\frac{1}{2}$ in 1988. The age range was limited because behavior problems were not assessed for children younger than age 4, and children already aged 7 or older in 1986 were born prior to the baseline 1979 interview. Our dependent variable is the factor-based scales using 1986 or 1988 maternal reports regarding the frequency with which children exhibit several forms of under- and overcontrolled behaviors. Home environments are similarly measured with factor-based scales using 1986 or 1988 maternal reports and interviewer observations regarding levels of cognitive stimulation, maternal warmth, and physical safety present in the home. We also measure both family structure in 1986 and 1988, as well as changes in family structure during the interval.

FINDINGS

Descriptive Findings

Table 5.1 conveys the descriptive characteristics for the sample with which we study the 1986 BPI. Relative to the more general sample of all NLSY children, our 4- to 6-year-olds showed slightly lower levels of behavior problems. Levels of parental characteristics are similar to those we found for the larger sample on which we studied PPVT-R, as are parental paid work and family characteristics. Only three independent variables show significant zero-order relationships with 1986 BPI. Stronger maternal self-concept, higher current maternal wages, and stronger home environments are associated with lower levels of children's behavior problems. Table 5.2 presents basic descriptive data for the sample of children for whom we study 1988 BPI. Reported levels of behavior problems are higher than in 1986, although still below the mean for the more general sample. As with the 1988 sample we used to study children's cognitive achievement, parental wages have risen and levels of occupational complexity increased slightly. While 21% of the mothers are not working in 1988, the distribution of maternal paid work effort among those still working reflects greater prevalence of full-time maternal paid work. Sixty percent of the sample has remained stably married, and 25% has been stably single. Eight percent of the sample has separated or divorced and 8% are recently married. Twenty percent have had an additional child. Home environments are stronger in 1988 than in 1986. Several independent variables are significantly associated with 1988 BPI at the zero-order level. Children of mothers with higher levels of schooling, higher current wages, and who are stably married show lower levels of behavior problems; better current home environments are also associated with fewer behavior problems. Children of mothers who are stably single and who bear additional children during the interval show higher levels of behavior problems.

Table 5.1. 1986 BPI Sample: 1986 Variable Means, Standard Deviations, and Correlations with BPI 1986 (*N* = 536)

Variable	Mean	Std. dev.	Correlation with BPI 1986
BPI 1986	−.80	11.43	
Child characteristics 1986			
Health problems	.05	.22	.08
Low birth weight	.06	.24	.04
Male	.50	.50	−.06
Age (in months)	62.52	10.21	−.05
Parental characteristics			
Mother			
Ethnicity			
Black	.18	.38	−.05
Mexican Hispanic	.05	.21	−.03
White	.74	.44	.06
Other Hispanic	.03	.18	.01
Education 1986	12.06	1.47	−.08
AFQT 1980	67.16	18.86	−.06
Positive self-concept	−.05	.83	−.19*
Family of origin			
Two parents at age 14	.79	.41	−.02
Grandmother education	10.71	2.67	−.03
Spouse			
Education 1986	12.14	1.65	−.09
Maternal work characteristics 1986			
Occupational complexity	−5.92	11.43	−.06
Hourly wage	5.62	2.83	−.11*
Work hours			
1–20	.15	.36	.02
21–34	.15	.36	−.07
35–40	.59	.49	.05
Over 40	.11	.31	−.02
Spouse work characteristics 1986			
Occupational complexity	−5.94	10.12	.05
Hourly wage	9.06	4.65	−.06
Work hours			
Under 35	.04	.19	.07
35–40	.60	.49	−.09
Over 40	.37	.48	.06
Family characteristics 1986			
Married	.67	.47	−.08
Number of children	1.82	.72	−.02
Home 1986	.22	.87	−.13*

*Significant at $p < .05$, two-tailed test.

Table 5.2.   1988 BPI Sample: 1988 Variable Means, Standard Deviations, and Correlations with BPI 1988 (*N* = 493)

Variable	Mean	Std. dev.	Correlation with BPI 1988
BPI 1988	−.28	13.51	
Child characteristics 1988			
Health problems	.02	.14	.05
Age (in months)	86.41	10.19	.03
Parental characteristics 1988			
Maternal education 1988	12.14	1.48	−.11*
Spouse education 1988	12.19	2.05	−.07
Maternal work characteristics 1988			
Occupational complexity	−4.34	10.48	−.03
Hourly wage	7.07	3.58	−.12*
Stopped working (since 1986)	.21	.41	−.06
Work hours			
1–20	.12	.33	.03
21–34	.10	.30	−.08
35–40	.64	.48	.09
Over 40	.14	.35	−.08
Spouse work characteristics 1988			
Occupational complexity	−3.45	10.33	.04
Hourly wage	10.89	7.18	−.02
Work hours			
Under 35	.05	.21	.09
35–40	.61	.49	−.05
Over 40	.34	.47	.01
Family changes 1986–1988			
Marriage patterns			
Stably married	.60	.49	−.17*
Marriage ended	.08	.26	.08
Marriage started	.08	.27	.02
Stably single	.25	.43	.13*
Additional children born	.20	.40	.10*
Family characteristics 1988			
Number of children	2.01	.79	.02
Home 1988	.55	.74	−.13*

*Significant at *p* < .05, two-tailed test.

Predicting Initial Levels of Behavior Problems

Table 5.3 allows us to show the extent to which we can understand variations in children's behavior problems as a function of parental and child background characteristics, parental paid work, and family structure and environment. The first panel controls for maternal and child background, while the second panel controls for child characteristics, 1986 parental paid work, and 1986 family characteristics. Panel 3 adds parental background characteristics to the variables controlled in Panel 2. Finally, Panel 4 incorporates our 1986 measure of children's home environments.

Panel 1 suggests children with health problems are at slight risk for increased behavior problems, while those with mothers who have stronger self-concepts have noticeably reduced risk. Panel 2 suggests that children whose mothers earn better wages are at lower risk for behavior problems. The effect of hourly earnings is maintained in Panel 3, which also suggests that children of married mothers are at reduced risk. Previously noted effects of child health, maternal self-concept, and marital status are maintained when we introduce controls for children's home environments. The negative effect of children's home environments suggests that stronger home environments reduce the risk of children's behavior problems.

Assessing Statistical Interactions Suggested by Theory

Maternal resources, strongly protective in the overall model, interact with maternal complexity and with family size. Benefits of positive maternal self-concept are more powerful under more difficult conditions—when mothers are working for pay in occupations that are low in complexity, and when family size is larger. Thus, the coefficient for self-concept is nearly −5 for mothers with three children and a job one standard deviation below the mean in complexity, but close to −1 for mothers with a single child and a job one standard deviation above the mean in complexity. Conversely, maternal complexity effects are more positive when maternal self-concept is low.

Family size also interacts with fathers' levels of occupational complexity, with effects of family size more adverse for fathers with lower-quality jobs. Finally, the effects of mothers' paid work hours vary depending on the paid work schedule of her spouse, with the combination of overtime schedules for both parents significantly more adverse than when only one parent works overtime hours for pay. The effects of mothers' paid work hours also vary depending on her education, with overtime hours more beneficial for better-educated mothers.

Table 5.3. 1986 BPI: The Impact of Child, Background, and Work, Family, and Home (N = 536)

Variable	Child & background 1		Child, work, & family 1986 2		Child, background, work, & family 1986 3		Child background, work, family, family changes, & home 1986 4	
	B	Beta	B	Beta	B	Beta	B	Beta
Child characteristics 1986								
Health problems	4.41^d	.08	3.77	.07	3.74	.07	4.08^d	.08
Parental characteristics								
Mother								
Positive self-concept	-2.41^a	-.18			-2.42^a	-.18	-2.17^b	-.16
Maternal work characteristics 1986								
Hourly wage			-.39^c	-.10	-.23	-.06	-.24	-.06
Family characteristics 1986								
Married			-1.68	-.07	-2.08^d	-.09	-1.95^d	-.08
Home 1986							-1.36^c	-.11
Constant	7.99		6.46^d		9.29		7.10	
R^2	.06		.05		.09		.09	
Adjusted R^2	.03		.02		.04		.05	

$^a p < .001$; $^b p < .01$; $^c p < .05$; $^d p < .10$; two-tailed test.
$^a p < .0005$; $^b p < .005$; $^c p < .025$; $^d p < .05$; one-tailed test.
* = reference category for categorical variable.

Note: Variables not significant in any panel are not displayed. All panels also control for the following child characteristics: Low birth weight, Male, and Child age 1986 (in months). Panels 1, 3, and 4 also control for the following background characteristics: Maternal ethnicity, Maternal education 1986, Maternal AFQT 1980, Two parents at age 14, Grandmother education, and Spouse education 1986. Panels 2–4 also control for the following 1986 work and family variables: Maternal occupational complexity 1986, Maternal work hours 1986, Spouse occupational complexity 1986, Spouse hourly wage 1986, Spouse work hours 1986, and Number of children 1986.

Assessing Statistical Interaction by Race and Gender

Chow tests for race and gender differences in effects were significant for both race and gender. Higher spouse wages have significantly more positive effects on boys' behavior problems than on those for girls, for whom the effect was nonsignificant. Protective effects of home environments were stronger for girls than for boys and weaker for black children than for other children.

PREDICTING 1988 BEHAVIOR PROBLEMS

Table 5.4 estimates both behavior problems in 1988 (Panels 1–3) and change in behavior problems between 1986 and 1988 (Panels 4 and 5). At the most general level, Table 5.4 allows us to investigate whether the factors that predicted levels of behavior problems when the children were 4–6 years old can help us understand variations in behavior problems when the children are 6–8. Specifically, the model in Panel 1 shows how levels of behavior problems in 1988 vary as a function of levels of child and parental resources. Panel 2 adds to these controls the effects of parental paid work and family composition in 1988. Panel 3 adds to these variables the influence of 1988 children's home environments. Panel 4 taps changes in behavior problems by including the 1986 levels of behavior problems as an explanatory variable in an equation that has 1988 level of behavior problems as a dependent variable. It also includes measures of both 1986 and 1988 parental paid working conditions, as well as direct measures of changes in family structure over the interval. Analogous to the equations estimating changes in children's home environments presented in Chapter 3, coefficients associated with the 1986 levels of independent variables can therefore be interpreted as the (lagged) effects of 1986 levels of these variables on changes in behavior problems from 1986 to 1988. Substantively, the model estimates changes in behavior problems as a function of background controls and changes in both parental paid working conditions and family composition. Finally, Panel 5 adds to the model in Panel 4 both 1986 and 1988 measures of children's home environments. With these initial levels also in the equation, the coefficients for 1988 paid work and home variables represent the effects of recent *changes* in occupational conditions and in home environments on changes in behavior problems (Kessler and Greenberg 1981). In sum, where Panels 1–3 develop estimates for the cross-sectional effects of current (1988) parental employment status and family size, the change equations estimate effects of changes in employment status

Table 5.4. 1988 BPI: The Impact of Child, Background, Work 1986, Work 1988, Family 1988, Family Changes 1986–1988, Home 1986, Home 1988, and BPI 1986 (N = 493)

Variable	Child & background (1) B	Beta	Child, background, work, & family 1988 (2) B	Beta	Child, background, work, family, & home 1988 (3) B	Beta	Child, background, work 1986 & 1988, family changes, & behavior problems 1986 (4) B	Beta	Child, background, work 1986 & 1988, family changes, home 1986 & 1988, & behavior problems 1986 (5) B	Beta
Parental characteristics										
Mother										
Positive self-concept	-3.11^a	$-.20$	-3.34^a	$-.21$	-3.11^a	$-.20$	-1.32^d	$-.08$	$-.99$	$-.06$
Maternal work characteristics 1986										
Work hours										
1–20							3.71^c	$.10$	3.76^c	$.10$
21–34							1.98	$.06$	2.21	$.06$
35–40*							—	—	—	—
Over 40							-2.93^d	$-.07$	-3.24^d	$-.08$
Spouse work characteristics 1986										
Occupational complexity							$-.15^c$	$-.09$	$-.15^c$	$-.09$
Work hours										
0–35							2.79	$.03$	2.40	$.03$
35–40*							—	—	—	—
Over 40							-2.70^d	$-.08$	-2.76^d	$-.08$
Maternal work characteristics 1988										
Stopped working (since 1986)			-3.09^c	$-.10$	-3.07^c	$-.10$	-2.73^c	$-.09$	-2.58^c	$-.08$

	Panel 1		Panel 2		Panel 3		Panel 4		Panel 5	
	b	β	b	β	b	β	b	β	b	β
Work hours							[e]		[e]	
1–20			.82	.02	1.05	.02	−.09	−.00	−.05	−.00
21–34			−4.48[c]	−.09	−4.33[c]	−.09	−4.46[c]	−.09	−4.39	−.09
35–40*			—	—	—	—	—	—	—	—
Over 40			−3.91[c]	−.09	−3.67[d]	−.09	−.92	−.02	−.62	−.01
Family characteristics 1988										
Married			−5.37[a]	−.19	−5.34[a]	−.19				
Number of children			1.59[c]	.10	1.47[d]	.09				
Family changes 1986–1988										
Marriage patterns										
Stably married*										
Marriage ended							3.49[d]	.07	3.44[d]	.07
Marriage started							2.62	.06	2.66	.06
Stably single							4.91[a]	.16	4.82[a]	.16
Additional children born							4.61[a]	.14	4.47[a]	.14
Behavior problems 1986							.55[a]	.48	.55[a]	.48
Constant	3.55		8.86		8.59		−1.47		−2.05	
R²	.05		.12		.13		.37		.37	
Adjusted R²	.03		.08		.08		.32		.32	

[a]p < .001; [b]p < .01; [c]p < .05; [d]p < .10; two-tailed test.
[a]p < .0005; [b]p < .005; [c]p < .025; [d]p < .05; one-tailed test.
[e]Set of dummy variables is not significant.
*Reference category for categorical variable.

Note: Variables not significant in any panel are not displayed. All panels also control for the following child and background characteristics: Child health problems 1988, Low birth weight, Male, Child age 1988 (in months), Maternal ethnicity, Maternal education 1988, Maternal AFQT, and Spouse education 1988. Panels 2–5 also control for the following 1988 work variables: Maternal occupational complexity 1988, Maternal hourly wage 1988, Spouse occupational complexity 1988, Spouse hourly wage 1988, and Spouse work hours 1988. Panels 4 and 5 also control for the following 1986 work and family variables: Maternal occupational complexity 1986, Maternal hourly wage 1986, Spouse hourly wage 1986, Spouse occupational complexity 1986, and Number of children 1986. Panels 3 and 5 also control for the 1988 Home environment. Panel 5 also controls for the 1986 Home environment.

and in family size over time by including dummy variables identifying patterns of employment status over time and the birth of additional children over the last 2 years. As in Chapter 3, we take the respective strengths of the change and nonchange models into account when interpreting our findings.

Multivariate Models

Panel 1 in Table 5.4 suggests that stronger maternal self-concept reduces children's risk of behavior problems in 1988, while Panel 2 suggests that relative to children of mothers who work full-time for pay, children of mothers who work for pay either high part-time hours or overtime have children with reduced risk of behavior problems. In addition, there is a protective effect for children whose mothers stopped paid work between 1986 and 1988. Finally, children of married mothers are at reduced risk while the risks are higher for children with larger numbers of siblings. Panel 3 suggests that controlling for children's home environments does not influence 1988 levels of children's behavior problems, nor does introducing this control change the findings we observed in Panel 2.

Panel 4 suggests the extent to which these same factors help us to understand short-term increases or decreases in behavior problems. Maternal self-concept has a weak protective effect against increases in behavior problems; 1986 paternal occupational complexity also has a protective effect, and mothers who quit paid work between 1986 and 1988 have children with lower increases in behavior problems. We also observe 1986 and 1988 maternal paid work hours effects on changes in behavior problems. Mothers who worked low part-time hours for pay have children with greater increases in behavior problems relative to mothers who worked full-time for pay, while mothers who worked overtime for pay, or who are currently working high part-time hours, have children with lower levels of increases. Paternal overtime paid work in 1988 places children at increased risk for behavior problems. Family changes have strong effects on changes in children's behavior problems over the 2-year interval. Relative to children with stably married mothers, children of mothers who entered into new marriages and who were stably single all had increases in behavior problems. As expected, the positive effect of 1986 levels of behavior problems on 1988 levels of behavior problems is strong, thus suggesting clear continuity in levels of behavior problems over time. Panel 5 suggests that changes in children's home environments have no influence on changes in behavior problems in the short term. The effects noted in Panel 4 are all maintained, except that introducing the controls for home environments washes out the maternal self-concept effect.

Assessing Statistical Interaction Suggested by Theory

Including interactive effects qualifies many of the findings in the additive model. The effect of mothers' stopping paid work depends on the kind of occupation she held and her paid work hours; specifically, stopping employment was beneficial only for children of mothers who had been working overtime hours and working at jobs low in complexity. With this interaction included in the equation, the "benefit" of early maternal overtime hours noted in the additive model disappears. The adverse effects of very low maternal paid work hours in 1986 persist; these effects are particularly strong for mothers who remain in the labor force.

Once more, we see evidence that maternal resources are particularly critical under more difficult conditions, with the benefits of positive maternal self-concept much stronger for those facing marital disruption and those having an additional child. Conversely, of course, the adverse impacts of these two events on children's later behavior problems vary depending on the resources mothers can bring to bear, with more adverse impacts for children whose mothers are not high in positive self-concept. Occupational variables also interact with these family transitions. Fathers' paid work hours in 1988 condition the impact of an additional child, with adverse effects for fathers working extensive overtime hours. There is no significant impact of fathers' paid work hours in 1988 after controlling for this contingent effect. Mothers' 1988 levels of occupational complexity also condition the impact of marital disruption, with this event much more adverse for mothers employed in less complex occupations.

Assessing Statistical Interaction by Race and Gender

Chow tests were not significant for race or gender differences in the 1988 behavior problems equations, suggesting that short-term changes in children's behavior problems are not generated by different processes for boys than for girls or for black children than for others.

SUMMARY AND DISCUSSION

We have argued that family social capital is an important resource through which parental paid working conditions influence the transmission of norms and behavior patterns across generations. We have also argued that changing family composition and changes in parental paid working conditions, both especially likely in "the floundering phase" of the life course, may influence social adjustment among school age children through changes in social capital. Finally, we consider the likelihood that relatively stable parental personal resources such as mastery and self-esteem will affect children's norm internalization in middle childhood. We initially asked whether children who manifest behavior problems in the later preschool years continue these patterns into middle childhood. Our findings show continuity in levels of reported behavior problems across this period, but more importantly help to identify the ways in which family social capital contributes both to stability and change in social behaviors.

Social capital embodied in maternal personal resources and social capital that is more or less abundant as a function of parental paid work hours are important avenues through which families transmit appropriate behavior norms across generations. We see that stronger maternal self-concept has protective effects against higher levels of behavior problems in both 1986 and in 1988, and also protects against increases in behavior problems across the interval until home environments are controlled. In addition, maternal self-concept is more important under adverse conditions such as when family size is large, mothers work for pay in low complexity occupations, if additional children are born or if there is marital disruption.

We also note that family structure has important additive effects. If mothers are married, children's behavior problems are lower in both 1986 and 1988, and behavior problems increase between 1986 and 1988 if mothers experience marital disruption, or are stably single. These findings are particularly compatible with Coleman's worries that reduction in social capital associated with single-parent households may hinder appropriate transmittal of behavioral norms across generations. Additional findings support this conclusion since stronger home environments protect against higher levels of behavior problems in 1986, while higher numbers of children in 1988 and additional siblings born between 1986 and 1988 are associated with increases in behavior problems.

These findings suggest support for Coleman's arguments regarding the importance of parent-child bonds as a resource in facilitating internalization of behavior norms, and help to suggest the specific mecha - nisms through which such capital may be working. We have noted that such mechanisms are associated with several sources in that parental personal characteristics, home and family composition, and parental paid working conditions all play a role. Thus "casting a broad net" around potential causes of child social behaviors appears appropriate.

Parental paid working conditions also influence levels of behavior problems, although the findings regarding parental time inputs into child socialization are not precisely compatible with Coleman's concerns about maternal employment. Findings from the 1986 analysis suggest that behavior problems are greater if both parents are working overtime, although maternal overtime hours are more beneficial if mothers are more educated. Findings from the 1988 analysis suggest that mothers who stop paid work between 1986 and 1988 protect their children from higher levels of behavior problems only if they had been working paid overtime hours or if they had been employed in low complexity occupations. In addition, paternal overtime hours have more deleterious effects if additional children have been born into the family. Finally, higher levels of paternal occupational complexity appear to protect children against behavior problems. Thus there is some support for our contention that the mechanisms of social control that parents experience on the job influence the parenting styles they use at home, with expectable consequences for child social behaviors. Overall, then, our findings suggest that parental paid working conditions can have deleterious effects on intergenerational norm transmission under certain conditions, but that it would be a mistake to conclude that challenging parental paid work, either in terms of higher levels of complexity or more extended hours, are uniformly harmful to children.

These findings also inform a larger theoretical context regarding social control as it applies to the process through which macrolevel paid work structures may influence the content of socialization within the family. We initially argued that occupational complexity forms a critical link between the types of social control parents experience on the job and the styles of parenting they exhibit at home. Although our findings suggest that paid working conditions associated with "good" jobs have positive implications for parents' investment in children and child outcomes, our findings also suggest other mechanisms through which family social capital influences child social behavior. Most important of these mechanisms are maternal self-concept and family structure, thus suggesting diversity in the causes of children's social behaviors. Such findings help us to refine our understanding of the transmission of behavioral norms across generations.

NOTE

1. Additional analyses support this view since early maternal self-concept and later (1987) self-esteem are highly correlated ($r = .47$). Substituting the more recent measure of self-esteem for the early self-concept measure used here makes no difference in our findings.

Chapter 6

Early Parental Work, Family Social Capital, and Early Childhood Outcomes

We have already demonstrated that current parental paid working conditions, and child and parental background characteristics can influence both social and cognitive child outcomes. We have argued that these findings inform thinking about how family social capital can influence children's lives. We now turn to a related question: that is, to what extent does parental paid work early in a child's life have discernible effects on child outcomes measured later?

Although we have shown that current circumstances in children's lives have effects on measurable child outcomes, some psychologists focus particular attention on the first few years of life as causative for subsequent child outcomes. We need to understand which set of influences is stronger. If effects from the child's first few years are present several years later, are they maintained when current circumstances are also considered? Similarly, are contemporaneous effects maintained when earlier circumstances are controlled? In addition, although there are sound theoretical reasons to focus on the first year of the child's life as a critical period in the socialization process, it has not been established that this year is more important than the second or third years of life. Hence, we evaluate whether "early" parental paid working conditions have differing effects on child outcomes depending on how the notion of early is conceptualized and measured. We investigate the effects of these paid working conditions on 1986 levels of PPVT-R, our measure of verbal facility, and 1986 levels of behavior problems, our measure of child social adjustment.

HOW IMPORTANT ARE EARLY INFLUENCES ON CHILD OUTCOMES?

Several arguments contribute to thinking about the effect of early parental employment on later child outcomes. At the macrolevel, policy analysts such as Kamerman (1991) and Ferber and O'Farrell (1991) suggest that parental leave policies in a large number of industrialized countries encourage direct parental care of children, usually by mothers, during infancy. The rationale for these policies might be that such care is optimal for children, although parental care is also less directly costly for society. In partial contrast, feminist and structural analyses have argued that the lack of widespread availability of infant child care is costly for women since it constrains women's paid work choices after motherhood and may even constrain the types of occupations for which they train; the implicit assumption is that quality child care could substitute for parental care during parents' hours of employment, with costs to women from lack of quality care important to the formulations.

From an important psychological perspective, however, Jay Belsky has argued that maternal employment during the child's first year of life may interfere with the establishment of appropriate attachment between the mother and the child (e.g., Belsky and Rovine 1988). He infers that insecurely and securely attached infants should differ on developmental outcomes as they mature, although the evidence is stronger for social outcomes (Matas, Arend, and Sroufe 1978; Lutkenhaus, Grossman, and Grossman 1985; LaFreniere and Sroufe 1985) than for cognitive outcomes (but see Vandell and Corasaniti 1991). But reliance on "attachment" may be unnecessary. More general views of development stress the importance of early influences on later development with the explicit assumption that such influences establish patterns that are long term. Coleman's notions of investment in family social capital are also tied more generally to the idea that investments at one point in time pay later dividends. We therefore evaluate whether early parental paid working conditions influence later developmental outcomes, without reliance on "attachment" as a key concept.

Clearly, research examining effects on children of mothers' employment during children's first few years has obvious social policy implications. If negative effects of higher levels of maternal employment are observed and are attributable to the inadequate quality of available supplemental child care, such effects could be prevented by improving availability and quality of child care for young children. If negative effects are interpreted to suggest, however, that maternal care is in principle nonsubstitutable, such findings could prompt policies that discourage mothers from delegating infant care to others; these might include supports for extended maternal leaves, or more punitively, reductions in the supply of child care for the very young and sanctions against mothers who seek employment. Alternatively, if additional research established that higher levels of maternal employment during children's early years had no significant negative or even positive consequences, the policy implications would differ. Under this scenario, policies promoting maternal employment would merit support, while policies discouraging such employment would merit reconsideration. In addition, such research can help to specify the conditions under which maternal employment may be beneficial, neutral or detrimental. Desai et al.(1989) find that maternal employment in infancy has negative effects on PPVT-R for boys in families with high income from other family members; we can provide additional evidence regarding employment effects interacting with maternal and child statuses to affect both cognitive and social child outcomes. We are most interested in whether early maternal employment interacts with current maternal paid working conditions in affecting these outcomes.

A few studies have approached these issues with some of these concerns in mind. Several have evaluated alternative measures of early life (Blau and Grossberg 1990; Vandell and Ramanan 1992), and have used large NLSY samples to allow for parameter estimation (Desai et al. 1989; Blau and Grossberg 1990; Belsky and Eggebeen 1991). Only Vandell and Ramanan (1992) study both cognitive and social outcomes; this study also clearly controls for both early and contemporaneous maternal paid work in multivariate models. However, even it fails to consider how paternal paid working conditions may affect child outcomes, and it uses a very small sample with little socioeconomic variation. Ours is unique in combining use of a large sample with the study of both cognitive and social outcomes, with clear consideration for paternal paid work influences, and explicit controls for both early and current paid working conditions for both parents.

Although differences in samples, design, and model specifications render comparisons of findings across these tentative, it is worth noting that several studies document negative effects of early maternal employment on later child cognitive outcomes. For example, Blau and Grossberg (1990) find that maternal employment during the child's first year of life has negative effects on PPVT-R, but employment in the second and later years has positive effects, so the net effect of the first 3–4 years is close to zero. Belsky and Eggebeen (1991) document negative effects of full-time maternal employment in year 1 or 2 on compliance, relative to children of mothers not employed in years 1–3, while Baydar and Brooks-Gunn (1991) document negative effects of maternal employment in the child's first year of life on both cognitive and social outcomes. In a study of cognitive achievement among older children, Vandell and Ramanan (1992) find early maternal employment facilitates math achievement while reading achievement is a positive function of recent maternal employment. Thus, research has documented both positive and negative effects of early maternal paid work, with greater inconsistency regarding the effects on cognition than those on social outcomes; the latter appear more consistently negative.

We employ the same basic theoretical ideas developed in earlier chapters in addressing the question of the effects of early parental employment. Following personality and social structure frameworks developed by Kohn and his colleagues (Kohn 1977; Kohn and Schooler 1982; Kohn et al. 1986; Miller et al. 1979; Schooler 1987; Kohn and Slomczynski 1990) we argue that the paid working conditions parents experience on the job influence their child-rearing values and provide a model of the kinds of behaviors they encourage in their children. Variation in parental paid work hours early in a child's life may also impact child outcomes. Psychologists are concerned with the *duration* of time that mothers spend with their children during infancy because mothers returning to paid work spend less time with their infants than mothers who remain at home. But following this argument, it is logical that, within a group of mothers who work outside the home in their child's first year, the duration of their paid work effort may make a difference. Mothers who work long hours for pay during their child's first year may be placing their children at greater risk for social maladjustment and cognitive delay than mothers who work shorter hours for pay. Indeed, in Chapter 4 we have demonstrated a nonlinear effect of contemporaneous maternal paid work hours on verbal facility among 3- to 6-year-olds, such that compared to mothers who work full-time hours for pay, children with mothers who typically work high part-time hours score significantly better, and children of mothers who routinely work paid overtime hours score significantly worse. There is no statistically significant difference between children of mothers who work full-time for pay and those of mothers who work low part-time hours for pay. In this analysis we consider whether such increments in the duration of maternal paid work hours in the child's first year(s) of life, as opposed to the fact of maternal employment-nonemployment during this time, influence later child outcomes.

The earnings that parents derive from their jobs typically provide the economic foundation for family welfare. Lower levels of earnings threaten the household material base used to support children, and also cause parental distress that hampers constructive parent-child interaction (Siegal 1984; Elder et al. 1985; Kessler et al. 1988; McLoyd 1989, 1990; Mirowsky and Ross 1986). This may be particularly true in the child's first year of life, when, owing to low levels of paid work experience among young parents, wage levels may be especially low. Increased levels of parental distress and limited material resources may hinder child social adjustment and limit cognitive development.

As in our analyses in Chapters 3–5, we also introduce controls for child and parental background characteristics. We expect that being married, and stably married over time, will be associated with more positive outcomes than being unmarried or unstably married. Following arguments regarding resource dilution in the family (Blake 1989), we also expect that greater numbers of children in the family will be associated with less favorable child outcomes. We also expect that better home environments will be associated with higher cognitive performance and lower levels of behavior problems (Bradley et al. 1988a; Moore and Snyder 1991; Rogers et al. 1991; Parcel and Menaghan 1993).

We investigate the effects of parental paid working conditions at two early points and one later point in time on two child outcomes, one social and one cognitive, in the presence of numerous background controls. This strategy allows us to cast a broad net around the problem of early effects on later child outcomes, without assuming that such effects are solely confined to one type of child outcome. It also allows us to compare the strength of any early effects with comparable measures from a second time point. Finally, it allows us to determine whether maternal and paternal effects are similar or different.

We allow marital status to vary and tap variation in paternal paid working conditions during this same period. Our models control for pre-existing maternal and child background characteristics that theory suggests should be associated with child outcomes, and evaluate the impact of parental paid working conditions early in the child's life. We also include contemporaneous parental paid working conditions, along with measures of temporally subsequent characteristics of family structure.

SAMPLE AND METHODS

Data

As noted in Chapter 2, following our focus on the effects of maternal paid working conditions, we select a sample of 3- to 6-year-old children with mothers who were employed at the time of assessment. We measure variation in their paid working conditions, and in the paid working conditions of their spouses if these mothers are married. We then follow this sample back in time to capture variation in early maternal paid working conditions, allowing for the fact that some mothers were not employed during this time in their children's lives. In doing so we build on earlier work in Chapter 4, where we demonstrated that contemporaneous maternal paid working conditions influence PPVT-R in this age group. Using the same sample allows us to provide a more rigorous test of these findings by controlling for early influences; similarly, it allows us to compare the strength of the early influences with simultaneous controls for the contemporaneous effects. These sampling criteria resulted in a sample of 768 employed mothers with young children, and it is this group for whom we study the cognitive outcome, PPVT-R. Our second sample is identical to the first, except that we omit the three year olds because, as noted in Chapter 5, our social outcome measure of maternal perceptions of child behavior problems is not assessed for children younger than 4 years old; this resulting sample is 528 employed mothers with 4- to 6-year- old children.

Measurement of Variables

Most of the variables we use in this analysis are described in Chapter 2. There are several additional measures unique to the models we present here; we summarize key points about these measures now. Parental occupational characteristics are measured at two key time points: early in the child's life and at the time of assessment in 1986. We use two alternative operationalizations to capture the effect of early parental paid working conditions: measures referring only to parental occupations in the child's first year of life, and summary measures that capture typical parental paid working conditions over the child's first 3 years of life. As in previous chapters, we dummied typical hours of paid work to permit detection of nonlinear relationships between paid work hours and the dependent variables. Mothers with no employment during year 1 or years 1–3 receive missing values for all paid work hours dummies for that period; absent fathers receive missing values for all paid work hour dummies when absent. Thus, paid work hours variables capture variations in paid work hours among employed parents.

FINDINGS

Descriptive Findings

Table 6.1 displays the means and standard deviations for the dependent variables included in the analysis plus those independent variables that are unique to this chapter. Average levels of parental occupational complexity appear unchanged over the interval; negative levels of complexity suggest that mean complexity levels are below average across all occupations. Two-thirds of the mothers were employed during the child's first year, and 90% had some employment during the child's first 3 years. Bivariate correlations, also shown in Table 6.1, are generally in the expected directions. We note that wages and occupational complexity for both parents are positively associated with PPVT-R. The scattered associations with BPI are mostly negative, i.e., better parental jobs are associated with lower levels of behavior problems. In addition, maternal employment status in year 1 and in years 1–3 has near-zero associations with child outcomes.

Multivariate Models: Modeling Effects on Verbal Facility

For both cognitive and social outcomes, we estimated multivariate models including both early and current paid work and family conditions, as well as controls. As Table 6.2 shows, we utilize two alternative specifications of early conditions: conditions in year 1 only (Panel 1), and conditions during years 1–3 (Panel 2). We also evaluate whether the effects of mothers' current paid work hours, prior paid work history, and background characteristics differ depending on the complexity of mothers' current occupation.

Most background and family effects on verbal facility are stable across both specifications of early conditions. Maternal background characteristics, including age, ethnicity, AFQT, and grandmothers' levels of educational attainment, have significant positive direct effects on the child's cognitive skills; fathers' levels of educational attainment also has a positive direct effect. Larger numbers of older siblings, as well as a younger sibling born within 3 years of the target child, have negative effects for verbal facility; sibs born at later intervals have no significant effect. Better home environments also predict greater child cognitive skills.

Current paid work conditions generally have stronger direct effects than early conditions. For both mothers and fathers, current routine overtime paid work schedules are more negative than full-time hours; for mothers, moderate part-time paid work (20–34 hours per week) is more positive than full-time paid work schedules. Higher current maternal wages has positive implications for children's PPVT scores, although this effect becomes insignificant ($t = 1.60$, $p < .15$) when paid work and family conditions during the first 3 years are controlled.

Fathers' early paid work conditions have little independent impact, except for the positive effect of fathers' wages in year 1. Variations in employed mothers' early paid work conditions also have no significant effects. There is a weak ($p < .10$) tendency for children whose mothers

Table 6.1. Early Sample: Child Years 1–3 Variable Means, Standard Deviations, and Correlations with 1986 PPVT-R and BPI (*N* = 768)

Variable	Mean	Std. dev.	Correlations with PPVT-R 1986	BPI 1986
PPVT-R 1986	94.66	17.29		
BPI 1986	−.80	11.47	−.13*	
Maternal work characteristics year 1				
Occupational complexity	−4.13	9.08	.11*	−.10
Hourly wage	5.55	2.69	.13*	−.08
No work hours	.32	.47	−.04	−.00
Work hours				
1–20	.20	.40	.13*	−.07
21–34	.24	.43	−.05	.06
35–40	.47	.50	−.09	−.00
Over 40	.09	.29	−.02	.01
Spouse work characteristics year 1				
Occupational complexity	−5.80	9.63	.13*	−.03
Hourly wage	8.71	4.74	.20*	.11
Work hours				
Under 35	.04	.20	.02	.12*
35–40	.63	.48	−.04	−.10
Over 40	.32	.47	.04	.05
Maternal work characteristics years 1–3				
Occupational complexity	−4.58	8.11	.17*	−.11*
Hourly wage	5.49	2.73	.16*	−.08
No work hours	.10	.30	.01	−.03
Work hours				
1–20	.14	.35	.03	.01
21–34	.33	.47	−.01	.04
35–40	.39	.49	−.02	−.05
Over 40	.14	.34	.01	.01
Spouse work characteristics years 1–3				
Occupational complexity	−5.83	8.25	.10*	−.04
Hourly wage	8.88	4.56	.14*	−.03
Work hours				
Under 35	.07	.25	−.05	.22*
35–40	.42	.49	−.06	−.15*
Over 40	.51	.50	.09*	.03
Family characteristics year 1				
Married	.74	.44	.21*	−.03
Number of older siblings	.42	.68	−.13*	−.07
Family changes years 1–3				
Additional children born	.19	.40	−.09*	−.00
Marriage patterns				
Unstably married	.18	.38	.04	.07

Table 6.1. (continued)

Variable	Mean	Std. dev.	Correlations with	
			PPVT-R 1986	BPI 1986
Married	.62	.49	.11*	−.04
Not married	.20	.40	−.18*	−.03
Family characteristics 1986				
Additional child at 4–7 years	.27	.44	.08*	.03
Number of younger siblings	.41	.56	−.00	.04

*Significant at $p < .05$, two-tailed test.
Note: Correlations with 1986 BPI are for sample size $N = 528$.

have forgone early employment to have higher PPVT scores, although as we note below, this effect varies depending on the complexity of mothers' current occupation. In addition, since these models may underestimate total effects of early conditions because later conditions are simultaneously considered, we also estimated models excluding current paid work and family conditions (equations not shown); effects of early mother and father paid working conditions are unchanged.[1]

Interactions by Current Maternal Occupational Complexity

Following our interest in whether maternal paid working conditions formed important bases for statistical interaction, we evaluated whether mothers' current occupational complexity interacted with mothers' background characteristics (education, AFQT, self-esteem, mastery), their prior paid work history (employed/not employed), or their current paid work hours. We found significant interactive effects with maternal AFQT and paid work history; to better describe these interactions, we solved for mean values and for plus and minus one standard deviation around the means. We find that a more complex occupation in 1986 increased the positive effects of higher initial intellectual skills. In particular, the benefits of mothers' greater cognitive skills for children's verbal facility were greater when her cognitive skills were continually practiced and reinforced on the job; mothers with similar AFQT but in simple, repetitive jobs were less able to promote their children's verbal facility.

The second interaction, with maternal paid work history, significantly qualifies the additive beneficial effect of mothers' forgoing early employment. That is, the effect of nonemployment is *adverse* for mothers whose current occupations are high in complexity, near zero for mothers in average occupations, and beneficial only for mothers whose

Family Social Capital and Childhood Outcomes

Table 6.2. 1986 PPVT-R: The Impact of Current and First Year or Years 1–3 Child, Maternal, and Spouse Characteristics, Family Configuration, and Maternal and Spouse Work Characteristics ($N = 768$)

Variable	(1)		(2)	
	B	Beta	B	Beta
Child characteristics 1986				
Shy in interview	-1.22^c	$-.07$	-1.03^c	$-.06$
Male	-1.69^d	$-.05$	-1.45	$-.04$
Parental characteristics				
Mother				
Ethnicity				
Black	-14.10^a	$-.33$	-14.86^a	$-.35$
White*	—	—	—	—
Mexican Hispanic	-6.83^b	$-.09$	-7.91^b	$-.10$
Other Hispanic	-8.05^b	$-.09$	-7.59^b	$-.08$
Age 1986	$.89^b$	.11	$.92^b$	.12
AFQT 1980	$.12^b$	.13	$.13^a$	.15
Family of origin				
Grandmother education	$.85^a$	.13	$.84^a$	.13
Spouse characteristics				
Education 1986	$.71^d$	.06	$.80^d$	.07
Maternal work characteristics year 1				
No work hours	2.14^d	.06		
Spouse work characteristics year 1				
Hourly wage	$.46^b$	.10		
Maternal work characteristics years 1–3				
No work hours			3.25^d	.06
Maternal work characteristics 1986				
Hourly wage	$.54^b$	.09	.33	.06
Work hours				
1–20	1.45	.03	2.06	.04
21–34	3.30^c	.08	4.60^b	.11
35–40*	—	—	—	—
Over 40	-2.85^d	$-.05$	-2.89^d	$-.06$
Spouse work characteristics 1986				
Work hours				
Under 35	-3.26	$-.03$	-3.51	$-.04$
35–40*	—	—	—	—
Over 40	-3.79^b	$-.09$	-4.37^b	$-.11$
Family characteristics year 1				
Number of older siblings	-3.12^a	$-.13$		
Family changes years 1–3				
Marriage patterns				
Unstably married			-1.58	$-.04$

Table 6.2. (continued)

Variable	(1)		(2)	
	B	Beta	B	Beta
Married			−4.15^c	−.12
Not married*			—	—
Number of older siblings			−2.88^b	−.12
Additional children born			−4.13^b	−.10
Home 1986	2.73^a	.15	2.83^a	.15
Constant	59.7^a		62.8^a	
R^2		.36		.37
Adjusted R^2		.33		.34

$^a p < .001$; $^b p < .01$; $^c p < .05$; $^d p < .10$; two-tailed test.
$^a p < .0005$; $^b p < .005$; $^c p < .025$; $^d p < .05$; one- tailed test.
^{e}Set of dummy variables is not significant.
*Reference category for categorical variable.
Note: Variables not significant in any model are not displayed. Both panels also control for the following child and background characteristics: Child health problems 1986, Low birth weight, Maternal education 1986, Maternal positive self-concept, Two parents at age 14, Spouse age 1986; and for the following 1986 work variables: Maternal occupational complexity 1986, Spouse occupational complexity 1986, Spouse hourly wage 1986, and Married 1986. Panel 1 also controls for the following Year 1 variables: Maternal occupational complexity year 1, Maternal hourly wage year 1, Maternal work hours year 1, Spouse occupational complexity year 1, Spouse work hours year 1, Married year 1; and for the Number of younger siblings 1986. Panel 2 also controls for the following Years 1–3 variables: Maternal occupational complexity years 1–3, Maternal hourly wage years 1–3, Maternal work hours years 1–3, Spouse occupational complexity years 1–3, Spouse hourly wage years 1–3, Spouse work hours years 1–3, and for Additional children born years 4–7.

current occupations are low in complexity. Since complexity of early and current employment are positively correlated, any benefits of forgoing employment appear largely limited to mothers with poorer occupational prospects; we return to this point in our discussion.

Characteristics of mothers' current occupations also interact with fathers' current paid work hours. Benefits of a more complex maternal occupation were diminished when fathers maintained overtime hours. This pattern echoes earlier findings suggesting that highly complex and challenging paid work has less positive effects when other demands, such as total number of children, are high or other supports, such as availability of a partner, are low. Finally, we again see evidence that maternal resources are particularly important under more stressful circumstances, with positive effects of mothers' cognitive skills stronger when fathers had jobs lower in complexity.

Interactions by Ethnicity and Gender

We also estimated separate models by child gender and ethnicity and conducted Chow tests to assess whether the separate equations explained a significantly greater proportion of variance than the equation pooling the two groups. Chow tests were significant for ethnicity but not significant for child gender. Subsequent evaluations of specific interactions by ethnicity found that current health problems had a significantly greater adverse effect on children's PPVT scores for black children than for others.

Multivariate Models: Modeling Effects on Behavior Problems

We next examine parallel models for children's behavior problems for the subset of children aged 4–6 in 1986. Table 6.3 displays the parallel additive equations with our alternative specifications of early time periods. Again, background and family effects tend to be stable across the two equations. Mothers with more positive self-concepts and those providing more positive home environments have children with fewer behavior problems. Mothers' marital history also has significant effects in the second equation; being currently married is beneficial to child social well-being. Neither spouse's current paid working conditions has significant additive effects, although as we note below, there are some interactive effects. No early maternal paid working conditions, nor early maternal employment status, have significant effects. However, for fathers, low paid work hours, either in the first year or across the child's first 3 years, have a strong adverse impact on children.

Interactive Effects of Occupational Complexity

As for PPVT-R, we evaluated whether mothers' occupational complexity interacted with mothers' background characteristics, prior paid work history, or current paid work hours. Paralleling the finding for PPVT-R, we find that a more complex maternal occupation increased the beneficial effects of higher initial intellectual skills. That is, the benefits of mothers' greater cognitive skills for children's social adjustment were greater when her cognitive skills were continually practiced and reinforced on the job; mothers with similar AFQT but in simple, repetitive jobs were less able to prevent behavior problems. For behavior problems, the interaction was slightly stronger ($p < .05$ versus $p < .10$) for

Table 6.3. 1986 BPI: The Impact of Current and Year 1 or Years 1–3 Child, Maternal, and Spouse Characteristics, Family Configuration, and Maternal and Spouse Work Characteristics ($N = 528$)

Variable	(1) B	(1) Beta	(2) B	(2) Beta
Child characteristics 1986				
Male	−1.84[d]	−.08	−1.38	−.06
Parental characteristics				
Mother				
Ethnicity				[e]
Black	−4.09[c]	−.14	−2.84[d]	−.10
White*	—	—	—	—
Mexican Hispanic	−3.27	−.06	−2.23	−.04
Other Hispanic	−.67	−.01	−.69	−.01
Positive self-concept	−2.03[b]	−.15	−2.38[a]	−.17
Spouse work characteristics year 1				
Work hours				
Under 35	6.85[c]	.11		
35–40*	—	—		
Over 40	1.28	.04		
Spouse work characteristics years 1–3				
Work hours				
Under 35			10.04[a]	.20
35–40*			—	—
Over 40			2.02	.08
Family characteristics 1986				
Married	−2.13[d]	−.09	−2.88[c]	−.12
Home 1986	−1.58[c]	−.12	−1.72[b]	−.13
Constant	1.14		−7.30	
R^2	.12		.15	
Adjusted R^2	.06		.08	

[a]$p < .001$; [b]$p < .01$; [c]$p < .05$; [d]$p < .10$; two-tailed test.

[a]$p < .0005$; [b]$p < .005$; [c]$p < .025$; [d]$p < .05$; one-tailed test.

[e]Set of dummy variables is not significant.

*Reference category for categorical variable.

Note: Variables not significant in any model are not displayed. Both panels also control for the following child and background characteristics: Child health problems 1986, Low birth weight, Maternal age 1986, Maternal education 1986, Maternal AFQT 1980, Two parents at age 14, Grandmother education, Spouse age 1986, Spouse education 1986; and for the following 1986 work variables: Maternal occupational complexity 1986, Maternal hourly wage 1986, Maternal work hours 1986, Spouse occupational complexity 1986, Spouse hourly wage 1986, and Spouse work hours 1986. Panel 1 also controls for the following year 1 variables: Maternal occupational complexity year 1, Maternal hourly wage year 1, Maternal no work hours year 1, Spouse occupational complexity year 1, Spouse hourly wage year 1, Married year 1, Number of older siblings year 1; and for the Number of younger siblings 1986. Panel 2 also controls for the following Years 1–3 variables: Maternal occupational complexity years 1–3, Maternal hourly wage years 1–3, Maternal no work hours years 1–3, Maternal work hours years 1–3, Spouse occupational complexity years 1–3, Spouse hourly wage years 1–3, Marriage patterns years 1–3, Number of older siblings years 1–3, Additional children born years 1–3; and for Additional children born years 4–7.

early maternal complexity than for the complexity of her current occupation, although the form of the interactions was the same.

We also evaluated whether effects of maternal resources interacted with paid work and family conditions. The adverse effects of mothers' current overtime paid work schedules were less severe when mothers had more education, and the effect of the rapid addition of a younger sibling was less negative the higher mothers' AFQT scores. Again, we see evidence that maternal resources are particularly protective when circumstances are more difficult, and conversely that the effects of difficult paid work and family circumstances are modified by higher resources. Finally, we again see some indications that mothers' and fathers' paid work conditions interact in their effects, with benefits of each parent's better early wages somewhat less when the other parent's wages were also high. This is consistent with earlier findings suggesting some diminishing returns of occupational conditions.

Interactions by Ethnicity and Gender

We again evaluated whether the final model varied by child ethnicity or gender. Chow tests for both ethnicity and gender were significant. The beneficial effects of a positive home environment were weaker for black children. Mothers' having experienced marital changes during the child's early years were significantly more adverse for boys than for girls; higher current father wages, on the other hand, conferred greater benefits on boys than on girls.

SUMMARY AND DISCUSSION

We recall from our summary of prior studies on the effects of early parental paid work on child outcomes that our investigation is the only one that provides inferences regarding the effects of paternal paid working conditions on child outcomes. Along with Vandell and Ramanan, we tap both social and cognitive outcomes, control for children's home environments, and study both early and current maternal paid working conditions. We combine these advantages with use of a larger sample and incorporation of paternal paid working conditions, and we explicitly consider how these data inform the functioning of family social capital.

Our findings suggest several conclusions. First, in contrast to Desai et al. (1989), Baydar and Brooks-Gunn (1991), and to a somewhat lesser extent Belsky and Eggebeen (1991), we find minimally negative effects of early maternal employment on child outcomes. The data suggest that mothers who do not work for pay in the child's first 3 years may, if their occupational prospects are poor, facilitate verbal fluency in their children; however, this effect is reversed for mothers with later occupations high in complexity. In addition, these findings are duplicated for children's behavior problems: the protective effect of maternal AFQT on behavior problems was increased when mothers worked for pay in high complexity occupations. Thus, the emphasis on mothers forgoing employment to prevent children's social maladjustment (e.g., Belsky and Eggebeen 1991) does not receive strong support. These findings suggest serious qualifications to the conclusions that maternal employment has more positive consequences for women with fewer cognitive and material assets, and is more problematic for mothers with greater assets (e.g., Desai et al. 1989). None of these studies has considered the *quality* of mother's experience on the job as tapped by occupational complexity. Our explicit consideration of such conditions suggests that employment has its strongest benefits for mothers with better jobs, and less benign implications for mothers restricted to routine, monotonous labor at low wages.

Second, our findings suggest that it is essential to consider the role of fathers when attempting to understand the effects of parental paid working conditions on child outcomes. Fathers' less than full-time paid work hours in the child's first year or averaged over the child's first 3 years of life is associated with elevated behavior problems. In addition, overtime paternal hours in 1986 are associated with lower levels of verbal facility. Clearly, our data support the notion that fathers' paid working conditions may be important pathways through which children absorb appropriate behavioral norms, as well as develop verbal skills that serve as the foundation for future cognitive attainment.

How much support do our findings provide for those who worry that maternal paid work outside the home weakens bonds of social capital between parents and children useful in transmitting behavioral norms across generations? Support for the narrowest conceptualization of this argument is weak given the general lack of maternal early paid working conditions effects on child outcomes. Clearly, heavy parental employment demands may limit social capital needed in the development of cognitive and social skills, since 1986 overtime hours for mothers as well as fathers appear to inhibit the development of verbal facility. However, the findings are incompatible with social policies that discourage maternal employment. Thus, social trends toward increased maternal employment cannot be shown to be uniformly deleterious to child outcomes.

Also deserving closer scrutiny is the notion that it is the sheer dura-

122   Family Social Capital and Childhood Outcomes

tion of time that parents spend with children that is important. If that
were the case, we would expect to see that more limited paid work
hours are uniformly advantageous to children. The effects of variations
in early maternal part-time paid work, however, are not significant as a
set in any of our models; the effects of current maternal hours are nonlinear for cognitive outcomes, with moderate part-time hours superior
to more limited schedules, and contingent on occupational complexity
for cognitive outcomes. At the same time, the fact that early paternal
underemployment is associated with increases in behavior problems
points to one clear negative outcome associated with lower parental
paid work hours. Paternal underemployment likely results in frustration
for both parents, which may limit their ability both to set appropriate
examples of self-control and to help children establish suitable standards for themselves. It is likely that despite the numerous controls we
have introduced, there are unmeasured differences between families
where fathers work part-time hours and families where this is not the
case. Additional research should investigate the robustness of the findings we have produced regarding the disadvantages of paternal part-
time hours.

We also need to consider the processes through which parental paid
working conditions may indirectly influence child outcomes through
children's home environments. Our findings support the notion that
social capital embedded in children's home environments will both promote verbal facility and reduce behavior problems. Since we also know
that parents' paid working conditions influence the quality of children's
home environments, taken together these findings suggest that parental
paid working conditions may have both direct and indirect effects on
children, with family social capital as represented by the home environment playing an important role. We return to this issue in Chapter 7.

At a more general level, these findings caution us against easy
assumptions regarding when the most critical periods of child growth
may be for particular outcomes. Our findings suggest that current
maternal paid working conditions affect later verbal facility, but that
early paternal paid work hours affect later levels of behavior problems.
These findings reinforce the usefulness of looking at the roles of both
parents in the socialization process, and provide useful input to policy
debates. In particular, arguments regarding the importance of the child's
first year of life are often associated with normative prescriptions
regarding the desirability of "traditional" nuclear families and a traditional division of labor in the home. We know that such models are
impossible for many families today, and that even when possible, are
inconsistent with many adult decisions regarding the allocation of time
to paid work and family. A more useful working hypothesis is that there

are likely multiple periods throughout a child's life where parental input, or social capital, is important in facilitating appropriate development; if a particular period is deficient either in terms of parental time or in the nature of adult inputs generally, such deficiencies may be compensable, depending upon the timing, extent and nature of remedial intervention. Although this hypothesis may be proved false in particular circumstances, it provides a relatively parsimonious view of the socialization process. It also appears fruitful to consider viewing parental inputs in terms of averages across longer periods than some earlier researchers have advocated. Such a strategy helps us to focus on the overall, long-term environment in which the child is reared, without the distraction of short-term variations in either parental inputs or child outcomes, each of which might be inconsistent with longer-term trends. In the next chapter, we consider simultaneously the effects of early, 1986, and 1988 work and family conditions on child outcomes.

NOTE

1. The second panel of Table 6.2 shows a negative relationship between mothers being stably married during the child's first 3 years of life and PPVT-R, while the sign of the zero-order relationship is positive. We attribute the multivariate findings to our controlling for numerous maternal background characteristics such as AFQT, age, and ethnicity, each of which is associated with both mother being stably married and child having a higher PPVT-R score. We have therefore "explained" the stably married effect with background controls to the point that the sign of the marriage coefficient itself is reversed from the bivariate.

Chapter 7

The Cumulative Effects of Work and Family Conditions on Cognitive and Social Outcomes: Early, Recent, and Current Effects Reconsidered

We began our study of parents' jobs and children's lives by identifying young children with employed mothers in 1986 and tracing the linkages between parents' resources and occupational and family circumstances on the one hand and the children's current home environments and cognitive and behavioral outcomes on the other. We then followed these children forward in time from 1986 to 1988, asking two related questions. First, do linkages between current conditions and current outcomes continue to hold when the children are slightly older? Second, do alterations in paid work and family circumstances account for changes over time in children's outcomes? Finally, in Chapter 6 we returned to our original time point in 1986, and examined how the picture changed when we took into account the paid work and family conditions of the first few years of the children's lives.

In this chapter, we first examine variations in mothers' initial cognitive and social resources and consider the effects of maternal background characteristics on those resources. Second, we examine continuities and discontinuities in paid work and family conditions over the early, 1986, and 1988 periods, tracing the linkages between conditions at various time points. Finally, we consider data from all three time points in explaining the 1988 levels of children's reading recognition, arithmetic reasoning, and behavior problems. This analysis provides additional evidence regarding the relative power of early versus more recent experiences in shaping children's outcomes, an issue we considered in the previous chapter. But as the discussion of continuities and discontinuities in paid work and family circumstances makes clear, early and later conditions are themselves closely linked, and treating these as rival sets of explanatory factors is in some ways misleading. Early conditions are powerful predictors of later ones; this very continuity presents con-

125

ceptual as well as statistical difficulties in estimating models that include parallel measures from the three time points. We examine how the simultaneous inclusion of multiple time points may lead us to underestimate the effects of some conditions, and also provide some reassuring evidence that most of our findings are robust across alternative specifications. We begin by focusing on mothers' initial resources.

THE SOCIAL ROOTS OF INDIVIDUAL MATERNAL RESOURCES: AFQT AND SELF

As we have seen throughout earlier chapters, mothers' cognitive skills and attitudes about themselves and their mastery over the world have significant impacts on their children's cognitive and social development, and these effects are particularly strong when paid work and family conditions are more difficult. To better understand the social roots of the mothers' own competencies, we estimated multivariate models predicting mothers' 1988 scores on the AFQT and on the measures of self-concept included in the survey.

We have argued that children's cognitive skills are shaped by the resources their families can provide and the demands on those resources. As Table 7.1 shows, mothers' own cognitive skills vary in parallel ways, with higher maternal education completed and fewer siblings in 1979 predicting higher AFQT scores in 1980. Family structure does not have a significant impact, as tapped by the presence of two parents at age 14. Finally, ethnicity and region also affect AFQT scores, with black mothers most disadvantaged on these measures and Mexican and other Hispanic mothers also lagging behind white mothers. With ethnicity and family background controlled, being reared in the South is associated with lower scores as well (see Parcel and Geschwender 1994, for parallel findings for children).

Because the mothers completed the AFQT when they ranged in age from 15 to 22, it is not surprising that maternal age is strongly correlated with higher AFQT scores. However, this largely reflects associated differences in completed education at the time the test was taken; when education completed by 1980 is included in the equation, maternal age has a nonsignificant negative effect. Ethnicity, region, family size, parental education, and maternal age and education together account for nearly half of the variation in the mothers' cognitive scores.

As the second panel of Table 7.1 shows, maternal self-concept has some of the same precursors since higher maternal education and fewer siblings predict more positive self-concept. As was true for cognitive

Table 7.1. AFQT and Positive Self-Concept: Predictions from Early Maternal Resources ($N = 781$)

Variable	Mothers' AFQT		Mothers' self-concept	
	B	Beta	B	Beta
Ethnicity				
Black	−16.44[a]	−.34	.09	.04
White*	—	—	—	—
Mexican Hispanic	−4.85[d]	−.05	−.08	−.02
Other Hispanic	−7.70[c]	−.07	.17	.04
Education 1980	4.95[a]	.42	.16[a]	.31
Grandmother education	1.35[a]	.18	.02[d]	.07
Number of siblings 1979	−.98[a]	−.13	−.02[d]	−.07
Lived in south at age 14	−4.77[a]	−.12	−.06	−.04
Constant	15.66[c]		−2.68[a]	
R^2	.47		.16	
Adjusted R^2	.47		.15	

[a]$p < .001$; [b]$p < .01$; [c]$p < .05$; [d]$p < .10$; two-tailed test.
[a]$p < .0005$; [b]$p < .005$; [c]$p < .025$; [d]$p < .05$; one-tailed test.
*Reference category for categorical variable.
Note: Both models include controls for Maternal age in 1986, Family composition at age 14, and Urban residence at age 14.

skills, family structure at age 14 had no direct effects on mothers' self-concept. Unlike the findings for cognitive skills, however, ethnicity and region had no significant effects on mothers' self-attitudes.

Not surprisingly, reflecting their common precursors, these two maternal resources are themselves interrelated; the overall correlation is .37, and each is a significant predictor when added in a final step to the equations noted above. Our analyses in earlier chapters have established the significant direct effects of these resources on children's outcomes, even with paid work and family conditions controlled. As we will see in the following section of this chapter, these resources also have direct effects on the paid work and family circumstances that mothers experience.

PATTERNING OF WORK AND FAMILY CONDITIONS

Our general strategy is to estimate a series of multivariate models estimating early, recent (1986), and current (1988) paid work and family conditions. All equations include parental background characteristics, ethnicity, and child characteristics established at birth, such as low birth

weight and gender as predictors. Equations for recent (1986) paid work
and family conditions also include paid work and family characteristics
in the early period; and equations for current (1988) paid work and family conditions include paid work and family conditions in both the early
and recent time periods. We do not permit prediction from one measure
of paid work or family conditions to another at the same time point; for
example, only earlier occupational complexity and wage levels may
affect recent (1986) overtime hours. Since occupational complexity and
wage levels are related indicators of the quality of employment, we also
do not include earlier or contemporaneous measures of one in equations
predicting the other. For example, 1988 occupational complexity would
be predicted as a function of background, early and 1986 family conditions, and early and 1986 measures of occupational complexity and paid
work hours. We first consider mothers' employment status and mothers' occupational conditions from the child's early years to 1988, then
fathers' occupational conditions over the same time period, before
examining marriage and childbearing patterns.

Explaining Continuities and Discontinuities
of Occupational Patterns: Mothers

All the mothers in our sample were employed in 1986 when we first
studied the relationship between their occupational conditions and their
3- to 6-year-old children's social and cognitive outcomes. As we have
noted, however, not all were employed during their children's early
years, and about 1 in 5 was not currently employed when followed 2
years later. Here we examine predictors of early maternal paid employment as well as predictors of the mothers' occupational conditions and
hours. We follow these mothers forward and consider how early
employment experiences affect their 1986 occupational conditions. We
then return to the question of predictors of maternal paid employment,
this time focusing on continuing work from 1986 to 1988 versus sus-
pending employment, and consider for those working in 1988 how their
occupational conditions are linked to their earlier experiences.

Predicting Early Maternal Paid Employment

Among our mothers, all employed in 1986, there is a steadily increasing pattern of maternal paid employment as we follow children over the
first 3 years. While about a third did not work for pay during the child's
first year, this falls to 19.2% who did not work for pay throughout the
child's first 2 years, and 9.9% who did not work for pay at all during
the child's first 3 years. The intensity of employment shows a similar

increase, as shown by increases in the proportion of mothers who worked for pay in all 4 quarters of the year from 28.8% in year 1 to 49.9% in year 2 and 57.5% in year 3.

What distinguishes mothers with higher and lower levels of paid employment? We estimated OLS equations for a set of outcomes; in cases where the outcome was dichotomous, we also compared these results with those obtained from logit models and found no substantial differences in significant effects. For ease of interpretation, we display the OLS results predicting not working for pay throughout the child's first 3 years and exiting employment between 1986 and 1988 in Table 7.2. Our set of predictors included mothers' background and resources (age, ethnicity, education, cognitive skills, and self-concept), birth characteristics of the target child (birth weight and gender), and early family circumstances (number of older children, birth of another child within 3 years, and early marital history). Models predicting the number of years (0 to 3) of the first 3 that contained some employment, contrasting those working for pay all 3 years (61% of our sample) with those working for pay less than that, and contrasting the 9.9% who did not work for pay at all during the child's first 3 years with all others reveal a basically similar pattern; we table the latter contrast in the first panel of Table 7.2. Those not working for pay at all during the child's first 3 years have significantly lower education and the child was more likely to have low birth weight. Interestingly, marital history also predicts the absence of paid employment, with mothers who remained *un*married throughout the child's first 3 years also more likely than others to remain without any paid employment as well, perhaps because they were more likely to be eligible for public support programs through the time period.

The equation predicting mothers' working for pay all 3 years (data not shown) also indicates that mothers' human capital characteristics are the most critical predictors, since mothers who were older, had completed more years of education, and had higher cognitive skills had higher levels of paid employment. Family constraints also mattered; mothers who had more older children when the target was born, those whose child had a low birth weight, indicative of more early health problems, and those who had another child within 3 years of the target child's birth were less likely to have paid employment in all 3 years.

Predicting Mothers' Later Employment

We have noted that 1 in 10 mothers did not work for pay at all during the child's first 3 years, and 1 in 5 was not working for pay in 1988. Nevertheless, only 3.8% of the mothers worked for pay only in 1986. Seventy-four percent of the mothers were employed in all three periods, 17% worked for pay early and in 1986 but were not working for pay in

Table 7.2. Mother's Employment Patterns: The Impact of Child, Background, Family, and Work Characteristics

Variable	No employment during child's first 3 years		Employment exit between 1986 and 1988	
	B	Beta	B	Beta
Child characteristics 1988				
Low birth weight	.16[a]	.12	.04	.02
Male	.01	.01	.06[c]	.08
Parental characteristics				
Mother				
Age 1988			−.01[d]	−.07
Education year 3	−.02[b]	−.13		
Education 1988			−.04[b]	−.14
Maternal work characteristics years 1–3				
No work hours			.15[b]	.11
Spouse work characteristics years 1–3				
Work hours				
Under 35	.01	.01	.13[d]	.07
35–40*	—	—	—	—
Over 40	.02	.03	−.04	−.04
Maternal work characteristics 1986				
Hourly wage			−.02[c]	−.11
Work hours				
1–20			.15[b]	.13
21–34			−.01	−.01
35–40*			—	—
Over 40			−.00	−.00
Family changes years 1–3				
Marriage patterns				
Unstably married	−.07[c]	−.10	.01	.01
Married	−.08[b]	−.14	.01	.01
Not married*	—	—	—	—
Number of older siblings	−.00	−.00	−.06[c]	−.10
Constant	.39[c]		1.13[a]	
R^2	.07		.13	
Adjusted R^2	.05		.08	
N	775		720	

[a]$p < .001$; [b]$p < .01$; [c]$p < .05$; [d]$p < .10$; two-tailed test.

[a]$p < .0005$; [b]$p < .005$; [c]$p < .025$; [d]$p < .05$; one-tailed test.

*Reference category for categorical variable.

Note: Variables not significant in any panel are not displayed. Both panels also control for the following background characteristics: Maternal ethnicity, Maternal AFQT, Maternal positive self-concept; and the following years 1–3 work and family characteristics: Additional children born years 1–3, Spouse occupational complexity years 1–3, and Spouse hourly wages years 1–3. Panel 1 also controls for the following background characteristics: Maternal age year 3, Two parents at age 14, Grandmother education, Spouse age year 3, and Spouse education year 3. Panel 2 also controls for the following 1988 child and background characteristics: Child health problems 1988, Spouse Age 1988, Spouse education 1988; and the following work variables: Maternal hourly wage years 1–3, Maternal occupational complexity years 1–3, Maternal work hours years 1–3, Spouse 1986 work characteristics, and Maternal occupational complexity 1986.

1988, and 5.5% did not work for pay at all during the child's first 3 years but were working for pay in 1986 and 1988. Early and later nonemployment are linked, with not working for pay at all in the child's early years a significant predictor of stopping work for pay between 1986 and 1988. What else distinguished the 1 in 5 mothers who were not working for pay 2 years later in 1988, in addition to having been less likely to work for pay earlier? Significant predictors are shown in the second panel of Table 7.2. Echoing the importance of education as a predictor of working for pay in the first 3 years, mothers with less education were more likely to stop working for pay; in addition, those who had been working for pay at lower-wage jobs in 1986 and who had been working for pay only very low part-time hours were more likely to discontinue employment. Having more older children also predicted discontinuation; unexpectedly, mothers with a target child who was a boy were also more likely to stop working for pay. Thus, mothers with less previous paid employment, poorer occupational prospects and experiences, and greater family demands tended to cease paid employment.

Predicting Mothers' Occupational Conditions

Among the 90% of mothers who had some employment during the target child's first 3 years, what shaped the quality and amount of their early employment? We estimated OLS models predicting occupational complexity, wage levels, and the likelihood of maintaining an overtime paid work schedule during those years. We then examined how early employment and early paid working conditions affected 1986 paid working conditions, when all sample mothers were employed. As noted earlier, models predicting early paid working conditions included maternal background characteristics, child gender and birth weight, and early family conditions. Marital history and spouse's occupational characteristics at prior time points were also added in a second step to evaluate whether these also affected paid maternal working conditions.[1] We highlight the direct effects of resources and the same condition at earlier time points in Figure 7.1.

Occupational Complexity. Not surprisingly, older mothers, better educated mothers, and those with fewer older children (presumably indicating greater prior paid employment) were working in more complex early occupations. With these effects controlled, more positive maternal self-concept also predicted more complex work, while black mothers had less complex occupations. Models including early marital history or characteristics of the spouse's employment showed no additional effects.

In turn, early occupational complexity was the single strongest predictor of 1986 complexity. Higher education and higher cognitive skills

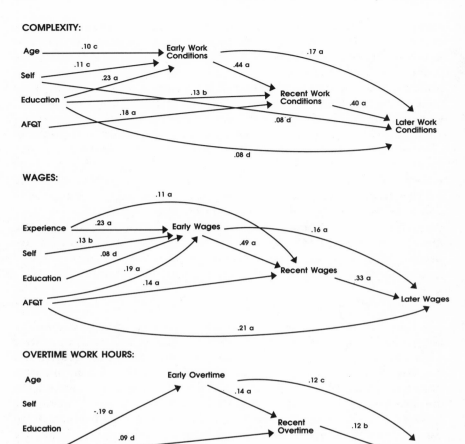

Figure 7.1.   Continuities in maternal occupational conditions: effects of
resources and prior conditions (standardized regression coefficients shown).
a: p < .001; b: p < .01; c: p < .05; d: p < .10; two-tailed test.
Note: Equations for early conditions include controls for paternal age and
education, child sex and birth weight, and early family conditions.
Equation for recent conditions also controls for early work and family
conditions. Equation for current work conditions also controls for recent
work and family conditions.

R^2 (and adjusted R^2) for each equation is:

Early complexity: .18 (.16) 1986 complexity: .38 (.36)   1988 complexity: .39 (.36)
Early wages: .24 (.22)   1986 wages: .39 (.36)   1988 wages: .38 (.34)
Early OT hours: .06 (.03)   1986 OT hours: .10 (.06)   1988 OT hours: .11 (.05)

Numbers of cases used are the maximums available for each time point.

also predicted work in more complex occupations, controlling for early occupational complexity. Other aspects of the early situation also had significant effects; specifically, not working for pay at all during the first 3 years, as well as working for pay with moderate part-time schedules, predicted lower occupational complexity in 1986. Overall, these models suggest strong continuity over time in occupational experiences and a strong continuing effect of both educational credentials and cognitive skills. They also suggest that greater early maternal investment in paid employment appears to have a significant positive effect on later opportunities.

For mothers employed in 1988, we see some fading of effects of early credentials and a strengthening of effects of recent paid working conditions. Both early complexity and recent (1986) complexity are very strong predictors of later complexity, and maternal education and self-concept have only weak ($p < .10$) direct effects on current complexity once early and recent occupational conditions are controlled.

Maternal Wage Levels. Our models predicting maternal wages are generally parallel to those just described for complexity. To control for the effects of employment experience on wage rates, however, we also included a continuous measure of mothers' total hours of paid employment from 1979 through the child's third year when predicting early wage rates, and from 1979 through 1986 when predicting recent and current wage rates. Predictors of early maternal wage level patterns are generally similar to those for early occupational complexity, with maternal self-concept and education significant; but maternal AFQT has a stronger impact on early wages than on complexity (for which it fell short of statistical significance), and early complexity but not early wages varies with race. Older mothers had occupations higher in complexity and wages, but maternal age has no significant effect on wages once the significant positive effect of total hours of paid employment is included. Even with employment experience controlled, mothers with more older children were earning lower wages. Unexpectedly, mothers whose target child is a boy also have higher early wages.

As with 1986 complexity, higher early wages predict higher 1986 wages, and having had no paid employment throughout the child's first 3 years predicts lower wages. Greater total hours of paid work experience also predicts higher 1986 wages. Some maternal resources continue to have direct effects even with early paid work conditions controlled; although education no longer has a direct effect on wages with early paid working conditions controlled, higher cognitive skills and more positive self-concept both predict higher 1986 wages. Finally, consideration of effects of marital and spousal patterns suggests that mothers who were more stably married had somewhat lower wages than other mothers. This is consistent with other research suggesting that married mothers who are employed experience less upward mobility than unmarried mothers (see Peterson 1989 for additional discussion).

Following these mothers forward to 1988, mothers' cognitive skills are the only maternal resource that continues to have a direct effect on 1988 wages even when early and recent conditions are controlled. Both early and recent higher wages predict higher current wages.

Work Hours.   If these patterns suggest that more advantaged mothers are investing more in labor force attachment and obtaining greater returns, the patterns of overtime employment, particularly in the early period, seem to reflect a greater push from family needs than a pull from economic opportunities. Mothers with low AFQT scores and those in unstable marriages are more apt to work early overtime schedules; black mothers are less likely to do so than whites. Predictors of more recent overtime schedules are more mixed. Early overtime paid work hours predicts to a greater likelihood of overtime paid work schedules in 1986, but controlling for that effect, mothers with higher AFQT and those whose early jobs were higher in complexity are more likely to be working for pay more than full-time in 1986. Being stably married throughout the first 3 years, on the other hand, makes mothers less likely than stably single mothers to be maintaining heavy paid work hours. The pattern is similar for current (1988) overtime schedules, which are more likely when early and 1986 paid work schedules were overtime. But they are also more likely when mothers are not currently married and when they have more older children and have also had a closely spaced subsequent birth. For all three time points, explained variance is low, but the findings suggest that mothers pursue overtime schedules for a complex set of reasons involving both greater economic needs and greater opportunities.

Explaining Continuities and Discontinuities
of Occupational Patterns: Fathers

Tracing fathers' occupational trajectories is additionally complicated because father presence and identity may change over the three time points. Data for the first 3 years may not refer to the same spouse as in 1986 or 1988. Thus, our models probably underestimate the continuities that would hold for the subset of 50% of our mothers who were stably married throughout the first 3 years of the child's life as well as in 1986 and 1988. We also lack parallel measures of fathers' cognitive skills or self-concept, and must rely on their age and education. Nevertheless, even this patchwork of data suggests high continuity of men's paid working conditions; effects of resources and prior occupational conditions are displayed in Figure 7.2.

Predicting Fathers' Occupational Conditions

Occupational Complexity. Predictors of early complexity are similar to those for mothers, with educational attainment having the strongest effects and black fathers characterized by paid work in less complex occupations given the same background characteristics; in addition, older maternal age was a positive predictor. There was strong continuity between early and 1986 occupational complexity ($r = .59$, beta $= .63$). Fathers' high early paid work hours predicted greater occupational complexity in 1986, consistent with the argument that greater early investment in employment has positive returns. Interestingly, however, low early hours also predicted greater occupational complexity, possibly reflecting greater investment in schooling during the early period. In addition, fathers with a low-birth-weight child had lower recent occupational complexity. Having a wife who worked for pay full-time was associated with greater father complexity than when wives worked for pay either moderate part-time or overtime hours.

Following fathers to 1988, we find that both early and recent complexity strongly predict higher current occupational complexity. Interestingly, mothers' early paid work conditions also predicted fathers' current occupational complexity, with mother not having worked for pay at all a negative predictor and mother working for pay in a more complex field during the child's early years a positive predictor. Since husbands and wives tend to be homogamous on human capital characteristics, these effects may proxy for unmeasured aspects of fathers' occupational capabilities.

Wage Levels. Fathers' wage patterns have generally similar predictors. Fathers' education is the key predictor of early wage levels, but black fathers earn lower early wage rates with age and education controlled. As found for fathers' early complexity, men married to older mothers have better early wages; it is possible that maternal age is proxying for other unmeasured aspects of fathers' occupational capabilities.

In turn, early wage levels are strongly predictive of later (1986) wages ($r = .64$ and beta $= .67$); education also had a direct effect. In addition, fathers who worked only part-time early work schedules have lower wages. Interestingly, family variables that were unrelated or negatively related to maternal job outcomes have positive effects for fathers, with having been stably married over the child's first 3 years and having had

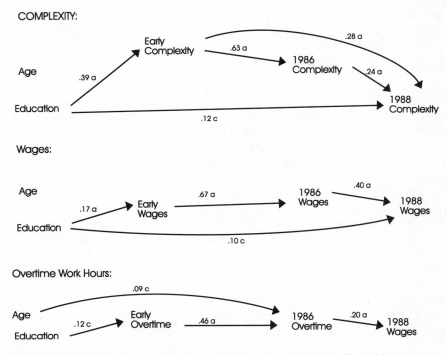

Figure 7.2. Continuities in father's occupational conditions: effects of resources and prior conditions (standardized regression coefficients shown).
a: p < .001; b: p < .01; c: p < .05; d: p < .10; two- tailed test.
Note: Equations for early conditions include controls for paternal age and education, child sex and birth weight, and early family conditions. Equation for recent conditions also controls for early work and family conditions. Equation for current work conditions also controls for recent work and family conditions.

R2 (and adjusted R2) for each equation is:

Early complexity: .22 (.20)   1986 complexity: .46 (.44)   1988 complexity: .34 (.29)
Early wages: .14 (.12)   1986 wages: .52 (.50)   1988 wages: .32 (.27)
Early OT hours: .06 (.04)   1986 OT hours: .26 (.23)   1988 OT hours: .13 (.07)

Numbers of cases used are the maximums available for each time point.

a closely spaced birth subsequent to the birth of the target child both emerging as significant positive predictors of fathers' 1986 wages.

Finally, following fathers forward to 1988, we again see fairly strong continuity from recent to current wage levels (*r* = .39, beta = .40). Higher father education continues to predict to higher wages in 1988. Fathers employed only part-time hours in the recent period had lower wages. An anomalous finding is that early part-time employment, net of the adverse impact of 1986 part-time employment, has a significant positive effect. Again, this may reflect lagged positive effects of schooling during the early period. Also unexpected is lower 1988 wages for fathers with a male target child.

Work Hours. Fathers' overtime paid work schedules are more normative than are mothers', and their predictors are more parallel to predictors of advantaged occupational placement; but again we see sign of economic need driving hours. Better educated and nonblack fathers are more likely to be working overtime schedules in the early years. Those with early overtime hours are more likely to be maintaining overtime schedules in 1986 ($r = .42$ and beta $= .46$); but those with higher early wages and a spouse with higher early wages are less likely to do so, as are those with a closely spaced birth. The pattern is similar for 1988 overtime hours, with working overtime hours 2 years earlier the single best predictor; again, those with a wife with higher early wages and those with a closely spaced subsequent child are less likely to do so.

Continuities and Discontinuities in Marital Histories

We now turn to the mothers' histories of marital union and childbearing. We first discuss changes in marital status over time, and then examine the birth of additional children. We first consider these issues descriptively, then report our findings from multivariate models. There is a small but steady decline over time over the first few years in the proportion of mothers married, with 73% married in years 1 and 2, and 69% married in year 3. However, this masks some movement in and out of marriage over this time period. Overall, only half of the mothers were married in all 3 of the child's first 3 years and in 1986 and 1988. Fourteen percent were not married at any of these time points, and a third experienced at least one marital transition over this time period. We may note that the category labeled unstably married during the child's first 3 years includes both mothers not initially married who became married in the child's second or third year (30% of the unstable group), mothers who were initially married but subsequently experienced disruption (58% of the unstable group), and a small number who had more than one change during the first 3 years (less than 2% of the unstable group).

Figure 7.3 displays the effects of maternal resources as well as the strong continuity over time in mothers' marital status in the first 3 years and from 1986 to 1988. Models contrasting mothers stably married during the child's first 3 years with others (shown in Figure 7.3) and those contrasting mothers remaining single all 3 years (data not shown) are generally consistent in suggesting that older mothers and those with

MARITAL STATUS:

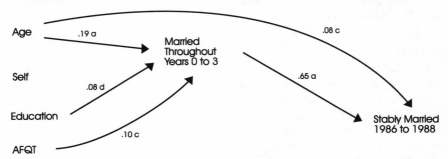

Figure 7.3. Continuities in maternal mother's marital status: effects of resources and prior status (standardized regression coefficients shown).
$a: p < .001; b: p < .01; c: p < .05; d: p < .10;$ two-tailed test.
Note: Equation for married through year 3 also controls for maternal ethnicity and child characteristics at birth. Equation for stably married 1986–1988 also controls for early work and family conditions.
R^2 (and adjusted R^2) for each equation is:
Married throughout years 0–3: .28 (.26)
Stably married 1986–1988: .38 (.36)
Numbers of cases used are the maximums available for each time point.

higher education and higher cognitive skills were more likely to be married in their children's early years; with these factors controlled, black mothers were less likely to be continuously married. In turn, mothers who had remained married throughout the child's first 3 years were much more likely to be married in 1986 ($r = .58$, beta = .79, equation not shown) and mothers married at least some of those years were also more likely to be married in 1986. These continuities are so strong that other effects are relatively weak or reversed, but black mothers remain less likely than others to be married, as are younger mothers.

Finally, models contrasting those stably married in both 1986 and 1988 with all others (Figure 7.3) suggest the same high levels of predictability from earlier marital status, with mothers stably married or intermittently married in the first 3 years more likely to be married in 1986 and 1988. In addition, the spouse's early paid work history predicts later marital patterns, with higher early spouse wages a positive predictor and early spousal part-time employment a negative predictor; early spousal overtime hours also tended to have a negative effect ($p < .10$) on later marriage. Black mothers are still less likely to be stably married from 1986 through 1988, controlling for earlier history.

Patterns of Family Building

We have noted that overall family size was fairly small in 1986, with a third of the children being the only children in their families; of the remaining children, more than three-fourths had only one sibling. Nearly 1 in 5 (19%) mothers had another child before the target child turned 3, and 27% had a child between that time and 1986. Finally, 22% had an additional birth between 1986 and 1988. Nevertheless, cumulated family size is generally not that high; average number of children in 1988 is 2.06; 25% of the children are still only children, 51% have one sibling, 19% have two siblings, and only 5% have three or more.

In our multivariate models, predictors of subsequent childbearing included mothers' background and resources; birth characteristics of the target child (birth weight and gender), and initial family size (number of older children). We also evaluated the effects of early and current marital history, and earlier paid work history, in subsequent steps for each equation. We estimated a series of models predicting the likelihood of additional births during the target child's first 3 years, births between that time point and 1986, and births between 1986 and 1988. Major findings are outlined in Figure 7.4.

While models predicting additional births in this accumulating fertility have generally low explained variance, some consistencies are apparent. Older mothers and those with fewer children older than the target child were more likely to have another child within the next 3 years; better educated mothers were somewhat less likely to do so ($p < .10$). Mothers who were stably married during the child's first 3 years were significantly more likely to have a closely spaced subsequent birth. Since such births have negative effects on children's early vocabulary development and later reading skills, this implies an indirect negative effect of early stable marriage. With mothers' marital history controlled, black children were also more likely to have a closely spaced younger brother or sister.

Older mothers and those more stably married in the early years were also more apt to have an additional child in the next few years, while having a higher number of older children and having had a child before the target child turned 3 were negative predictors. Similarly, those married in 1986, those who had fewer older children, and those who had not had a recent birth prior to 1986 were more likely to have another baby between 1986 and 1988. Parents' paid work histories did not have effects on subsequent fertility except for the final interval. But for births between 1986 and 1988, fathers' occupational conditions influenced the likelihood of another birth, with higher occupational complexity in 1986

FAMILY BUILDING:

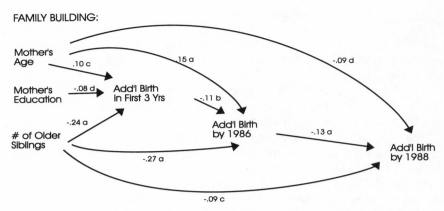

Figure 7.4.   Patterns of family building: effects of maternal resources and prior
    fertility (standardized regression coefficients shown).
a: $p < .001$; *b:* $p < .01$; *c:* $p < .05$; *d:* $p < .10$; two-tailed test.
Note: Equation for each time period also controls for maternal ethnicity, AFQT
    and positive self-concept, spousal characteristics, work and family
    conditions at earlier time points.

R^2 (and adjusted R^2) for each equation is:

Additional child within 3 years: .05 (.04)
Additional child by 1986: .10 (.06)
Additional child between 1986 and 1988: .12 (.07)

Numbers of cases used are the maximums available for each time point.

and a pattern of overtime work hours during the target child's first few
years associated with a greater likelihood of another birth. Thus, overall, older mothers and mothers spending a greater proportion of time
married were more likely to have another baby; a recent birth made subsequent births less likely.

These models examine the incremental steps contributing to total fertility. We also predicted the total number of children in the family by
1988 (data not shown). We estimated a series of four equations, beginning with maternal background and birth characteristics of the target
child, and adding in subsequent steps marital history, parents' early
paid working conditions, and parents' recent (1986) paid working conditions. Since the latter two steps may be simultaneous with the births
of children that are contributing to the total, we focus here on early predictors. Consistent with the findings just noted, we find that older mothers and less well-educated mothers had more children; these effects persist across all equations. Mothers stably married through the child's first
3 years had higher eventual family size than all others; having been single in 1986 and 1988 was also associated with lower total family size.

With age and marital history controlled, black mothers also had more children than whites. It is noteworthy that in all models, neither mothers' own early employment status nor their occupational conditions had significant direct effects on additional childbearing. Rather, the key predictors were marital status and prior fertility.

ASSESSING CUMULATIVE MODELS
OF 1988 CHILD OUTCOMES

In Chapters 4 and 5, we estimated effects of 1986 paid working conditions on 1986 cognitive and social outcomes, then followed the children forward to 1988 and asked how changes occurring between 1986 and 1988 in paid work and family conditions helped to explain 1988 outcomes net of 1986 levels of vocabulary skills and behavior problems. Here we focus on absolute levels of 1988 outcomes and evaluate how taking into account both early paid work and family conditions during the child's first 3 years and more recent conditions in 1986 and 1988 may qualify our earlier conclusions. These models include parental background resources (age and education and, for mothers, AFQT and self-concept), child background (ethnicity, gender, birth weight, and current health problems), and paid work and family conditions in the early years, in 1986, and in 1988. For ease in presenting results, we refer to 1988 conditions as *current* and 1986 conditions as *recent; early* refers to conditions during the child's first 3 years. To evaluate the possible mediating impact of home environments, we estimate models both with and without home environments controlled. As in earlier chapters, we also evaluate interactive effects. Table 7.3 displays the additive findings for 1988 PIAT reading, 1988 PIAT mathematics, and 1988 behavior problems. For each dependent variable, the first panel shows additive effects without controlling for home environments, and the second includes additive effects of 1986 and 1988 home environments. We note that many effects significant in the additive models are qualified when interactive effects are included.

Resources and Conditions: Effects on Reading Achievement

Child background and maternal resources play a similar role for reading and mathematics achievement, with boys, children with low birth weights, and those whose mothers had more limited cognitive skills far-

Table 7.3. 1988 PIAT Read, PIAT Math, and BPI: The Impact of Child, Background, Maternal and Spouse Work Characteristics for Years 1–3, 1986 and 1988, Family Characteristics 1986, Family Changes Years 1–3 and 1986–1988, Home 1986, and Home 1988 (N = 721)

	Read 1988				Math 1988				BPI 1988			
	1		2		3		4		5		6	
Variable	B	Beta	B	Beta	B	Beta	B	Beta	B	Beta	B	Beta
Child characteristics 1988												
Low birth weight	-4.41c	-.09	-4.86b	-.09	-5.56b	-.11	-6.14a	-.12				
Male	-2.05c	-.09	-1.88c	-.08	-1.62c	-.07	-1.42d	-.06				
Parental characteristics												
Mother												
Ethnicity												
Black					-4.55a	-.15	-3.33c	-.11				
White*	—		—		—		—		—		—	
Mexican Hispanic					-4.83c	-.09	-3.37d	-.06				
Other Hispanic					-2.09	-.03	-1.57	-.02				
Age 1988	-.27	-.05	-.39d	-.07								
AFQT 1980	.20a	.33	.20a	.34	.14a	.23	.15a	.24				
Positive self-concept	.92d	.07	.42	.03	-.28	-.02	-.93d	-.07	-2.71a	-.17	-2.25b	-.14
Spouse												
Education 1988					-.46d	-.07	-.49d	-.08				
Maternal work characteristics years 1–3												
Occupational complexity	.11d	.07	.09	.06	.40d	.08	.48c	.09				
Hourly wage												
No work hours									-3.96c	-.10	-3.91d	-.09
Work hours												

	C1	C2	C3	C4	C5	C6	C7	C8	C9	C10	C11	C12
1–20					.11	3.91b	.10	3.58b				
21–34					.01	.18	.00	.05				
35–40*					—	—	—	—				
Over 40					-.06	-2.00	-.07	-2.54d				
Spouse work characteristics years 1-3												
Occupational complexity	.07	.11	.08	.13d	.11	.18c	.10	.16c				
Work hours												
Under 35	-.07e	3.33d	-.08	-4.05c	-.10	-5.13c	-.08	-4.22c	.15	8.42b	8.40b	.15
21–34												
35–40*	—	—	—	—	—	—	—	—	—	—	—	—
Over 40	-.05	-1.30	-.05	-1.39	-.01	-.39	-.01	-.19	.08	2.32	2.23	.08
Maternal work characteristics 1986												
Work hours												
1–20									.12	4.37c	4.48c	.12
21–34									.02	.85	1.23	.03
35–40*									—	—	—	—
Over 40									-.06	-2.37	-2.93	-.07
Spouse work characteristics 1986												
Work hours												
0–35					-.05	-3.15	-.02	-1.48				
35–40*					—	—	—	—				
Over 40					-.12	-3.58b	-.12	-3.44b				
Maternal work characteristics 1988												
Occupational complexity	-.09	-.11c	-.09	-.11c					-.12	-3.65c	-3.44c	-.11
Stopped work (since 1986)	.06	1.66d	.06	1.58								
Work hours												
1–20					-.07	-2.92c	-.09	-3.45c	-.00	-.09	-.00	-.00e
21–34					.05	1.94	.05	1.68	-.10	-4.60c	-4.47d	-.09
35–40*					—	—	—	—	—	—	—	—
Over 40					.09	-3.42c	.07	2.90c	-.08	-3.53d	-2.96	-.07

Table 7.3. (continued)

Variable	Read 1988				Math 1988				BPI 1988			
	1		2		3		4		5		6	
	B	Beta	B	Beta	B	Beta	B	Beta	B	Beta	B	Beta
Spouse work characteristics 1988												
Hourly wage	.22c	.10	.23c	.11								
Family changes years 1–3												
Marriage patterns												
Unstably married					2.04	.07	1.01	.03				
Married					−1.29	−.05	−1.56	−.07				
Not married*	—	—	—	—	—	—	—	—				
Number of older siblings	−1.55c	−.09	−.72	−.04								
Additional children born	−2.31c	−.08	−1.91d	−.07	−2.73b	−.09	−2.14c	−.07				
Family characteristics 1986												
Additional child at 4–7 years	−2.15c	−.08	−1.77d	−.07	−1.83c	−.07	−1.38	−.05				
Family changes 1986–1988												
Marriage patterns												
Stably married*	—	—			—	—			—	—	—	—
Marriage ended									4.88c	.10	4.67c	.10
Marriage started									4.98c	.11	5.28c	.11
Stably single									6.97a	.23	7.00a	.23
Additional children born									4.97a	.15	4.82b	.15

	(1)	(2)	(3)	(4)	(5)	(6)
Home 1986		1.35[b] .11		2.10[a] .16		−1.31[d] −.09
Home 1988		1.64[b] .11		1.76[b] .12		
Constant	94.71[a]	96.64[a]	90.67[a]	93.75[a]	4.51	1.96
R^2	.25	.27	.29	.32	.20	.21
Adjusted R^2	.19	.21	.23	.27	.11	.12

[a] $p < .001$; [b] $p < .01$; [c] $p < .05$; [d] $p < .10$; two-tailed test.

[a] $p < .0005$; [b] $p < .005$; [c] $p < .025$; [d] $p < .05$; one-tailed test.

*Set of dummy variables is not significant.

[e] Reference category for categorical variable.

Note: Variables not significant in any model are not displayed. All panels also control for the following child and background characteristics: Child Health Problems 1988, Maternal Education 1988, Spouse Age 1988; and the following work variables: Maternal occupational complexity 1986, Maternal hourly wage 1986, Maternal hourly wage 1988, Spouse hourly wage years 1–3, Spouse occupational complexity 1986, Spouse hourly wage 1986, Spouse occupational complexity 1988, and Spouse work hours 1988. Panels 1 and 2 also control for Maternal ethnicity, Spouse education 1988, Maternal hourly wage years 1–3, Maternal hourly wages years 1–3, Maternal number work hours years 1–3, Maternal work hours 1986, Maternal work hours 1988, Spouse work hours 1986, Marriage patterns years 1–3, Marriage patterns years 1986–1988, and Additional children born 1986–1988. Panels 3 and 4 also control for Maternal age 1988, Maternal occupational complexity years 1–3, Maternal number work hours years 1–3, Maternal work hours 1986, Maternal occupational complexity 1988, Maternal stopped working since 1986, Spouse hourly wage 1988, Number of older siblings years 1–3, Marriage patterns 1986–1988, and Additional children born 1986–1988. Panels 5 and 6 also control for Low birth weight, Male, Child age in months 1988, Maternal ethnicity, Maternal age 1988, Maternal AFQT in 1980, Spouse education 1988, Maternal occupational complexity 1988, Maternal occupational complexity years 1–3, Spouse occupational complexity years 1–3, Spouse work hours 1986, Spouse hourly wage 1988, Marriage patterns years 1–3, Number of older siblings years 1–3, Additional children born years 1–3, and Additional child at 4–7 in 1986. Panel 6 also controls for Home environment 1988.

ing more poorly. In addition, mothers' more positive self-concept conveys an advantage for children's reading skills, although it has no direct effect on mathematics.

Marital history had little impact on children's reading skills, but sibling structure did have significant effects. In particular, a younger sibling spaced fairly closely had a negative impact, and a greater number of older siblings also had an adverse impact on reading. Occupational conditions tended to have weak positive effects, with both parents' early occupational complexity having positive effects, and fathers' current wage levels also being positive. Variations in paid work hours are generally nonsignificant, except that an early pattern of fathers working for pay less than full-time is associated with poorer reading skills. One anomalous finding is a negative direct effect of higher current maternal occupational complexity on children's reading skills.

Interactions

Once more, tests for interaction qualify some of these findings. Effects of current maternal occupational complexity differ for mothers who have a new baby, since it is only for this subgroup that higher complexity is problematic. Marital termination, nonsignificant overall, has more negative effects when mothers are currently working for pay only part-time than when they are full-time paid workers. Childbearing and paid work effects also interact in that the effects of mothers' current paid work hours differ for new mothers, with very low part-time worse for new mothers than for others. Finally, mothers' and fathers' recent occupational complexity had less positive effects the higher was the other parent's occupational complexity, suggesting some diminishing returns of positive parental occupational conditions.

Effects of Home Environments

Both recent and current home environments have significant positive additive effects on reading skills; we do not find significant interactions by family background, paid work, and family conditions in these effects. To the extent that the quality of home environments mediates the effects of other variables, their direct effects should become weaker when home environments are included in the model. However, the inclusion of home environments alters very few direct effects of other variables; we do find that the effect of maternal self-concept now drops below significance and effects of siblings become weaker. We return to this issue in our concluding chapter.

Interactions by Ethnicity and Gender

We conducted Chow tests for the final model including home environment measures and all significant interactive effects. Chow tests were not significant for ethnicity but were significant for gender. We find that the effects of fathers' early complexity are significantly more positive for boys than for girls, for whom they are nonsignificant. The proportion of variance explained in the final model incorporating interactive effects, effects of home environments, and interactions by gender accounts for 30% of the variance in children's 1988 reading skills (adjusted $R^2 = .24$).

Resources and Conditions: Effects on Mathematical Reasoning

The second two panels of Table 7.3 display results for the additive equations predicting children's 1988 PIAT arithmetic skills. We see that boys and children with low birth weights score lower than their counterparts on the 1988 PIAT arithmetic subscale. Mothers' own poorer early cognitive skills as tapped by the AFQT also predict lower child scores. These findings are consistent with those for children's reading skills. As noted above, we found no significant ethnic differences in PIAT reading skills, but ethnic background does have significant effects on children's arithmetic skills, with black and Mexican-American children having lower average skills than white children. Family experiences also shape children's development of mathematics skills. Specifically, while mothers' marital history during the first 3 years has no direct effect, the recent end of mother's marriage is associated with poorer math skills in 1988. As was true for reading skills, sibling structure affects arithmetic skills. That is, although neither the number of siblings older than the target child nor a recent birth within the last 2 years has a significant impact, both the birth of a young sibling during the child's first 3 years and the birth of a younger brother or sister in the subsequent few years have negative effects.

Mothers' not working for pay at all during the first 3 years has no impact, but early wages have a positive effect, and early complexity effects are also positive although they do not reach statistical significance ($p < .13$); more recent maternal complexity or wages are not significant. Both early and current paid work hours have a significant impact, with low part-time hours better than full-time during the early years but worse than full-time in the current period; current overtime hours also have a positive impact, an unexpected finding. Fathers' early complexity has positive effects, but no father wage variables reach significance. Both early and recent (1986) father paid work hours are significant, with early part-time patterns negative and more recent overtime schedules also negative.

Interactions

There was some evidence that maternal resources played a stronger role when conditions were more difficult, since higher maternal education had more positive effects for mothers currently in low-wage jobs. Mothers' stopping work for pay, insignificant overall, had positive effects when mothers had been working overtime schedules in 1986. As was true for reading skills, the effects of mothers' current (1988) paid work hours varied depending on whether mothers had recently had a new baby in that moderate part-time schedules were significantly more positive for new mothers than for others. Finally, again echoing the finding for reading skills, mothers' and fathers' recent occupational complexity interact, with diminishing returns when both jobs are high in complexity.

Effects of Home Environments

Paralleling the findings for children's reading skills, both recent and current home environments have significant positive effects on mathematics scores, and the proportion of variance explained increases significantly when home environments are included in the equation. Relatively few effects are altered, although the effect of younger siblings becomes weaker, the coefficient for siblings born after the first 3 years is no longer significant, and the effect of early maternal overtime paid work schedules becomes significantly negative. The only interaction with home environments is with fathers' current paid work hours, since a positive current home environment is less powerfully predictive of better math skills when the father is currently working for pay extensive overtime work schedules.

Interactions by Ethnicity and Gender

Chow tests were nonsignificant for ethnicity but significant for gender. Examination of and testing of gender differences showed two differences. First, the birth of a closely spaced sibling, significantly negative overall, had a significantly more powerful effect on boys than on girls, for whom it was nonsignificant. Second, the effects of mothers' stopping work for pay between 1986 and 1988, which was more positive if mothers had been working for pay long hours, was more positive for girls than for boys. The final model incorporating interactive effects, additive and interactive effects of home environments, and interactive effects by gender accounts for 37% of the variance (adjusted $R^2 = .32$).

Resources and Conditions: Effects on Behavior Problems

We now evaluate effects of early, recent, and current conditions on 1988 levels of behavior problems. In Chapter 5, we had traced effects of 1986 to 1988 conditions on changes in behavior problems over the same time period; here our focus is on tracing effects of early, recent, and current paid work and family conditions on absolute levels in 1988. For comparison with models presented in earlier chapters, we use the sample of children aged 4 to 6 in 1986. Results for the additive equations are shown in the final two panels of Table 7.3.

Maternal self-concept has a strong direct effect on children's level of behavior problems in 1988, consistent with findings in early models reported in Chapters 5 and 6. No other background or child characteristics reach significance in the initial additive model. Marital history plays a stronger role than for the cognitive outcomes in two ways. First, both ending a marriage and starting a new marriage in the last 2 years is associated with higher behavior problems compared to children whose mothers remained married at both recent time points. Second, mother being unmarried at both recent time points is also associated with higher behavior problems. There is a weak anomalous adverse impact of mother being married through the first 3 years, produced by the high collinearity between early and later marital status. We had found that births of closely spaced younger siblings had negative impacts on math and reading outcomes, but it is only mother having an additional child in the last 2 years that is associated with higher behavior problems.

Mothers' occupational complexity has no significant effects, but both having no paid employment in the child's early years and having stopped working for pay in the most recent period have beneficial implications in the additive model; as we shall see shortly, these effects are altered when we include interactive effects. There are also some effects of mothers' paid work hours, with very low part-time paid work in the recent (1986) period associated with higher behavior problems in 1988 than when mother was working for pay a full-time schedule in 1986; in addition, current (1988) paid work schedules that are moderate part-time or overtime are more protective than current (1988) full-time paid work. Fathers' occupational complexity and wage levels also have no significant effects; but again we see that fathers' part-time paid employment in the early years has adverse implications for children's outcomes.

Interactions

Inclusion of significant interaction terms produces several significant changes in our conclusions. We again see that maternal resources are more critical under more difficult circumstances, with effects of mothers' positive self-concept more powerful when mothers have ended their marriage or had another baby during the last 2 years. The quality of the mother's current employment also buffers the adverse effects of marriage ending, with effects more benign for mothers whose current occupations are higher in complexity. Finally, the effect of mothers' stopping work for pay between 1986 and 1988 is not invariant, since it is more beneficial for mothers whose 1986 jobs had been lower in challenge and complexity and involved extensive overtime hours. With these interactions included, effects of mothers' early paid employment, recent hours, and current hours become nonsignificant; in addition, children with low birth weight now have significantly higher behavior problems, a finding that persists in all subsequent equations.

Effects of Home Environments

In contrast to the strong effects of both recent and current home environments on 1988 arithmetic and reading scores, and the significant protective effects of 1986 home environments on 1986 behavior problems reported in Chapters 5 and 6, we find that home environments have very little impact on current behavior problems. Even the weak ($p < .10$) effect of recent home environments shown in the second panel of Table 7.3 becomes nonsignificant when the interactions just discussed in the previous paragraph are included. Neither 1986 nor 1988 home environments have statistically significant effects on 1988 behavior problems, and tests for interaction by maternal resources and paid work and family conditions do not qualify this conclusion.

Interactions by Ethnicity and Gender

In contrast to our nonsignificant findings of interactions between home environments and maternal resources, paid work conditions, or family conditions, we find that effects of home environments vary by gender and ethnicity. The effect of 1986 home environments is significantly stronger for girls, for whom it does have a significant protective effect, than for boys, for whom it is not significant. Conversely, the number of older siblings also has little impact for boys, but tends to increase behavior problems for girls. There is also an interaction between ethnicity and gender, with boys reported to have significantly more behavior problems than girls among black children than among other ethnic groups. Finally, recent marital transitions—both marital disruption and beginning a new marriage—which had overall adverse effects, have weaker effects for black children than for others. Proportion of variance explained by the final model including all significant interactions is .34 (adjusted R^2 = .24).

COMPARING ALTERNATIVE SPECIFICATIONS

These models of 1988 child outcomes include measures of paid work and family conditions in the child's early years and in 1986 and 1988. Given the high continuity in marital status and in occupational conditions, the simultaneous inclusion of measures from all three time points may make it difficult to sort out causal impacts. To evaluate possible problems, we also estimated two sets of additive models and analyzed changes in signs and significance under alternative specifications. The first series was a cumulative model. Step one included only parental background and child characteristics; subsequent steps added early paid work and family conditions, recent (1986) paid work and family conditions, and finally current (1988) paid work and family conditions. We were particularly concerned with understanding when variables significant in earlier steps became nonsignificant or changed sign when related variables measured at other time points were also permitted to have an effect.

This set of analyses was generally reassuring. While direct effects of education generally became nonsignificant when early occupational conditions were entered, other child and background effects were robust throughout the series. Sibling and marriage effects were also generally invariant across models. The exception was for the effects of marital history on behavior problems. In particular, early marital history had no significant impact in models containing only the early variables or early and 1986 variables, but the full model produced anomalous significant effects opposite in direction to those observed earlier. We conclude that these effects are produced by multicollinearity among the full set of predictor variables. To check this, we also constructed a series of dummy variables capturing stability and change in mother's marital history from the child's birth to 1988; these detect no adverse effects of greater early exposure to marriage.

Most maternal occupational effects were also consistent across models. Effects of fathers' early paid working conditions, however, tended to be stronger when first entered in the model and then become nonsignificant in later steps. This occurred consistently for fathers' wages, which as we have noted is highly correlated over the three time points. For all three dependent variables—reading, mathematics, and behavior problems—higher fathers' wages in the early years had significant beneficial effects, which became nonsignificant when more recent measures of wages were also included. The latter measures were nonsignificant and often inconsistent in direction. Coefficients for early spouse part-time employment also became weaker but remained significant, while the parallel measures for later time points were generally nonsignificant. Overall proportions of variance explained continued to increase with the inclusion of data from additional time points, but relatively few of the new variables were statistically significant, and some of the formerly significant effects drop below significance. This pattern suggests that the effect of these variables is being diluted across the variables tapping the same construct across time. The more highly correlated are measures over time, the more this is likely to occur. Thus, it is not surprising that such problems are more serious with the most stable variables.

The second series of equations provided additional support for this interpretation. It focused particularly on the three sets of paid work variables; it began with a model containing parent and child background and added the full set of marital and childbearing variables. In three alternative models, we then added mother and father paid work variables from one of the three possible time points. We were particularly concerned with identifying variables that had consistent effects in single-time-point models but that all became nonsignificant or had opposing signs in more saturated models.

It is interesting that addition of paid work variables from any time point produced roughly equivalent increases in explained variance. Early and recent wage variables for both mothers and fathers were stronger and more consistent when not in the same models. For example, positive effects of mothers' early wages on mathematics skills fell from .51 ($p < .01$) in models including only early paid working conditions to .40 ($p < . 10$) in models with three measures of paid working conditions; positive effects of mothers' recent wages on math skills were .27 ($p < .10$) in models including only recent paid working conditions, but nonsignificant in the final model; and similar changes from significant to nonsignificant effects were observed for effects of fathers' early wages on behavior problems and fathers' recent wages on reading skills. Fathers' work hours variables showed similar losses in significance. For example, low work hours measured at any time point had significant negative implications for children's reading skills; but in the final model only the early measure remains significant. Fathers' early and recent paid overtime work has negative effects in separate models, but no paid overtime work variable remains significant in the final model. Again, we see suggestions that the very continuity of occupational conditions may lead us to underestimate their effects when we cast measures tapping the same construct but at various time points into competition with one another. While overall explained variance increases over that achieved by data from any single time point, collinearity among our measures weakens individual effects and makes it difficult to be confident about any claims that effects vary over differing time points. We are on stronger ground in making more general claims that a pattern of low wages of either parent or of extensive part-time employment of fathers has negative implications for their children's cognitive and social development.

SUMMARY AND DISCUSSION

In this chapter, we have considered the social roots of initial maternal resources, the linkages among mothers' and fathers' paid work and family experiences over time, and the effects of paid work and family conditions at three time points on children's cognitive and social outcomes. We find that mothers' initial resources are themselves predicted by more advantaged family circumstances in their own families of origin. Given the power of these maternal resources in influencing maternal paid work and family conditions and in shaping outcomes for the next generation, we suggest that future research give greater attention to the precursors to these two major maternal resource measures and to examining their influence on one another.

Second, we find strong continuities over time in both maternal and paternal paid work conditions. Mothers with higher human capital are more likely to be employed and to be employed at better wages and in more complex occupations; and earlier conditions shape later ones. We see a similar pattern for fathers, with especially high continuity in wage levels. Marital ties are also relatively stable over time, with those initially married much more likely to be married at later time points, and those initially unmarried likely to remain so. Although mothers' own occupational experiences have little impact on later marital disruption, marriages to men who work for pay part-time or at low-wage jobs in the early years are less likely to persist.

Finally, our cumulative models of early, recent, and later paid work and family conditions are largely consistent with findings reported in earlier chapters. We continue to find that initial maternal cognitive and psychosocial resources have significant effects in shaping paid work and family conditions, especially at earlier time points. In addition, these resources have direct effects on children's cognitive and social outcomes even with early, later, and current paid work and family conditions controlled. In particular, mothers' cognitive skills are strong predictors of their children's math and reading skills, while mothers' self concept is more important for reading and for the prevention of behavior problems. These resources also interact with paid work and family conditions, blunting the adverse impact of difficult circumstances.

Children's own vulnerabilities also play a role, with low birth weight implicated in more adverse cognitive and social outcomes; boys also have poorer average reading and math skills than do girls, while children from black and Hispanic families lag behind other children in math skills but not in other areas. Gender and ethnicity also qualify the effects of other variables. Family circumstances also matter, with the numbers of siblings particularly critical for the development of cognitive skills, and mothers' marital history more critical for the avoidance of behavior problems.

Finally, and most central to our story, both parents' economic activities affect their children's well-being. The quality of employment, as tapped by occupational complexity and wage levels, has generally positive effects on children's outcomes, although these effects are often contingent on other conditions. The hours of mothers' paid work have few consistent effects, but both fathers' paid part-time employment and routine overtime schedules have adverse implications for children's cognitive and social outcomes.

Contingent effects of paid working conditions are generally of two kinds. The first include interactions between paid work and family conditions, with, for example, challenging paid working conditions less beneficial for mothers who are also facing the challenges of high numbers of children or a recent additional birth. The second includes interactions between fathers' and mothers' paid work conditions; examples are our earlier findings that the combination of two overtime schedules, two part-time schedules, or two highly complex occupations are more negative than an additive model would predict.

In the next chapter, we discuss how consideration of conditions at multiple time points has helped to inform our understanding of social influences on children's development, and review the evidence regarding the mediating role of home environments in that process. We also discuss variations in those processes by ethnicity and gender, and draw policy implications from our findings.

NOTE

1. For consistency with earlier models, we use the continuous measure of years of education in these models. Because educational credentials such as a high school diploma or college degree are likely to affect employers' decisions

to hire workers for specific occupations and at particular wage rates, we also reestimated these models using a nonlinear specification for education, contrasting respondents with less than a high school education and those with more than a high school diploma with high school graduates. In general, the set of dummies and the continuous measures yielded the same conclusion regarding significant education effects, and substituting these dummy variables in models predicting occupational complexity, wages, and hours did not alter effects for other variables.

Chapter 8

Conclusions: Work, Family, and Young Children's Lives

Our study of parents' jobs and children's lives is grounded in the argument that the occupational and economic conditions that parents face have significant implications for their children's lives. In developing our argument regarding how and why parents' occupational experiences should shape their children's lives, we have drawn heavily on Kohn and Schooler's work socialization arguments, Coleman's formulation of social capital, and Becker's arguments regarding allocation of effort between work and family. We have argued that children's home environments are an important pathway through which parents transmit family and social class advantage to their children, and that adequate examination of the causal chains linking parental social background and children's outcomes must include likely interactive effects among our explanatory variables. In this concluding chapter, we summarize the emerging conclusions from our empirical work, and suggest some directions for future research.

WORK, FAMILY, AND RESOURCES: CONTINGENT EFFECTS

In Chapter 1 we raised several questions regarding the effects of parental working conditions, the effects of family structure, and the effects of both parental and child characteristics on children's lives. Our analytic methods allowed us to control for the effects of a number of variables simultaneously, thus potentially suggesting the relative importance of these respective effects. We also allowed for the possibility that the effects we observed were variable, or contingent upon the statuses of other variables. Consistent with this latter possibility, we have observed repeatedly in our analyses that neither individual resources, occupational conditions, family circumstances, nor home environments have uniform effects. Parental characteristics and resources qualify the effects of family and work variables; and work conditions have differing impact depending on the family demands and stressors simultaneously impinging on parent-workers.

Four general patterns receive support across models. First, parental resources are particularly powerful when work and family conditions are more difficult. Conversely, parental resources blunt the adverse effects of difficult work and family conditions. For example, children's PPVT scores are less adversely affected by fathers' having jobs that are lower in occupational complexity when mothers have higher cognitive skills. Similarly, for children's behavior problems we find that the beneficial effects of mothers' positive self-concept are more powerful when mothers have ended their marriage or had another baby during the last 2 years.

Second, the effects of workplace conditions vary depending on parental family circumstances. An example is the observed interaction between mothers' 1988 occupational complexity and the birth of an additional child in equations predicting reading skills, in which increases in occupational complexity had less positive effects when mothers were also dealing with an additional child than when they were not. Similarly, fathers' overtime work hours in 1988 had more adverse implications for children's behavior problems when the family had recently added another child. For children's behavior problems, the quality of the mother's current employment buffers the adverse effects of marriage ending, with effects more benign for mothers whose current occupations are higher in complexity and more adverse for mothers working in less complex occupations.

Third, effects of one parent's working conditions vary depending on the working conditions of the other parent. For example, the combination of two parents working only part-time work schedules had more negative impacts on the quality of children's 1986 home environments than when only one parent worked part-time; the combination of two parents on overtime work schedules was associated with significantly more 1986 behavior problems than when only one parent worked overtime hours. Mothers' higher wages were particularly beneficial for children's PPVT scores when fathers worked relatively few hours. These findings suggest that when two parents are present, one may offset or buffer the negative effects of the others' work problems. One may also modify the beneficial impacts of one partner's working conditions; however, benefits of maternal complexity are significantly lower for PPVT when fathers are working overtime schedules and for PIAT math and reading when fathers' occupations are also high in complexity.

Finally, occupational quality and employment status effects are also interactive. We find that maternal entrances to and exits from the labor force have differing consequences depending on the quality of maternal employment. For example, in our analysis of the effects of early and 1986 work patterns on children's PPVT, we find that mothers' forgoing employment during the child's first 3 years had more adverse impacts for those who obtained employment in complex occupational settings than for those whose later employment was less complex and challenging. Similarly, mothers' exit from employment between 1986 and 1988 was more beneficial for children's math skills when the mothers had been working overtime work schedules in 1986. For children's behavior problems, the effect of mothers' stopping work between 1986 and 1988 was also more beneficial for mothers whose 1986 jobs had been lower in challenge and complexity and had involved extensive overtime hours.

These examples suggest that there is no simple answer to questions concerning the benefits or dangers of maternal employment. Much depends on the quality of that employment, the demands of partners' occupations, and the demands of other children. It is clear that both mothers' and fathers' work may be more or less helpful to children depending on other resources on which parents may draw and other responsibilities they must shoulder.

FAMILY RESOURCES AND DEMANDS: EFFECTS ON CHILD OUTCOMES

As noted above, our analysis explicitly took into account the likelihood that family size and structure would have direct effects on child well-being. These hypotheses take on additional importance because testing them brings evidence to bear on perspectives stressing the role of resource dilution in family welfare. Our findings suggest that there are effects of both marital history and childbearing on both cognitive and social outcomes. It is somewhat surprising that the timing and number of children has significant effects even in this sample, which has relatively low variability in total family size. These effects differ for the cognitive and social outcomes, with recent additions to the family having more adverse implications for behavior, but the number of older siblings and the births of closely spaced younger siblings more negative for the development of cognitive skills. These effects are less adverse for mothers who are higher in cognitive and social resources to begin with and those who are in more advantaged occupational and economic circumstances.

These findings help to specify the general conclusion that other children in the family household tend to dilute the resources available to any single child and to stretch the mother's time and energy. They also suggest that cognitive skills measured at any single point in time may reflect earlier environmental shortfalls in time and attention that have cumulative effects on the development of skills essential for school performance. Future research needs to evaluate more fully such potential lagged effects of earlier conditions.

It is interesting that sibling composition is more consequential for children's cognitive outcomes than the presence or absence of a father or stepfather. As we noted earlier when we described our methods, our models include dummy variables tapping father absence at various time periods, and substitute average values for work conditions for absent fathers. When contrasted to the complexity, wages, and hours of the average father in our sample, father presence per se tends to have virtually no impact on cognitive outcomes for children. The exception occurs for marital change rather than marital status. Specifically, recent marital disruption tends to compromise later home environments and hurt arithmetic skills; in addition, a new marriage has a deleterious effect on girls' reading skills, one of the few strong gender differences we observe.

Children's behavior problems are more responsive to men's presence. In particular, mother remaining unmarried or ending her marriage has substantial effects on increases in children's behavior problems and in the absolute levels of behavior problems; in addition, mother starting a new marriage is associated with higher levels of behavior problems in 1988. Taken together, these findings suggest that while the presence of a spouse generally improves the overall economic resources available to families, it may not consistently increase the total resources of time and attention available to children as much as one might expect.

EFFECTS OF PARENTAL WORK: MOTHERS VERSUS FATHERS

We had hypothesized that higher wages and employment in occupations higher in complexity would have generally beneficial consequences for children's social and cognitive outcomes. We explicitly raised the question as to whether maternal or paternal working conditions had the strongest effects on children's well-being. Our findings suggest that for both mothers and fathers, effects of wages and complexity are generally in the expected direction, and we do not observe consistent differences in the size of mothers' effects versus fathers' effects. Thus, our actual findings are supportive of our hypothesis in its broadest form, but they suggest that these benefits are in many cases contingent on other conditions. In particular, the findings suggest that jobs high in occupational complexity present challenges that absorb the time and emotional energy of adult workers in ways that are not readily combined with large numbers of children, recent births of additional children, or marriage to a partner facing a similar set of occupational challenges and opportunities. These difficulties are apparent for both mothers and fathers. Social policies that might reduce such conflicts continue to lag far behind the massive changes in labor force participation and family composition that have occurred in the last half-century; designing and implementing effective support for working parents remains difficult, and our findings suggest that this lag has discernible consequences for the next generation.

When we turn to work schedules, findings for mothers and fathers diverge somewhat. Effects of maternal work hours are scattered, with many models showing no effects of variations in her work hours. For example, models predicting PPVT-R suggest some benefits of moderate part-time schedules while others suggest negative implications of very low maternal part-time schedules, especially when accompanied by the birth of an additional child or when fathers are also employed only part-time. A few other models suggest adverse effects of maternal overtime schedules, e.g., on children's 1986 PPVT scores and on 1986 behavior problems only if the father is also working overtime.

Effects of part-time work schedules are more clearly negative for men than for women. For fathers, low work hours tend to be have consistently negative implications since low hours have negative effects on home environments especially if mother also works part-time or her self-concept is low, and on PPVT unless mothers' wages are high. A pattern of low work hours during the child's first few years also has direct negative effects on later reading and math skills, and as noted in the previous chapter this pattern is also linked to later marital disruption, which has direct effects on increased behavior problems. We speculate that such patterns are far more likely to be involuntary, negatively sanctioned by others, and interpreted in terms of failure to meet normative breadwinner expectations. Effects of fathers' overtime schedules, in contrast, have no impact on children's home environments or reading skills but do have negative impacts on children's PPVT and later arithmetic skills; fathers' overtime work schedules increase behavior problems only if mothers are also working overtime (in 1986) or they have just added another child to the family (in 1988). Thus, under most circumstances, fathers' overtime hours have little impact on home environments or behavior problems, although they do have some adverse implications for some cognitive outcomes under some specifications.

The most consistent finding here across parents is that both mothers' and fathers' overtime schedules appear to retard vocabulary development in their young children; since this knowledge is linked in turn to later reading and arithmetic skills, this suggests that either parent's high absorption in employment may carry cognitive costs for their children. In contrast, it is only when both parents are working long work hours or when fathers continue to work long hours despite their wives' absorption in the care of a new baby that we can discern increases in behavior problems. The patterns are consistent with the hypothesis that dilution in the resources available to children has negative implications for their development.

HOME ENVIRONMENTS AS A MEDIATING PATHWAY FOR EFFECTS OF SOCIAL CONDITIONS ON COGNITIVE AND SOCIAL OUTCOMES FOR CHILDREN: A REASSESSMENT

When we began our study of parents' jobs and children's lives, we argued that work and family conditions affected children's cognitive and social outcomes. We speculated that this effect was partly a function of parental work shaping the quality of children's home environments. However, the demonstration of such mediation is more demanding than the demonstration of, for example, the direct effects of sibship size on child cognition. For home environments to mediate the effects of work and family on children's outcomes, three relationships must hold: (1) social conditions must affect home environments; (2) home environments must affect children's outcomes; and (3) direct effects of social conditions on children's outcomes must diminish when home environments are included. Here we review what we have found regarding these three relationships.

Do Social Conditions Affect Home Environments?

In Chapter 3, we reported models predicting 1986 home environments, 1988 home environments, and change in home environments between 1986 and 1988. As we had theorized, we found that current work and family circumstances affected the quality of children's home environments, with higher maternal occupational complexity and smaller family size predicting better home environments in 1986. These variables, as well as parents' wage levels and fathers' part-time 1986 work schedules, also have lagged effects on later home environments in 1988 and on change from 1968 to 1988; and recent family changes—the birth of an additional child and the combination of marital disruption and stopping paid employment—also affect short-term change. Parental resources, including education and self-concept, interact with work and family conditions, and work and family changes also interact with one another, in shaping the quality of home environments.

It is interesting that the conditions observed 2 years earlier have lagged effects, yet 1988 working conditions have little impact either on 1988 home environments or on the direction or degree of change. In contrast, recent changes in family composition do impact family environments. This difference in timing of work and family effects suggests that family changes have more immediate impacts on the warmth and nature of parent-child interaction, while occupational conditions have more slowly accumulating effects via alterations in parental attitudes and values. In any case, it is clear that work and family conditions do have significant effects on children's family environments.

Do Home Environments Affect Child Outcomes?

As we discussed in Chapters 4 and 5, we found that the quality of children's current home environments had a significant effect on 3- to 6-year-olds' receptive vocabularies and on 4- to 6-year-olds' levels of behavior problems. These effects also held when we also controlled for early work and family conditions in Chapter 6. However, we did find that the benefits of positive home environments for children's lower behavior problems were weaker for black children compared to whites, and weaker for boys than for girls.

The quality of home environments also had strong positive effects on 1988 cognitive outcomes. As we discussed in Chapters 4 and 7, when we followed the children forward in time, both recent and current home environments had positive effects on children's reading and math skills when they were 5–8 years old. This pattern of findings is consistent with expectations.

In contrast, home environments had only weak and contingent effects on later behavior problems; as discussed in Chapter 7, significant effects were observed only for the 1986 measure of home environments, suggesting lagged effects on children's social behavior, and these effects were weaker for black children and for boys. These findings suggest that the aspects of home environment observed here—cognitive stimulation, expressed warmth, and organization of the physical environment—are less closely related to children's social and emotional outcomes as they grow older. However, in related analyses utilizing somewhat differing samples of mothers with children aged 5–8 in 1988 (Parcel and Menaghan 1993; Menaghan 1994), the quality of the home environment did have a significant impact on the level of older children's behavior problems and on changes over time (Parcel and Menaghan 1993). Moreover, more positive home environments were *most* strongly linked to lower behavior problems when both mothers' and fathers' occupations were high in complexity and opportunities for self-direction (Menaghan 1994). Differences in model specification make direct comparison of these studies with the current analyses difficult, but these findings suggest caution in concluding that home environments become less salient for older children. Further research is needed to adjudicate this issue.

If subsequent research does show that effects on behavior problems are nonsignificant for older children, we suggest two explanations. First, it is possible that family influences more generally are less powerful when children are older and spending more of their time at school. A second possibility is that the aspects of home environments that are critical in preventing or reducing behavior problems shift over time. Our measure of home environments does not tap how parents establish family rules or respond to rule violations, how much effort parents exert in monitoring children's activities or friendships, how aware they are of children's school progress or peer problems, or how consistent they are in facilitating emotional self-regulation and behavioral self-control. Such active socialization efforts are likely to be increasingly important as children grow older and as direct supervision must be supplemented by more indirect efforts to help children to internalize behavioral norms. This argument is consistent with recent studies establishing the importance of parental monitoring (Crouter, MacDermid, McHale, and Perry-Jenkins 1990) and authoritative management approaches (Baumrind 1991) for older children. Thus, our measure of home environments may not fully capture the aspects of parent-child interaction that are most critical in shaping older children's behavior. This is an important issue deserving of further study.

Why should we observe weaker effects of home environments for boys than for girls? We suggest that the unmeasured aspects of parent-child interaction we have just noted may be more closely correlated to those aspects we *do* measure for girls than for boys. Prior research suggests that girls are generally more closely supervised and more consistently discouraged from aggressive, acting-out behavior than boys; and such parental efforts are associated with other measures of parental warmth and involvement such as those tapped here. For boys, who have been described as "overvalued but undersocialized," parental warmth and cognitive stimulation may not covary as closely with effective parental socialization strategies. Future research on children's home environments that considers a more comprehensive set of dimensions should help to illuminate this issue.

A somewhat similar pattern may underlie differing effects of home environments by race. Other studies have suggested that black socialization patterns differ from white patterns in several key ways. The overt expression of warmth is somewhat lower and physical punishment for misbehavior is somewhat more common. We have noted that on average black mothers score lower on the measure of home environments included here; and we find that variations on this measure are less powerful in predicting black children's behavior problems. It is possible that this measure is less effective at capturing the dimensions of black mothers' behavior that are most relevant for preventing emotional and social difficulties. Future research should investigate such differences more fully.

Do Home Environments Mediate Effects of Social Context?

It is clear that social conditions do affect children's home environments, and that the quality of home environments does shape children's outcomes, although their effects on cognitive outcomes are stronger and more consistent than for social outcomes. The final requirement for evidence of mediation is that controlling for the mediating variable reduces the direct effects of other variables. This is the weakest link in our argument for mediation. When we have compared models before and after controlling for the quality of children's home environments, we fail to see the diminished direct effects that would suggest that home environments are functioning as important mediators of work or family conditions or of parental resources. In particular, although occupational variables do affect home environments, it is never the case that controlling for home environments changes the effects of occupational variables. The small changes that are observed are found for family composition and for parental psychosocial resources.

Thus, we conclude that mediational processes are relatively weak, at least for the aspects of home environments captured here; effects of family size and maternal self-concept operate in part by affecting the stimulation, warmth, and organization of the home environment, but occupational and economic conditions have effects that follow other pathways. Taking the stimulation, warmth, and organization of the home into account improves our prediction of children's outcomes and increases our understanding of factors shaping those outcomes, but does not explain the effects of occupational and economic conditions.

INITIAL PARENTAL SOCIAL ADVANTAGES
AND CHILDREN'S OUTCOMES

The questions we raised in Chapter 1 acknowledged the likely importance of parental and child characteristics on child outcomes. Although in accounting for variation in children's cognitive and emotional outcomes, we have focused particular attention on the direct effects of work and family conditions, we have also investigated the extent to which parental social characteristics will directly affect child well-being. In Chapter 7 we introduced the additional complication that parental working conditions are themselves endogenous variables affected by parents' social background and resources. For example, mothers who have more education, higher cognitive skills, and more positive self-concept are more likely to be employed at any given time point, more likely to remain employed, and more likely to be employed at better jobs at higher wages. Such effects hold not only for early working conditions but for improvements in working conditions over time. Similarly, fathers' educational attainment contributes to more positive early occupational conditions and to greater improvements over time. Mothers' cognitive and educational resources are also associated with a greater likelihood of being married during the child's first few years and to greater marital stability over time. Although mothers' own occupational experiences have little impact on later marital disruption, marriages to men who work part-time or at low-wage jobs in the early years are less likely to persist. Marital homogamy predicts that mothers with lower educational attainment themselves are more likely to be married to men with poorer occupational prospects; thus, women who are disadvantaged are also more likely to be rearing children alone.

It is noteworthy that these individual parental resources are themselves predictable from social variables in ways consistent with our argument that outcomes for the next generation are shaped by the resources their families can provide and the demands made on those resources. Specifically, fewer siblings and higher educational attainment in the grandparental generation are key predictors of these young mothers' own resources.

A major pathway by which early social advantage in one generation affects the well-being of the next is through its impact on the occupational conditions parents face and the family lives they construct. The models we estimate control for the independent direct effects of early, recent, and contemporaneous work and family conditions on children's home environments and family outcomes. In most of our models, the direct effects of self-concept, educational attainment, and maternal cognitive skills diminish when work and family variables are added. Even with these variables controlled, however, these enduring parental resources typically retain significance, with maternal self-concept particularly critical in forestalling children's behavior problems and maternal cognitive skills a key predictor of children's cognitive outcomes. These findings suggest that we must also consider other pathways by which parental resources affect the next generation. These in all likelihood include patterns of family interaction, and variations in occupational demands and challenges, that are not fully captured in the measure of home environments and in the occupational and wage variables we utilize here. The significant direct effects of maternal cognitive skills on children's vocabulary, reading, and arithmetic performance may also in part reflect direct genetic linkages. The persistence of direct effects of cognitive and social resources in these models thus offers a challenge for future research in this area to account for the effects we have observed.

ETHNIC AND GENDER DIFFERENCES IN PROCESSES AFFECTING CHILDREN

A major motivating issue in this research has been whether the processes we have observed uniformly hold for children of differing social characteristics. Accordingly, in each analysis, we have systematically investigated possible differences by ethnicity and child gender. Such differences are surprisingly few. In particular, ethnic differences are generally weak and scattered. This absence of differences calls attention to the specific characteristics of the sample we have chosen, i.e., young mothers who had relatively early births but were employed when their children were aged 3–6. We know that nonwhite women are more likely to become mothers at an earlier age than whites; that nonwhites tend to complete fewer years of education and if employed have poorer occupational prospects. In our sample, both white and nonwhite mothers have experienced early births and limited educational attainment; and all were employed in 1986. We observe only weak differences in age at first birth and no white-nonwhite differences in education and, as just noted, observe little systematic variation in the strengths of effects in multivariate models. These findings suggest that prior studies reporting sharp ethnic differences may reflect in part the confounding of age at childbearing and employment status with ethnic membership. This is an important hypothesis for further study.

We also find relatively few differences for boys and girls; these suggest that marital status/presence of a father may affect young boys more than young girls; in addition, the findings suggest that fathers' occupational conditions may have more powerful effects on sons. These differences are consistent with other research suggesting that fathers are more involved in interaction with young sons than with their daughters. These differences, however, are relatively small.

LIMITATIONS OF OUR INVESTIGATION

We also recognize that there are limitations to this research that constrict the degree to which we can generalize our findings. First, the sample we have studied, while generally representative and containing good variation in both explanatory and dependent variables, is not fully representative of all families with children in the 3–6 and 5–8 year ranges. This is because the NLSY mothers in 1986 were themselves a select group— those who had become mothers relatively early in their adult lives. Those women who were postponing childbearing in order to attend school or obtain additional job training and experience had no opportunity in this sample. Many of these women are likely to hold occupations higher in complexity and in rates of remuneration than the mothers we studied, thus contributing to greater variation in these variables and associated background characteristics, as well as paternal characteristics. A fully representative sample of working mothers and children 3–6 and 5–8 years old would contain these families as well. Greater variation in explanatory variables might increase their explanatory power. Thus, such an analysis might reveal even stronger effects of parental work than we have observed here.

The second major qualification is that, despite our interest in studying the longitudinal nature of parental work and child well-being, we have only begun to consider these issues within a comprehensive longitudinal framework. We have studied child outcomes and children's home environments at two points in time—1986 and 1988—thus confining our analysis to that of relatively short-term changes in these outcomes. Such analyses do not suggest whether the effects we observe involving parental work, the home environments, family structure, and parent and child background would be stronger or weaker had the outcomes been studied over a longer period of time. We have studied parental working conditions at these two time points as well, in addition to considering the effects of early parental work. Here again it would be ideal to observe the effects of such working conditions on child outcomes as these children mature, as well as to understand the effects that parental work during these later years may have on older children and adolescents. We cannot rule out the possibility that some of the contingent effects we have described would disappear, or become intensified. Our findings, however, provide an important baseline against which to evaluate this future work.

THE DANGERS AND DIVIDENDS
OF MATERNAL EMPLOYMENT

We now return to the overarching question that motivated our study. Are there dangers or dividends to maternal employment? This issue is tied directly to our concern that we study these processes within an explicitly longitudinal framework. Our findings suggest that dangers of early maternal employment may have been overstated and overgeneralized, and that such arguments neglect to adequately consider the positive consequences of maternal employment for children and their families. To appreciate the potential for such benefit, it is important to recognize that these models suggest strong continuity over time in mothers' occupational experiences and a strong continuing effect of both educational credentials and cognitive skills. They also suggest that greater early maternal investment in paid employment appears to have a significant positive effect on her later opportunities. And greater later occupational rewards in turn have benefits for family well-being and individual children's outcomes. Thus, for the mothers who are able to maintain favorable employment circumstances over time, such activities may constitute resources for her family both financially, as well as in the social capital that she brings to family interaction and child rearing. Conversely, low employment early on hinders mothers' achievement of better jobs and better wages in subsequent years. These families will not have access to the resources we have argued can facilitate family welfare. Such adverse effects must be considered in any calculation of costs and benefits to families or to children.

A particular challenge is to consider advantages and disadvantages both to mothers and to children within a framework that is explicitly longitudinal. Conventional arguments suggest that the child's long-term welfare is importantly influenced by the socialization environment created by the family during the child's infancy and preschool years. In stereotypic families, these environments are chiefly the responsibility of mothers, although fathers may contribute labor and certainly do contribute to the household material base. Such models portray the child's long-term development as critically affected by environments and events that take place in these early years. Maternal work experience, however, is not seriously viewed with this same longitudinal perspective. Work is portrayed as something to which the mother can return

when her children are older; although researchers acknowledge the negative implications of discontinuities in experience and earnings, these are
viewed as compensable given the relatively modest levels of investment
most women have made anyway. There are similar arguments regarding
disrupted earnings. What is neglected in this view is that such disruption reduces the level of financial resources the mother can bring to her
family not only when she is not working, but also after she returns to
employment. This is particularly true if her skills have atrophied during
the period when she has not been employed and she therefore returns to
work in an occupation of lower complexity and remuneration than the
position she occupied previously. And we do not know how such
arrangements affect children. Specifically, we have not studied, over a
number of years, the impact of varying maternal work schedules and
working conditions on both child cognitive and social outcomes. It may
be that despite the time pressures that employed mothers with young
children face, their work force investments pay off in long-term child
welfare both because of enhanced material well-being but also because
of the social capital that such employment brings to family socialization.

These findings suggest that the costs to women of forgoing employment may be underestimated. But these costs are also variable. In contrast to arguments that children whose mothers are higher in human
capital have the most to gain from their mothers' avoidance of early
employment, we find that forgoing employment is less beneficial to this
group than to less advantaged mothers. In contrast, when employment
is likely to be at repetitive jobs offering little challenge or opportunities
for self-direction or problem solving, the trade-offs involved in arrang-
ing child care and pursuing employment may be excessive. These findings suggest that debates about maternal employment in general may be
seriously flawed if they do not consider the quality of employment that
mothers can obtain, the demands they are managing in their families,
and the resources that individual mothers are able to bring to their
tasks. They also suggest that social solutions to the dilemmas facing
many working parents need to be similarly sensitive to the wide variations in resources and conditions that families face.

HOW DO OUR FINDINGS INFORM THEORY?

Another way to view our findings is to ask what evidence they provide in support of the theoretical perspectives we used to guide the
analysis. We recall that Kohn's arguments regarding occupational complexity suggested that parents whose jobs were high in complexity used

child-rearing techniques that stressed self-direction and internalization of behavioral norms, with attendant positive implications for child outcomes. Parents whose jobs were low in complexity used child-rearing strategies stressing obedience and conformity to externally imposed standards, which may produce higher levels of behavior problems and lower levels of cognitive attainment. We recall that Kohn's empirical work was not aimed at demonstrating a connection between parental occupational complexity and child outcomes, and instead emphasized connections between parental work and child socialization environments. Do our findings support the causal extension of this hypothesis to show effects on child outcomes themselves?

There is no evidence to suggest that there are consistent effects of parental occupational complexity on either child social or cognitive outcomes; more often, the effects of complexity are contingent on levels of other paid work and family variables. However, there is substantial evidence that parental occupational complexity has important effects on children's home environments. Because these home environments consistently predict both child cognition and levels of behavior problems, we infer some evidence for an indirect effect of complexity on these child outcomes. This is not inconsistent with Kohn's arguments regarding the content of parental socialization being influenced by parental paid work, with such socialization in turn influencing child well-being. The measure of children's home environments that we have used in this analysis, while not specifically constructed to tap child-rearing practices, is likely nonetheless to be positively associated with such patterns of parent-child interaction. Taken together, we think that the findings regarding the effects of parental complexity on children's home environments and the effects of home on child social and cognitive outcomes provide some support for Kohn's thesis. Our findings suggest that the generally positive effects Kohn envisions, however, may hold only when the total set of paid work and family demands do not overwhelm them.

What implications do our findings have for Coleman's arguments regarding the importance of family social capital for the growth and well-being of children? We think that our findings provide substantial support for this notion. First, to the extent that children's home environments represent an important form of family social capital, our findings suggesting the importance of these home environments for both child cognition and child social adjustment are clearly consistent with Coleman's thesis about the importance of social capital within the family. Second, findings in support of "resource dilution" owing to increased numbers of children also support these arguments. The findings suggest that parents have a finite amount of energy and resources to devote to child rearing, in this case to parent-child interactions that constitute social capital. If these interactions are to be spread across greater numbers of siblings, then each child necessarily gets less. Reductions in this form of social capital have negative effects on child outcomes.

Not all of our findings are consistent with Coleman's worries regarding maternal employment interfering with family social capital to the detriment of children. Coleman argues that nonmaternal child care may interfere with the formation and functioning of family social capital, while we find that such care has no discernible effects on either child cognitive or social outcomes. In addition, if Coleman's concerns regarding the dangers of maternal employment were fully borne out empirically, we would have seen consistent negative effects of maternal work on child outcomes, while instead, as noted above, these effects are most evident when other resources important to family functioning are weak or overextended. Finally, our analysis of the effects of early parental work on child outcomes suggests only weak cautions regarding the dangers of early maternal work on children. Although we did find that the children of mothers who worked in the child's first 3 years had lower PPVT-R scores than children of mothers who did not work during that time, these effects hold only for mothers whose later levels of occupational complexity are low. That they are so qualified suggests that cautions regarding the dangers of early maternal work have been overgeneralized. In addition, that we demonstrated effects of paternal as well as maternal working conditions on child outcomes suggests that the emphasis upon mothers' work interfering with the formation and use of social capital is incomplete. Future research considering the impact of family social capital on child well-being should explicitly consider the roles of mothers and fathers in these processes.

We are also interested in what our findings might suggest for Becker's analysis of the new home economics. As we indicated earlier, his perspective is a very fertile one, thus suggesting many hypotheses that cannot be evaluated in a single investigation. We have, however, observed how variation in the working conditions, family structure, and social characteristics within a group of inefficient families produces variation in child cognitive and social outcomes. Studying such variation is not a direction that his models suggest for study, although given the increase of this family form, the issue becomes a logical one. In one particular respect, however, our models do inform his thinking. Becker directs our attention to maternal allocation of work effort between the marketplace and the home. We might argue that those mothers who work fewer hours for pay are more closely approximating families in which mothers are not employed, i.e., efficient families. If this is true, then we would expect this efficiency to pay off in improved child outcomes. As noted above, however, the effects of low maternal work hours are not uniformly positive. Although having mothers not work in the child's first 3 years is associated with increased PPVT-R when children are 3–6 years old if the mothers' occupational prospects are poor, the reverse is true if her occupational prospects are good. Among working mothers, very low work hours are associated with lower levels of verbal facility, and in general do not seem to be particularly influential in influencing a variety of other outcomes. As with Coleman, Becker's argument regarding the effects of the allocation of maternal work effort is one-sided. That we have found effects of paternal work hours on child well-being suggests that his models need to be adapted to consider how the allocation of fathers' time to paid employment and to family work can be influential. Our findings regarding the negative implications of excessive overtime hours within the family are broadly consistent with the notion that such families may not be maximally efficient. However, Becker's models largely neglect the complication that the long-term implications of such arrangements may be negative, positive, or mixed. Additional research should address the extent to which negative outcomes for children early on contribute to unfavorable child outcomes as they mature, or whether the additional work hours are functioning as a parental investment in work that has long-term benefits for the children that are detectable as they grow older.

Finally, our findings can also inform general questions about the transmission of inequality across generations. Sociologists have documented that most of the association between fathers' and sons' occupational statuses is mediated by the level of schooling sons attain. More recently, however, economists have argued that the correlation between fathers' and sons' income levels is higher than previously reported (Solon 1992; Zimmerman 1992), thus suggesting greater levels of intergenerational income transmission than had previously been reported (Becker 1988). Our findings provide several pieces of evidence to support the notion that the intergenerational transmission of inequality is nontrivial in magnitude. First, we find positive associations among parental background characteristics and the working conditions that parents experience. We also find positive associations between maternal personal resources and marital status. These findings suggest that there is clear nonrandom sorting of mothers to work and family contexts, contexts that in turn do influence both child cognition and child social adjustment. Second, we know that children's home environments are important determinants of child well-being, and that maternal background and work arrangements influence the quality of these environments. Although home environments do not mediate the effect of background on child outcomes, they still play an important role in transmitting inequality across generations. That parental background characteristics and work arrangements continue to exert direct effects when home environments are controlled suggests additional aspects of home and community environments, unmeasured in this analysis, that are influencing the life chances of the next generation. Clearly, these findings point to several avenues through which parents influence children, avenues through which advantage and disadvantage can travel. These avenues also are likely to play a role in the transmission of inequality as children mature.

HOW DO OUR FINDINGS INFORM CURRENT POLICY?

Our findings support neither the liberal nor the conservative position in its strictest form. Almost inevitably, when social science findings are produced within a multivariate context such as we have used, the results will provide more qualified findings than any extreme political view is likely to endorse. Rather, the most accurate summary of our findings as an instrument for policy would support several elements of each perspective.

Looking at the liberal perspectives first, we produce no evidence to suggest that nonmaternal child care is damaging to children. The evidence to suggest that early maternal employment is damaging to children is scant, being confined to those circumstances when other parental resources are weak or overextended. We have also produced evidence to suggest that maternal employment can be helpful to the family. Obviously, maternal employment contributes to family financial well-being, and given the level of wages earned by the spouses in our sample, mothers' wages frequently make the difference between poverty-level earnings and a materially sufficient life-style. In addition, however, our findings also suggest that the working conditions mothers experience on the job can be an asset to the socialization environments that children experience in the home. If the mother holds a job with high levels of complexity, such a resource promotes a stronger home environment, which in turn promotes stronger child cognitive and social outcomes. At the same time, however, if the job she holds is low in complexity, this has negative implications for the home environment she creates and for her child's well-being. Under these conditions, we need to examine whether the increment in family income is a sufficient advantage to offset the likely disadvantages of working in a job that is associated with weaker home environments and child outcomes.

Additional analysis should investigate whether home environments among nonemployed mothers are stronger than those of mothers employed in low-complexity jobs, controlling for other economic and social resources that the mother and spouse provide. Kohn argues that when mothers are not employed, the complexity level of the father's job is important in influencing whether the child is socialized in an environment emphasizing self-direction and internalized standards, or whether parents stress obedience to externally imposed norms. But empirical evidence for this hypothesis is scanty. Such investigation would help to determine whether any form of maternal employment is a net asset to families, or whether such employment is only advantageous if the mother can, in addition to bringing home a paycheck, also make positive contributions to the social capital she constructs with her children. Support for the latter scenario would be more consistent with the conservative than with the liberal policy agenda. Such investigations are complicated by the fact that each parent's human capital resources are associated with those of their spouse, as are their working conditions. Still, answers to these questions could be very useful to informing policy regarding the conditions under which maternal work helps or harms families.

Turning to the conservative agenda, our findings do suggest that the home environments parents create for children are very important to supporting both their cognitive and their social development. Although long parental work hours are not associated with weaker children's home environments as might be inferred from conservative arguments, the findings do suggest that when the resources parents use to create and maintain positive home environments for their children are absent, weak, or overextended, children's everyday experiences may suffer. The long list of contingent effects that we enumerated above also alerts us to the fact that while maternal employment is not necessarily harmful, neither is it uniformly a boon to families. In particular, both parents and policymakers need to be attentive to the *combinations* of circumstances that may result in maternal employment functioning more as a cost than an asset to the family. An example of such circumstances would be when both parents work overtime hours, since our findings suggest that these arrangements may hinder the development of children's verbal facility. Another example would be that increase in maternal complexity had less salutary effects on children's reading when maternal resources were also being devoted to caring for an additional child, or that increases in paternal overtime hours were associated with increased child behavior problems when family size increased. These examples suggest that policymakers with either a liberal or conservative bent will find it essential to qualify their most general pronouncements to take the complexities of family life and change into account. Such efforts should pay dividends in the precision with which the advantages and disadvantages of maternal employment are portrayed.

Historically, much of the policy debate has concerned the extent of support that society should provide to single-female-headed households. More recently, additional arguments have revolved around the extent to which "workfare" may provide a sounder, longer-term solution by providing work experience for mothers instead of providing welfare penalties for paid employment. Our findings do not suggest that the processes we have studied are noticeably different for married and unmarried mothers. Regarding the relative sizes of family structure effects, the effects of increased numbers of children are more negative than the effects of maternal marital status. In addition, there are no contingent effects involving maternal working conditions and marital status. More generally, however, our findings suggest that it may be important to consider the nature of jobs that women will be holding under workfare policies. Given our demonstration that the working conditions mothers face influence the home environments they provide for their children and the children directly, it is legitimate to ask whether workfare jobs will be an asset or a hindrance to families. If they are jobs that provide the types of work experiences on which mothers can build in terms of work advancement, the influence is likely a positive one, particularly if family earnings are stable and higher than under traditional welfare policies. In addition, to the extent that children are exposed to an adult role model who conveys positive values regarding the value of work in social life, this arrangement would seem beneficial in conveying these norms, a form of social capital, to the next generation. We have argued, however, that parental jobs that are low in occupational complexity and/or that require extensive overtime hours may actually hinder child well-being. If the jobs women hold under workfare entail these conditions, we would expect some negative effects, particularly if we consider that maternal time in the home will drop as paid employment increases. Whether these effects would be more than offset by the benefits of such arrangements is a critical question that deserves close empirical scrutiny.

CAN OUR FINDINGS GUIDE PARENTS
IN MAKING CHOICES FOR THEIR FAMILIES?

We also think it important to consider the extent to which our findings may be useful to the millions of parents who are facing the questions we raised earlier regarding the relative trade-offs in the allocation of effort to paid employment and to family life. Parallelling our conclusions regarding implications for policy, the guidance cannot follow simple prescriptions or admonitions. Parents are also hindered in making choices given that they cannot foresee with certainty whether their marriages will survive, whether their jobs will change, and if so, within a context of increasing or decreasing responsibility and reward. They also cannot foresee precisely how easy or difficult varying combinations of work and family responsibilities might be.

Despite these difficulties, several prescriptions seem appropriate. First, longer parental work hours likely entail some risks, particularly when family resources are under pressure from increasing family size or the spouse's demanding work schedule. Here the likely trade-offs might involve consideration of whether the increased hours are essential to basic family economic welfare and to employment stability and/or advancement, or whether they merely hasten the acquisition of goods that might be purchased on a somewhat slower timetable. Even if the former scenario holds, parents may need to explicitly consider how to minimize the potential for children receiving less parental time than would likely be the case under more moderate work hours.

Second, parents need to consciously recognize the importance of the home environments they create for their children. We have shown that these home environments are important both for cognitive achievement as well as for social adjustment. For families with both parents working, or for single-female-headed households, parents may need to place priority on creating appropriate home environments at the expense of meeting some of their own needs. Such investments in the home environment may, in the long term, yield greater child well-being. While child well-being is obviously a valuable asset to society, the most immediate benefactors of improved social adjustment and stronger cognitive outcomes are the parents. Although it may be difficult to take this type of long-term perspective when family circumstances are creating pressures to meet immediate needs, that may be the point at which such perspective is most crucial.

Finally, parents need to be attuned to their abilities to handle the combinations of work and family arrangements that they undertake, either voluntarily and involuntarily. For parents whose personal resources are low, either in terms of cognitive skills or self-concept, families may be better off with lower total levels of work and family commitments. Even those with higher levels of personal resources should recognize that these resources are not limitless, and that overtime work hours for both parents or the birth of additional children may result in at least temporary diminution in child well-being. Questions remain, of course, regarding whether such temporary difficulties, which surely are common even in families with adequate personal and financial resources, necessarily have any deleterious long-term effect. We have no evidence

that they do. On the other hand, we have shown how personal characteristics are associated with less advantageous working conditions of parents, suggesting that, over time, inequality among one generation of parents may be transmitted in part through the quantity and quality of
social capital that parents form with their children. We think these findings form an important piece of the larger puzzle regarding such inequality, and hope that they serve as a foundation both for future
research and as one source of guidance for parents and for social policy.

Appendix

Supplemental Child Care Arrangements: Determinants and Consequences

Our study has focused on children with employed mothers and examined how occupational and family conditions influence children's outcomes. Because mothers are young children's usual caregivers, their employment generally necessitates some arrangement for children's care. In some cases, another member of the household can provide care, while in others, hired caregivers come to the child's home or children are transported to other homes or to formal child care centers. Yet our models of the effects of parents' jobs on children's cognitive and social outcomes have not controlled for variations in nonmaternal care arrangements experienced. How do we know that our models do not mistakenly attribute to parental working conditions effects that should be attributed to child care arrangements? The purpose of this appendix is to provide some evidence regarding this issue.

We first review previous literature examining determinants of child care and linking aspects of care to children's outcomes. Second, we describe the measures of child care that could be constructed for the NLSY children we study. Because child care arrangements are themselves endogenous variables affected by other variables in our models, we next examine the determinants of care arrangements observed in our sample. Finally, we discuss the bivariate associations between child care measures and children's 1986 and 1988 cognitive and social outcomes, and investigate whether they have significant independent effects when added to our multivariate models. To anticipate our conclusions, we find that child care measures have only weak bivariate associations with child outcomes and in almost all cases have no independent effect on child outcomes; we conclude by discussing why this is so.

CHILD CARE ARRANGEMENTS: RESEARCH AND THEORY

As maternal employment has increased, so has research on the consequences for children of time spent in supplemental care arrangements.

Reviews have described this work in terms of "waves" of research moving from simple group contrasts to increasingly complex analyses of contingent effects (see, for example, Belsky 1984b; Scarr and Eisenberg 1993). The earliest wave contrasting day-care/non-day-care children sought to assess whether day care (and the maternal employment associated with it) had negative effects in contrast to mother care at home. Researchers found few consistent differences between groups of children. The "second wave" of day-care research moved beyond such group contrasts to assess the effects of variations in child care arrangements on child outcomes. These studies sought to identify linkages between features of care (such as group size, caregiver-child ratios, and caregiver training) and children's everyday experiences, and between those experiences and developmental outcomes (Ruopp and Travers 1982; Clarke-Stewart 1982). More recent studies have considered both the quality of supplemental care and the quality of parental care, as well as characteristics of the child such as health and temperament.

Scarr and Eisenberg (1993) also describe an emerging wave of research that includes attention to variables that affect the quality of parental and other care; these more distal influences include parental employment conditions, the quality of social relationships available to parental and other caregivers, and caregivers' wages and staff turnover, which affect the child indirectly via their effects on the adults interacting with the child.

Key Aspects of Care: Group Size
and Socialization Ratios

In formal group care arrangements, caregiver-child ratios are viewed as a key indicator of the quality of care. As the ratio of children to the number of parents/caregivers increases, the effectiveness of socialization efforts generally declines. Two processes are involved here. First, caregivers spend less time in direct, sustained interaction with any single child. Second, a larger group of children is more likely to organize into a context of socialization itself, developing goals and norms different from, and often antithetical to, those of the caregiver (Gecas 1981:196). Research conducted in child care centers has generally confirmed this expectation. In particular, small group size and good caregiver-child ratios are associated with more flexible scheduling and caregivers engaging in more facilitative social stimulation, expressing more positive affect, and being less restrictive and negative; the children spend less time in solitary activities, are less frequently unhappy, and are more frequently involved in sustained activity. In turn, more frequent and more positive adult-child and peer interaction is associated with higher cognitive and social competence (Ruopp and Travers 1982; Clarke-Stewart 1982). McCartney (1984) has demonstrated that the higher adult-child verbal interaction associated with better caregiver-child ratios is a key predictor of child language facility.

While much of the research on quality of care has been conducted in group care settings, actual child care arrangements in the United States include extensive reliance on informal, often ad hoc, arrangements with neighbors or nearby relatives, or "coverage" by other members of the family household (Hofferth and Phillips 1987). Such informal arrangements typically have a single adult caregiver and a small number of children; the restricted variation in group size and number of caregivers makes it difficult to link these features of care to child outcomes, and the large numbers of "sites" for care hamper observational studies of children's everyday care experiences as well. Thus, we are on weaker ground in expecting small variations in features of care in informal settings to tap important differences in the quality of care or to have large effects on child outcomes.

Other research has focused on comparisons among types of child care (e.g., formal centers versus family day-care homes) and types of caregivers (e.g., relatives versus nonrelatives). For most children in the small families that prevail in the United States today, ratios of children to adults will be larger in formal care arrangements and in arrangements outside their own families than they experience at home; this suggests that formal care arrangements on average would have more negative effects than other arrangements. However, it is likely that the effects of formal center or school settings versus own home or home of a relative or neighbor vary depending on the relative economic and psychosocial characteristics of the two types of settings. Since neighborhoods and nearby relatives are likely to share the socioeconomic standards and cultural milieu of the child's family, informal relative/neighbor arrangements may reflect other inequalities between families. If formal centers and schools offer expanded opportunities relative to child household characteristics, exposure to them should have positive effects. Thus, effects of type of care probably vary with quality of care in both the maternal and nonmaternal setting.

Determinants of Child Care Arrangements

It is likely that families with differing resources have children in differing types and quality of care, but few child care studies explore *whose* children are apt to experience better or worse arrangements. Some studies do focus on determinants of *type* of care chosen—formal, group care in centers or schools versus informal arrangements in the neighborhood or in the child's own home. Formal arrangements are more common when female heads' wage rates are higher (Robins and Spiegelman 1978; Duncan and Hill 1975, 1977), in the South, and in larger cities (Stolzenberg and Waite 1984). Predictors of child care arrangements also vary depending on children's ages. For example, Leibowitz, Waite, and Witsberger (1988) find that better-educated mothers and those with higher earnings are more likely to arrange at-home care for children under age 3 but formal center care for children 3 years old and over.

Since quality varies within all types of care, the type of care is probably less critical than quality of care within each type. Only a few studies have examined determinants of the *quality* of care. Phillips, McCartney, and Scarr (1987) report that among Bermudan families using child care centers, parental values about child development were related to the quality of the child care center in which their children were enrolled. In particular, parents who valued social skills more highly and put a lower value on conformity enrolled their children in centers judged to be of higher quality. As Kohn's (1977) framework would suggest, mothers with more prestigious occupations (a dimension that co-varies with occupational self-direction) placed a lower value on conformity (Kathleen McCartney, personal communication). Parents in such occupational settings are also more likely to earn adequate incomes, which permits them to purchase higher-quality care. These findings suggest that higher-quality parental employment predicts higher-quality child care arrangements, at least among those who use formal care.

We argue that characteristics of employment such as wages and hours, characteristics of families such as number of children and presence of other adults, and parental characteristics such as education, positive self-concept, and cognitive skills influence the quality and continuity of the supplemental care arrangements mothers make (for reviews of this literature, see Menaghan and Parcel 1991; Scarr and Eisenberg 1993). Studies of child care arrangements that do not control for such linkages may be misleading. For example, if mothers with higher educational attainment, working in more complex occupations at higher earnings, and rearing fewer children—all characteristics predictive of better child outcomes—are disproportionately represented in a particular type of care, then children in that care type are likely to have better outcomes. This does not necessarily mean that the type of care per se has a significant impact on the child independent of other associated characteristics of the mother or the family.

ASSESSMENT OF CHILD CARE EFFECTS:
THE NLSY DATA

Measures

The NLSY interviews queried mothers about the arrangements employed mothers had made in the 4 weeks prior to the 1986 interview; we developed measures of type of care and location of care, as well as indicators of quality (child/adult ratio), stability (number of different arrangements), and duration (usual hours per week). The ratio of adult children to caregivers in the child's primary nonmaternal care arrangement is used here as an indicator of the quality of supplemental care; for multivariate analyses, this variable is transformed to a standard score with children for whom ratio data are missing being assigned the mean. In addition, we distinguished four types of care: formal group care in centers or schools, informal arrangements with relative caregivers, informal arrangements with nonrelative caregivers, and other arrangements.

We also constructed summary measures of child care arrangements during the child's first 3 years of life. There were two sources of data for this information: questions asked at each interview round, and a set of retrospective questions included in the 1986 mothers' supplement. Each of these has limitations. The annual child care information was not collected unless the mothers had been employed during the 4-week period prior to the interviews; thus, it is missing for many mothers who *were* employed earlier in the year, with mothers with more intermittent or sporadic employment during the year most likely to be missing on these questions. In addition, in several calendar years, information about child care was collected only for the child who was the youngest child in the household at that interview, creating gaps in data for individual children.

We therefore relied on the retrospective questions that were asked of *every* mother and for *each* of her children. These data also have limitations. The questions tap only the type and location of care recalled, and do not include indicators of quality such as child/adult ratio or duration of various arrangements, limiting any assessment of variation in quality of early child care. These retrospective reports are also vulnerable to underreporting of early nonmaternal care. When we compare mothers' employment data (collected at each annual interview) during the child's first 3 years with reported child care usage, we find that 47% of mothers who were employed during their child's first year reported no regular child care arrangement in the retrospective survey; percentages are a bit lower (38 and 32%) but still substantial for mothers employed during the second and third years. This suggests that many mothers have forgotten or failed to report nonmaternal care that occurred while they were employed.

We compared mothers' annual reports of child care with their retrospective accounts for the children for whom both sets of reports were available; these analyses suggest that patterns of annual and retrospective nonresponse appear most common for more sporadically employed mothers and those who did not make out-of-home or nonrelative arrangements. It appears that many mothers who went off to work leaving the child at home in the care of a spouse or another member of the family household tend not to think of this as an "arrangement" when asked about what arrangements they made for the care of their children while they were employed. As we report in the following section, even with this likely underreporting of in-home relative care, reported care by grandmothers, fathers, and other relatives is the predominant form of care reported, particularly in the first year.

Determinants of Supplemental Care Arrangements

Table A.1 displays basic statistics for the early and 1986 child care variables for our sample of children who were 3 to 6 years old in 1986. Given other studies (e.g., Mott 1991) suggesting benefits of regular, out-of-home arrangements, we focus in particular on patterns of out-of-home care. The mothers' retrospective reports regarding child care arrangements during the first 3 years of life suggest that only a minority of the children (29%) had some regular care arrangement outside their own homes during the first years of life, although more than half (60%) had some such experience during their first 3 years of life. Overall, the average number of years in which some out-of-home care was experienced was 1.23.

In the more recent period (1986), when the children were between 3 and 6 and all of the children's mothers were employed, 62% of the children had out-of-home care as their primary care arrangement; and this includes school attendance for those old enough to attend kindergarten or first grade. Nearly half (43%) were cared for by their fathers or other relatives; a third (34%) were in a formal group setting such as a nursery school, day-care center, or elementary school; 13% were cared for by nonrelatives such as neighbors or "family day care" providers; and 8% were cared for in other arrangements, including mothers taking their children to their workplace. The ratio of children to caregivers was not asked if children were in regular school (kindergarten or first grade);

for the other children, the average ratio was just under 4 children, reflecting the predominance of informal arrangements with neighbors and relatives.

As Table A.1 shows, the children's care arrangements clearly vary with their mothers' cognitive and psychosocial resources and the characteristics of her employment. Mothers who have higher cognitive skills, higher educational attainment, and higher-paying work are more likely to make arrangements for care out of the home, both in the child's first 3 years and later. They are also more likely to have a nonrelative caregiver. Mothers with more positive self-concept are also more apt to use out-of-home care in the child's early years. Associations with mothers' occupational complexity tend to be weaker than those for wages but are in the same direction. Associations with fathers' occupational and complexity are generally weak, suggesting that mothers' earnings and job experiences are more critical in determining children's care arrangements. The only significant association with fathers' occupational conditions is that fathers' high wages are associated with lesser reliance on care by father or another relative in 1986.

Finally, Table A.1 also shows the associations between the quality of children's home environments and their nonmaternal care arrangements. These associations are fairly weak but consistent. Greater use of out-of-home care during the child's early years, and lesser reliance on relatives in the recent period, are associated with higher-quality home environments in 1986 and 1988. We interpret this association as reflecting their common precursors in greater maternal resources and higher-quality employment.

Lower ratios of children to caregivers have generally been viewed positively in studies of children in formal care arrangements. Comparing across types of care, however, formal care arrangements have higher average numbers of children and larger ratios of children to caregivers, while care by relatives or by neighbors typically occurs in smaller groups. Reflecting the association between formal care and group size, we find that children of more advantaged mothers (with higher cognitive skills, higher educational attainment, more positive self-concept, and more complex occupations) experience higher average care ratios.

Effects of Child Care Arrangements:
Bivariate and Multivariate Analyses

Table A.2 shows bivariate associations between early and recent care arrangements and 1986 and 1988 child outcomes. We have noted that more advantaged mothers are more likely to make out of home arrange-

Table A.1. Children's Nonmaternal Care Experiences: Basic Statistics and Bivariate Associations with Family Background and Parental Employment (N = 781)

| | | | Correlations | | | | | | | | |
| | | | Maternal | | | | | Paternal | | Home environment | |
	Mean	Std. dev.	Educ.	AFQT	Self	Complexity	Wages	Complexity	Wages	1986	1988
Early care											
Number of years in out-of-home care in first 3 years	1.23	1.19	.23*	.15*	.11*	.12*	.32*	.04	.04	.08*	.15*
Any out-of-home care in first 3 years (1 = yes)	.60	.49	.18*	.10*	.07	.07	.24*	.06	.06	.08*	.16*
Any out-of-home care in first year (1 = yes)	.29	.45	.17*	.13*	.10*	.03	.24*	.06	.00	.05	.09*

Recent care at age 3–6 (1986)

Out-of-home care	.62	.48	.11*	.03	-.05	.21*	.14*	.03	.03	.02	.03
Ratio of children to caregivers (before Z-score)	3.81	3.57	.09*	.05	.12*	.08*	.06	.03	.06	.06	.13*
Primary type of care											
Formal center or school (1 = yes)	.34	.47	.11*	-.01	.00	.16*	.08*	.01	.07	.03	.08*
Care by nonrelative (1 = yes)	.13	.33	.08*	.11*	.03	.09*	.11*	.01	-.04	.00	.04
Care by relative (includes father) (1 = yes)	.43	.50	-.12*	-.06	-.05	-.13*	-.07	-.02	-.11*	-.08*	-.15*
Other arrangement (1 = yes)	.08	.27	.01	.02	.05	-.15*	-.14*	.08	.12*	.06	.03

*Significant at $p < .05$, two-tailed test.

Note: In correlations with early care arrangements, parental working conditions refer to early conditions. In correlations with 1986 care arrangements, parental working conditions refer to 1986 conditions. N for 1988 data is 721.

ments and less likely to rely on relatives for care; these variables tend to be associated in the bivariate analysis with better cognitive outcomes. Even before controlling for parental resources and family economic and occupational conditions, however, associations between child care variables and child outcomes are quite weak, with nearly all correlations below .10. Child ratios are either nonsignificant or have positive effects on 1988 cognitive skills.

Effects in multivariate models are also small and nonsignificant. In initial analyses of contemporaneous employment and child care arrangements on 1986 child outcomes, we found that characteristics of the child's current child care arrangement failed to influence either receptive vocabulary knowledge (PPVT-R) or behavior problems. We found no significant effects of form of care (informal/formal), location of caregiver to child, relation of care, or ratio of caregivers to children (Parcel and Menaghan 1990). Because ratio and type of care were correlated, we also estimated effects of child care type without controls for ratios; type of care remained nonsignificant. The location of care (child's home versus elsewhere) also did not have a significant impact.

We also evaluated the possibility that exposure to formal group settings in child care centers or schools would increase verbal facility more strongly for children from minority, particularly Hispanic, ethnic backgrounds. However, tests for interaction of ethnicity and formal care were not significant. Thus, *current* child care arrangements had little discernible impact on children's outcomes at ages 3–6.

However, other studies suggest that amount or location of nonmaternal care in infancy and early childhood may have lagged effects on child outcomes. For example, Mott (1991) suggests that regular out-of-home care has beneficial effects for children's cognitive skills, particularly for girls, while Belsky and Rovine (1988) find negative effects as supplemental care exceeds 20 hours a week. To test whether *early* child care experiences would provide additional explanatory power and to evaluate the robustness of our results when variations in early child care and early work conditions are controlled, we reestimated the final 1986 models described in Chapter 6 with controls for care in the first year, care in the first 3 years, and current care. Maternal work hours during the child's first 3 years, already in the models, tapped duration of nonmaternal care; we also included variables tapping whether children received regular out-of-home care in the first year, in any of the first 3 years, or currently, and the number of years of any out-of home care during the first 3 years. These were evaluated in alternative specifications. In no case did any of the early or current child care variables make a significant contribution to equations predicting 1986 PPVT-R or behavior problems; in addition, controlling for these arrangements did not alter our other findings.

Finally, we considered whether care arrangements during the early years or in 1986 had any lagged effects on reading, mathematics, or behavior problems in 1988, when the children were moving into their early school years. We added early and 1986 child care variables to the final 1988 equations reported in Chapter 7, evaluating effects in alternative specifications and in complete models. Again, given the correlation between ratio and type of care, we also reestimated effects of type of care in models that did not control for ratio, and effects of ratio in models that did not control for type of care. We found virtually no significant effects of early or recent child care; the single exception is a significant *adverse* impact of number of early years in out-of-home care on 1988 reading skills. This effect is inconsistent with the bivariate association and with prior findings and may reflect collinearity among the predictors.

SUMMARY AND DISCUSSION

While much of the current debate contrasts maternal care with other arrangements, viewing the former as desirable and the latter as potentially damaging, "mother care" and "other care" (Scarr 1984) have much in common. As we have reviewed elsewhere, similar features of maternal and nonmaternal care settings affect caregiving behaviors, and the same caregiving behaviors are associated with better child cognitive and emotional outcomes in each setting (Menaghan and Parcel 1991). It is variations in the *quality* of care in each setting that should be most consequential for child outcomes.

This does not necessarily mean, however, that these two contexts will have equal effects. Socialization theory suggests several reasons why the effects of nonmaternal child care arrangements may be less powerful than the effects of structurally similar family experiences. In general, socialization is more effective in situations of high affectivity and in which the socializing agents have considerable power or control over the initiates, where there is a smaller socialization ratio of children to adults, and where children spend more time (Gecas 1981). Children's nuclear family settings are more likely than other settings to be characterized by more intense, affectively charged interaction and they typically have large socialization ratios. In addition, even children in "full-time" nonmaternal care spend much larger amounts of time in their families than in such arrangements. Since the effects of children's environments will vary with the amount of the child's exposure to each arrangement, since the amount of time spent at home outweighs time with other caregivers, and since family environments are more affectively charged than other socialization settings, the effects of family

Table A.2. Children's Nonmaternal Care Experiences: Basic Statistics and Bivariate Associations with Cognitive and Social Outcomes

| | | | Correlations | | | | |
| | | | Cognitive outcomes | | | Behavior problems | |
	Mean	Std. dev.	PPVT-86	Read 1988	Math 1988	1986	1988
Early care							
Number of years in out-of-home care in first 3 years	1.23	1.19	.09*	.03	.09*	-.05	-.03
Any out-of-home care in first 3 years (1 = yes)	.60	.49	.09*	.06	.11*	.01	.01
Any out-of-home care in first year (1 = yes)	.29	.45	.06	-.04	.02	-.01	-.02
Recent care at age 3–6 (1986)							
Out-of-home care	.62	.48	-.01	.06	-.00	.04	.03
Ratio of children to caregivers (before Z-score)	3.81	3.57	.00	.07	.09*	.04	.06
Primary type of care							
Formal center or school (1 = yes)	.34	.47	.01	.07	.06	.09	.09
Care by nonrelative (1 = yes)	.13	.33	.02	.02	-.07	-.05	-.05
Care by relative (includes father) (1 = yes)	.43	.50	-.08*	-.09*	-.04	-.03	-.07
Other arrangement (1 = yes)	.08	.27	.05	.03	.06	.00	.07

*Significant at $p < .05$, two-tailed test.

Note: Basic statistics and correlations with cognitive outcomes are for children 3–6 years old. Correlations with BPI are for children 4–6 years old. Numbers of cases used are the maximums available for each dependent variable.

environments on child outcomes are likely to be larger than the effects of other caregiving settings. As reported in previous chapters, we have found significant effects of home environments, especially on cognitive outcomes, but we have generally not found strong effects of supplemental child care arrangements. Our results are consistent with the argument that for most children, the quality of care in the home environment may be more important than the characteristics of the alternative care arrangements they experience, given their greater exposure to the former, its more affectively charged climate, and its small socialization ratios. This is a critical hypothesis that deserves additional, rigorous investigation.

Our findings suggest that the quality of maternal care as measured by home environments and the quality of nonmaternal care have common precursors and are positively correlated. The already advantaged (occupationally, economically, socially, and psychologically) are also more able to arrange good supplemental care for their children, while less-advantaged mothers are more likely to be limited to poorer child care arrangements as well. Except in the small numbers of cases of care subsidized by third-party payments, children from families with limited economic and psychological resources are unlikely to encounter compensating nonmaternal arrangements. Despite the positive contributions to child development that superior care arrangements *could* make for children whose home environments place them at risk for developmental problems, such compensating experiences are probably rare. Rather than compensating for initial differences and disadvantages, nonmaternal care arrangements are apt to *reflect* other existing inequalities among families. For this reason as well it may be difficult to isolate a significant independent effect of child care variables when multivariate models also include measures of family resources capturing such inequalities.

Our near-complete failure to find any effect of child care quality or type reflects in part the limitations in the child care arrangement data available to us. In particular, it is unclear that child ratios tap quality dimensions as well in the informal settings prevalent in our sample as they do in formal child care centers, where caregiver-child ratios have been found to predict child outcomes. Even with better indicators of child care arrangements, however, we have suggested that strong effects are unlikely in models that also control for background characteristics and the quality of the child's home environment. Earlier cross sectional studies of child care "effects" may have overstated causal effects since few controlled for characteristics of parents and children that are associated with the amount and quality of supplemental care that children experience. Studies that do control for such selection effects generally find that type of care per se is not a powerful predictor of child outcomes; social class, family background variables, and the quality of adult-child relationships are the best predictors of cognitive skills and social competence for children in all types of care, including maternal care. Effects of care variables that have been observed are also highly contingent, varying by factors such as family economic status, child temperament and gender, and mothers' preferences for employment. In the most recent of the numerous reviews of the child care literature, Scarr and Eisenberg (1993:636) conclude, "The effects of nonmaternal care per se, if any, are small, so that from a practical standpoint it is impossible to predict the short-term effects of child care for any child. Long-term effects are even less likely to be predicted once appropriate controls for family background and later experiences have been applied." Our own results are consistent with this conclusion.

References

Achenbach, Thomas M., and Craig Edelbrock. 1981. "Behavioral Problems and Competencies Reported by Parents of Normal and Disturbed Children Aged Four through Sixteen." *Monographs of the Society for Research in Child Development,* Serial No. 188, 46, whole No. 1.

Achenbach, Thomas M., and Craig Edelbrock. 1983. *Manual for the Child Behavior Checklist and Revised Child Behavior Profile.* Burlington: Department of Psychiatry, University of Vermont.

Achenbach, Thomas M., Stephanie H. McConaughy, and Catherine T. Howell. 1987. "Child/Adolescent Behavioral and Emotional Problems: Implications of Cross-Informant Correlations for Situational Specificity." *Psychological Bulletin* 101:213–32.

Ainsworth, M. 1973. "The Development of Infant-Mother Attachment." Pp. 35–47 in *Child Abuse: An Agenda for Action,* edited by B. M. Caldwell and H. N. Ricciuti. New York: Oxford University Press.

Alexander, K. L., J. Fennessey, E. L. McDill, and R. J. D'Amico. 1979. "School SES Influences—Composition or Context?" *Sociology of Education* 52:222–37.

Andrisani, Paul J. 1978. *Work Attitudes and Labor Market Experience.* New York: Praeger.

Astone, Nan, and Sara McLanahan. 1991. "Family Structure, Parental Practices, and High School Completion." *American Sociological Review* 56:309–20.

Baker, Paula C., and Frank L. Mott. 1989. *NLSY Child Handbook 1989: A Guide and Resource Document for the National Longitudinal Survey of Youth 1986 Child Data.* Columbus: Center for Human Resource Research, Ohio State University.

Baumrind, D. 1991. "Parenting Styles and Adolescent Development." Pp. 746–58 in *The Encyclopedia of Adolescence,* edited by J. Brooks-Gunn, R. Lerner, and A. C. Peterson. New York: Garland.

Baydar, Nazli. 1988. "Effects of Parental Separation and Reentry into Union on the Emotional Well-Being of Children." *Journal of Marriage and the Family* 50:967–81.

Baydar, Nazli, and Jeanne Brooks-Gunn. 1991. "Effects of Maternal Employment and Child-Care Arrangements on Preschoolers' Cognitive and Behavioral Outcomes: Evidence from the Children of The National Longitudinal Survey of Youth." *Developmental Psychology* 27:932–45.

Becker, Gary S. 1988. "Family Economics and Macro Behavior." *American Economic Review* 78:1-13.

Becker, Gary S. [1981] 1991. *A Treatise on the Family,* rev. ed. Cambridge, MA: Harvard University Press.

Beller, Andrea. 1984. "Trends in Occupational Segregation by Sex and Race, 1960–1981." Pp. 11–26 in *Sex Segregation in the Workplace: Trends, Explana-*

tions and Remedies, edited by B. F. Reskin. Washington, DC: National Academy Press.

Beller, Andrea, and Kee-ok Kim Han. 1984. "Occupational Sex Segregation Prospects for the 1980s." Pp 91–114 in *Sex Segregation in the Workplace: Trends, Explanations and Remedies*, edited by B. F. Reskin. Washington, DC: National Academy Press.

Belsky, J. 1984a. "The Determinants of Parenting: A Process Model." *Child Development* 555:83–96.

Belsky, J. 1984b. "Two Waves of Day Care Research: Developmental Effects and Conditions of Quality." Pp. 1–34 in *The Child and the Day Care Setting: Qualitative Variations and Development*, edited by R. C. Ainslie. New York: Praeger.

Belsky, Jay, and David Eggebeen. 1991. "Early and Extensive Maternal Employment and Young Children's Socioemotional Development: Children of the National Longitudinal Survey of Youth." *Journal of Marriage and the Family* 53:1083–98.

Belsky, J., and M. Rovine. 1988. "Nonmaternal Care in the First Year of Life and the Security of Infant-Parent Attachment." *Child Development* 59:157–67.

Ben-Porath, Yoram. 1982. "Economics and the Family—Match or Mismatch? A Review of Becker's *A Treatise on the Family*." *Journal of Economic Literature* 20:52–64.

Berk, Sarah Fenstermaker. 1985. *The Gender Factory: The Apportionment of Work in American Households*. New York: Plenum.

Bielby, Denise D., and William T. Bielby. 1988. "She Works Hard for the Money: Household Responsibilities and the Allocation of Work Effort." *American Journal of Sociology* 93:1031–59.

Bielby, William T., and James N. Baron. 1984. "A Woman's Place is with Other Women: Sex Segregation within Organizations." Pp. 27–55 in *Sex Segregation in the Workplace: Trends, Explanations and Remedies*, edited by B. F. Reskin. Washington, DC: National Academy Press.

Blake, Judith. 1989. *Family Size and Achievement*. Berkeley: University of California Press.

Blau, Francine D. 1987. "Gender." Pp. 492–97 in *The New Palgrave: A Dictionary of Economics*, Vol. 2, edited by J. Eatwell, M. Milgate, and P. Newman. London: Macmillan.

Blau, Francine D., and Marianne A. Ferber. 1986. *The Economics of Women, Men, and Work*. Englewood Cliffs, NJ: Prentice-Hall.

Blau, Francine D., and Adam J. Grossberg. 1990. "Maternal Labor Supply and Children's Cognitive Development." *NBER Working Paper Series*. Working Paper No. 3536. Cambridge, MA: National Bureau of Economic Research.

Bluestone, Barry, and Bennett Harrison. 1982. *The Deindustrialization of America: Plant Closings, Community Abandonment and the Dismantling of Basic Industry*. New York: Basic Books.

Bowlby, J. 1969. *Attachment*. New York: Basic Books.

Bradley, Robert H. 1985. "The HOME Inventory: Rationale and Research." Pp. 191–201 in *Recent Research in Developmental Psychopathology, Book Supplement to the Journal of Child Psychology and Psychiatry*, edited by J. Lachenmeyer and M. Gibbs. New York: Gardner.

Bradley, Robert H., and Bettye M. Caldwell. 1977. "Home Observation for Measurement of the Environment: A Validation Study of Screening Efficiency." *American Journal of Mental Deficiency* 81:417–20.

Bradley, Robert H., and Bettye M. Caldwell. 1979. "Home Observation for Measurement of the Environment: A Revision of the Preschool Scale." *American Journal of Mental Deficiency* 84:235–44.

Bradley, Robert H., and Bettye M. Caldwell. 1980. "Home Environment, Cognitive Competence, and IQ among Males and Females." *Child Development* 51:1140–48.

Bradley, Robert H., and Bettye M. Caldwell. 1984a. "The HOME Inventory and Family Demographics." *Developmental Psychology* 20:315–20.

Bradley, Robert H., and Bettye M. Caldwell. 1984b. "The Relation of Infants' Home Environments to Achievement Test Performance in First Grade: A Follow-Up Study." *Child Development* 55:803–9.

Bradley, Robert H., and Bettye M. Caldwell. 1987. "Early Environment and Cognitive Competence: The Little Rock Study." *Early Child Development and Care* 27:307–41.

Bradley, Robert H., Bettye M. Caldwell, and Richard Elardo. 1979. "Home Environment and Cognitive Development in the First Two Years of Life: A Cross-Lagged Panel Analysis." *Developmental Psychology* 15:246–50.

Bradley, Robert H., Bettye M. Caldwell, and Stephen L. Rock. 1988a. "Home Environment and School Performance: A Ten-Year Follow-Up and Examination of Three Models of Environmental Action." *Child Development* 59:852–67.

Bradley, Robert H., Bettye M. Caldwell, Stephen L. Rock, Holly M. Hamrick, and Pandia Harris. 1988b. "Home Observation for Measurement of the Environment: Development of a Home Inventory for Use with Families Having Children 6 to 10 Years Old." *Contemporary Educational Psychology* 13:58–71.

Bronfenbrenner, Urie, William F. Alvarez, and Charles R. Henderson, Jr. 1984. "Working and Watching: Maternal Employment Status and Parents' Perceptions of Their Three-Year-Old Children." *Child Development* 55:1362–78.

Cargile, S. D., and J. E. Woods. 1988. "Strengthening Black Students' Academic Preparedness for Higher Education." *Journal of Black Studies* 19:150–62.

Caspi, Avshalom, and Glen H. Elder. 1988. "Emergent Family Patterns: The Intergenerational Construction of Problem Behavior and Relationships." Pp. 218–40 in *Understanding Family Dynamics*, edited by R. Hinde and J. Stevenson-Hinde. New York: Oxford University Press.

Caspi, Avshalom, and Glen H. Elder, Jr., and Daryl J. Bem. 1987. "Moving Against the World: Life-Course Patterns of Explosive Children." *Developmental Psychology* 23:308–13.

Caspi, Avshalom, Glen H. Elder, Jr., and Daryl J. Bem. 1988. "Moving Away from the World: Life Course Patterns of Shy Children." *Developmental Psychology* 24:824–31.

Center for Human Resource Research. 1988. *National Longitudinal Survey Handbook 1988.* Columbus: Center for Human Resource Research, Ohio State University.

Cherlin, Andrew J. 1993. "Nostalgia as Family Policy." *Public Interest* 110:77–84.

Clarke-Stewart, Allison. 1982. *Daycare.* Cambridge, MA: Harvard University Press.

Clausen, John. 1991. "Adolescent Competence and the Shaping of the Life Course." *American Journal of Sociology* 96:805–42.

Cohen, Ayala. 1983. "Comparing Regression Coefficients Across Subsamples: A Study of the Statistical Test." *Sociological Methods & Research* 12:77–94.

Coleman, James S. 1988. "Social Capital in the Creation of Human Capital." *American Journal of Sociology* 94:S95–120.

Coleman, James S. 1990. *Foundations of Social Theory*. Cambridge, MA: The Belknap Press of Harvard University Press.

Conger, Rand D., John A. McCarty, Raymond K. Yang, Benjamin B. Lahey, and Joseph P. Kropp, 1984. "Perceptions of Child, Child-Rearing Values, and Emotional Distress as Mediating Links between Environmental Stressors and Observed Maternal Behavior." *Child Development* 55:2234–47.

Crouter, Ann C., Jay Belsky, and Graham B. Spanier. 1984. "The Family Context of Child Development: Divorce and Maternal Employment." Pp. 201–38 in *Annals of Child Development*, Vol. 1, edited by G. J. Whitehurst. Greenwich, CT: JAI Press.

Crouter, Ann C., Shelley M. MacDermid, Susan M. McHale, and Maureen Perry-Jenkins. 1990. "Parental Monitoring and Perceptions of Children's School Performance and Conduct in Dual and Single-Earner Families." *Developmental Psychology* 26:649–57.

Cyert, Richard M., and David C. Mowery, eds. 1987. *Technology and Employment: Innovation and Growth in the U.S. Economy*. Washington DC: National Academy Press.

Desai, Sonalde, P. Lindsay Chase-Lansdale, and Robert T. Michael. 1989. "Mother or Market? Effects of Maternal Employment on the Intellectual Ability of 4-Year-Old Children." *Demography* 26:545–61.

Downey, Geraldine, and Phyllis Moen. 1987. "Personal Efficacy, Income, and Family Transitions: A Longitudinal Study of Women Heading Households." *Journal of Health and Social Behavior* 28:320–33.

Duncan, Greg, and C. R. Hill. 1975. "Modal Choice in Child Care Arrangements." Pp. 235–58 in *Five Thousand American Families: Patterns of Economic Progress*, Vol. 2, edited by G. J. Duncan and J. N. Morgan. Ann Arbor, MI: Institute for Social Research.

Duncan, Greg, and C. R. Hill. 1977. "The Child Care Mode Choice of Working Mothers." Pp. 379–88 in *Five Thousand American Families: Patterns of Economic Progress*, Vol. 5, edited by G. J. Duncan and J. N. Morgan. Ann Arbor, MI: Institute for Social Research.

Dunn, Lloyd, and Leota Dunn. 1981. *PPVT-R Manual*. Circle Pines, MN: American Guidance Service.

Dunn, Lloyd, and Frederick Markwardt. 1970. *PIAT Manual*. Circle Pines, MN: American Guidance Service.

Easterbrooks, M. Ann, and Wendy A. Goldberg. 1985. "Effects of Early Maternal Employment on Toddlers, Mothers, and Fathers." *Developmental Psychology* 21:774–83.

Edwards, Richard. 1979. *Contested Terrain*. New York: Basic Books.

Ehrhardt, Anke A. 1985. "The Psychobiology of Gender." Pp. 81–96 in *Gender and the Life Course*, edited by A. Rossi. Hawthorne, NY: Aldine de Gruyter.

Elardo, Richard D., and Robert H. Bradley. 1981. "The Home Observation for Measurement of the Environment (HOME) Scale: A Review of Research." *Developmental Review* 1:113–45.

Elder, Glen H., Jr., Tri van Nguyen, and Avshalam Caspi. 1985. "Linking Family Hardship to Children's Lives." *Child Development* 56:361–75.

England, Paula. 1981. "Assessing Trends in Occupational Sex Segregation, 1900–1976." Pp. 273–95 in *Sociological Perspectives on Labor Markets*, edited by I. Berg. New York: Academic Press.

England, Paula. 1992. *Comparable Worth: Theories and Evidence*. Hawthorne, NY: Aldine de Gruyter.

Eysenck, H. J., and L. Kamin. 1981. *The Intelligence Controversy*. New York: Wiley.

Farel, A. M. 1980. "Effects of Preferred Maternal Roles, Maternal Employment, and Socioeconomic Status on School Adjustment and Competence." *Child Development* 51:1179–86.

Ferber, Marianne A., and Brigid O'Farrell, with La Rue Allen, eds. 1991. *Work and Family: Policies for a Changing Workforce*. Washington, DC: National Academy Press.

Fischer, Mariellen, Jon E. Rolf, Joseph E. Hasazi, and Lucinda Cummings. 1984. "Follow-Up of a Preschool Epidemiological Sample: Cross-Age Continuities and Predictions of Later Adjustment with Internalizing and Externalizing Dimensions of Behavior." *Child Development* 55:137–50.

Forgatch, M. S., G. R. Patterson, and M. L. Skinner. 1988. "A Mediational Model for the Effect of Divorce on Antisocial Behavior in Boys." Pp. 135–54 in *Impact of Divorce, Single Parenting, and Step-Parenting on Children*, edited by E. M. Hetherington and J. D. Arestah. Hillsdale, NJ: Erlbaum.

Furstenberg, Frank F., Jr., Christine W. Nord, James L. Peterson, and Nicholas Zill. 1983. "The Life Course of Children of Divorce: Marital Disruption and Parental Contact." *American Sociological Review* 58:656–67.

Furstenberg, Frank F., Jr., and Judith A. Seltzer. 1986. "Divorce and Child Development." *Sociological Studies of Child Development* 1:137–60.

Gecas, Viktor. 1979. "The Influence of Social Class on Socialization." Pp. 365–404 in *Contemporary Theories About the Family*, Vol. 1, edited by W. R. Burr, R. Hill, F. I. Nye, and I. L. Reiss. New York: Free Press.

Gecas, Viktor. 1981. "Contexts of Socialization." Pp. 165–99 in *Social Psychology*, edited by M. Rosenberg and J. H. Turner. New York: Free Press.

Gecas, Viktor. 1989. "The Social Psychology of Self- Efficacy." *Annual Review of Sociology* 15:291–316.

Geerken, Michael, and Walter R. Gove. 1983. *At Home and At Work: The Family's Allocation of Labor*. Beverly Hills: Sage.

Gill, Richard T. 1993. "Family Breakdown as Family Policy." *Public Interest* 110:84–91.

Golden, M., L. Rosenbluth, M. Grossi, H. Policare, H. Freeman, and M. Brownlee. 1978. *The New York City Infant Day Care Study: A Comparative Study of Licensed Group and Family Day Care Programs and the Effects of These Programs on Children and Their Families*. New York: Medical and Health Research Association of New York City, Inc.

Gottfried, Adele, Allen Gottfried, and Kay Bathurst. 1988. "Maternal Employment, Family Environment, and Children's Development: Infancy through the School Years." Pp. 11–56 in *Maternal Employment and Children's Development*, edited by A. E. Gottfried and A. W. Gottfried. New York: Plenum.

Graham, Philip J., and Michael Rutter. 1968. "The Reliability and Validity of the Psychiatric Assessment of the Child II: Interview with the Parent." *British Journal of Psychiatry* 114:581–92.

Gurin, Patricia, and Orville G. Brim, Jr. 1984. "Change in Self in Adulthood: The Example of Sense of Control." Pp. 281–334 in *Life-Span Development and Behavior*, Vol. 6, edited by P.B. Baltes and O. G. Brim. New York: Academic Press.

Haskins, R. 1985. "Public School Aggression among Children with Varying Day-Care Experience." *Child Development* 56:689–703.

Haurin, R. Jean. 1992. "Patterns of Childhood Residence and the Relationship to Young Adult Outcomes." *Journal of Marriage and the Family* 54:846–60.

Haveman, Robert, Barbara L. Wolfe, and James Spaulding. 1991. "Educational Achievement and Childhood Events and Circumstances." *Demography* 28:133–57.

Heer, David M. 1985. "Effects of Sibling Number on Child Outcome." *Annual Review of Sociology* 11:27–47.

Hetherington, E. Mavis, Martha Cox, and Roger Cox. 1978. "The Aftermath of Divorce." Pp. 149–76 in *Mother/Child Father/Child Relationships*, edited by J. H. Stevens, Jr., and M. Matthews. Washington, DC: National Association for the Education of Young Children.

Hofferth, Sandra L., and Deborah A. Phillips. 1987. "Child Care in the United States, 1970 to 1995." *Journal of Marriage and the Family* 49:559–71.

Hoffman, Lois W. 1989. "Effects of Maternal Employment in the Two-Parent Family." *American Psychologist* 44:283–92.

Howell, Frank M., and Lynn W. McBroom. 1982. "Social Relations at Home and at School: An Analysis of the Correspondence Principle." *Sociology of Education* 55:40–52.

Jacobs, Jerry 1989. *Revolving Doors: Sex Segregation and Women's Careers*. Stanford, CA: Stanford University Press.

Johnson, Robert J., and Howard B. Kaplan. 1988. "Gender, Aggression, and Mental Health Intervention during Early Adolescence." *Journal of Health and Social Behavior* 29:53–64.

Kamerman, Sheila B. 1991. "Child-Care Policies and Programs: An International Overview." *Journal of Social Issues* 47:179–96.

Katsillis, John, and Richard Rubinson. 1990. "Cultural Capital, Student Achievement, and Educational Reproduction: The Case of Greece." *American Sociological Review* 55:270–79.

Kellam, Sheppard G., Jeannette D. Branch, Khazan C. Agrawal, and Margaret E. Ensminger. 1975. *Mental Health and Going to School*. Chicago: University of Chicago Press.

Kessler, Ronald, and David F. Greenberg. 1981. *Linear Panel Analysis: Models of Quantitative Change*. New York: Academic Press.

Kessler, Ronald, J. Blake Turner, and James S. House. 1988. "Effects of Unemployment on Health in a Community Survey: Main, Modifying, and Mediating Effects." *Journal of Social Issues* 44:69–85.

Ketterlinus, Robert D., Sandra Henderson, and Michael E. Lamb. 1991. "The Effects of Maternal Age-at-Birth on Children's Cognitive Development." *Journal of Research on Adolescence* 1:173–88.

Kim, Jae O., and Charles W. Mueller. 1978. *Factor Analysis: Statistical Methods and Practical Issues*. Sage University Paper Series on Quantitative Applications in the Social Sciences, series no. 07-014. Beverly Hills: Sage.

Kingston, Paul W., and Steven L. Nock. 1987. " Time Together among Dual-Earner Couples." *American Sociological Review* 52:391–400.

Kohlberg, Lawrence, Jean LaCrosse, and David Ricks. 1972. "The Predictability of Adult Mental Health from Childhood Behavior." Pp. 1217–84 in *Manual of Child Psychopathology*, edited by B. B. Wolman. New York: McGraw-Hill.

Kohn, Melvin L. 1977. *Class and Conformity, A Study in Values*, 2nd ed. Chicago: University of Chicago Press.

Kohn, Melvin L., and Carmi Schooler. 1973. "Occupational Experience and Psychological Functioning: An Assessment of Reciprocal Effects." *American Sociological Review* 38:97–118.

Kohn, Melvin L., and Carmi Schooler. 1978. "The Reciprocal Effects of the Substantive Complexity of Work and Intellectual Flexibility: A Longitudinal Assessment." *American Journal of Sociology* 84:24–52.

Kohn, Melvin L., and Carmi Schooler. 1982. "Job Conditions and Personality: A Longitudinal Assessment of Their Reciprocal Effects." *American Journal of Sociology* 87:1257–86.

Kohn, Melvin L., and Carmi Schooler. 1983. *Work and Personality: An Inquiry Into the Impact of Social Stratification*. Norwood, NJ: Ablex.

Kohn, Melvin L., and Kazimierz M. Slomczynski. 1990. *Social Structure and Self Direction: A Comparative Analysis in the United States and Poland*. Cambridge, MA: Basil Blackwell.

Kohn, Melvin L., Kazimierz M. Slomczynski, and Carrie Schoenbach. 1986. "Social Stratification and the Transmission of Values in the Family: A Cross-National Assessment." *Sociological Forum* 1:73–102.

LaFreniere, Peter J., and L. Alan Sroufe. 1985. "Profiles of Peer Competence in the Preschool: Interrelations between Measure, Influence of Social Ecology, and Relation to Attachment History." *Developmental Psychology* 21:56–69.

Lamb, Michael E., ed. 1981. *The Role of the Father in Child Development*, 2nd ed. New York: Wiley.

Langman, Lauren. 1987. "Social Stratification." Pp. 211–49 in *Handbook of Marriage and the Family*, edited by M. B. Sussman and S. K. Steinmetz. New York: Plenum.

Laosa, Luis. 1981. "Maternal Behavior: Sociocultural Diversity in Modes of Interaction." Pp. 125–67 in *Parent-Child Interaction: Theory, Research and Prospects*, edited by R. W. Henderson. New York: Plenum.

Lee, Valerie E., Jeanne Brooks-Gunn, and Elizabeth Schnur. 1988. "Does Head Start Work? A 1-Year Follow-Up Comparison of Disadvantaged Children Attending Head Start, No Preschool, and Other Preschool Programs." *Developmental Psychology* 24:210–22.

Leibowitz, Arleen, Linda J. Waite, and C. Witsberger. 1988. "Child Care for Preschoolers: Differences by Child's Age." *Demography* 25:205–20.

Lennon, Mary Clare. 1987. "Sex Differences in Distress: The Impact of Gender and Work Roles." *Journal of Health and Social Behavior* 28:290–305.

Lichter, Daniel T., Felicia B. LeClere, and Diane K. McLaughlin. 1991. "Local Marriage Markets and the Marital Behavior of Black and White Women." *American Journal of Sociology* 96:843–67.

Lillard, Lee, and Michael Brien. 1994. "Education, Marriage and First Conception in Malaysia." *Journal of Human Resources* (Autumn).

Lillard, Lee, and Robert J. Willis. 1994. "Intergenerational Educational Mobility: The Effects of the Family and State in Malaysia." *Journal of Human Resources* (Autumn).

Luster, Tom, Kelly Rhoades, and Bruce Haas. 1989. "The Relation between Parental Values and Parenting Behavior: A Test of the Kohn Hypothesis." *Journal of Marriage and the Family* 51:139–47.

Lutkenhaus, Paul, Klaus E. Grossman, and Karin Grossman. 1985. "Infant-Mother Attachment at Twelve Months and Style of Interaction with a Stranger at the Age of Three Years." *Child Development* 49:547–56.

Maccoby, Eleanor E., and Carol N. Jacklin. 1974. *The Psychology of Sex Differences.* Stanford, CA: Stanford University Press.

MacKinnon, Carol E., Gene H. Brody, and Zolinda Stoneman. 1982. "The Effects of Divorce and Maternal Employment on the Environments of Preschool Children." *Child Development* 53:1392–99.

MacKinnon, Carol E., Gene H. Brody, and Zolinda Stoneman. 1986. "The Longitudinal Effects of Divorce and Maternal Employment on the Home Environments of Preschool Children." *Journal of Divorce* 9:65–78.

Marks, Nadine, and Sara McLanahan. 1993. "Gender, Family Structure, and Social Support among Parents." *Journal of Marriage and the Family* 55:481–93.

Matas, Leah, Richard A. Arend, and L. Alan Sroufe. 1978. "Continuity of Adaptation in the Second Year: The Relationship between Quality of Attachment and Later Competence." *Child Development* 49:547–56.

McCartney, Kathleen. 1984. "Effects of Day Care Environment on Children's Language Development." *Developmental Psychology* 20:244–60.

McLanahan, Sara, and Karen Booth. 1989. "Mother-Only Families: Problems, Prospects, and Politics." *Journal of Marriage and the Family* 51:557–80.

McLanahan, Sara S., and Jennifer L. Glass. 1985. "A Note on the Trend in Sex Differences in Psychological Distress." *Journal of Health and Social Behavior* 26:328–36.

McLeod, Jane D., and Michael J. Shanahan. 1993. "Poverty, Parenting, and Children's Mental Health." *American Sociological Review* 56:351–66.

McLoyd, Vonnie C. 1989. "Socialization and Development in a Changing Economy." *American Psychologist* 44:293–302.

McLoyd, Vonnie C. 1990. "The Impact of Economic Hardship on Black Families and Children: Psychological Distress, Parenting, and Socioemotional Development." *Child Development* 61:311–46.

Mechanic, David. 1980. *Mental Health and Social Policy,* 2nd ed. Englewood Cliffs, NJ: Prentice-Hall.

Menaghan, Elizabeth G. 1983a. "Coping with Parental Problems: Panel Assessments of Effectiveness." *Journal of Family Issues* 4:483–506.

Menaghan, Elizabeth G. 1983b. "Individual Coping Efforts: Moderators of the Relationship between Life Stress and Mental Health Outcomes." Pp. 157–91 in *Psychosocial Stress: Trends in Theory and Research,* edited by H. B. Kaplan. New York: Academic Press.

Menaghan, Elizabeth G. 1990a. "The Impact of Occupational and Economic Pressures on Parental Well-Being." Paper presented at the Annual Meeting of the Society for the Study of Social Problems, Washington, DC, August.

Menaghan, Elizabeth G. 1990b. "Social Stress and Individual Distress." Pp. 107–41 in *Mental Disorder in Social Contexts,* edited by J. Greenley. Greenwich, CT: JAI Press.

Menaghan, Elizabeth G. 1991. "Work Experiences and Family Interaction Processes: The Long Reach of the Job?" *Annual Review of Sociology* 17:419–44.

Menaghan, Elizabeth G. 1994. "The Daily Grind: Work Stressors, Family Patterns, and Intergenerational Outcomes." Pp. 115–147 in *Stress and Mental Health: Contemporary Issues and Future Prospects,* edited by W. Avison and I. Gotlib. New York: Plenum.

Menaghan, Elizabeth G., and Toby L. Parcel. 1991. "Determining Children's Home Environments: The Impact of Maternal Characteristics and Current Occupational and Family Conditions." *Journal of Marriage and the Family* 53:417–31.

Miller, Joanne. 1988. "Jobs and Work." Pp. 327–59 in *Handbook of Sociology,* edited by N. J. Smelser. Beverly Hills: Sage.

Miller, Joanne, Carmi Schooler, Melvin L. Kohn, and Karen A. Miller. 1979. "Women and Work: The Psychological Effects of Occupational Conditions." *American Journal of Sociology* 85:66–94.

Miller, Karen A., Melvin L. Kohn, and Carmi Schooler. 1985. "Educational Self-Direction and the Cognitive Functioning of Students." *Social Forces* 63:923–44.

Mirowsky, John, and Catherine E. Ross. 1983. "Paranoia and the Structure of Powerlessness." *American Sociological Review* 48:228–39.

Mirowsky, John, and Catherine E. Ross. 1984. "Mexican Culture and Its Emotional Contradictions." *Journal of Health and Social Behavior* 25:2–13.

Mirowsky, John, and Catherine E. Ross. 1986. "Social Patterns of Distress." *Annual Review of Sociology* 12:23–45.

Mirowsky, John, and Catherine E. Ross. 1989. *Social Causes of Psychological Distress.* Hawthorne, NY: Aldine de Gruyter.

Moen, Phyllis. 1989. *Working Parents: Transformations in Gender Roles and Public Policies in Sweden.* Madison: University of Wisconsin Press.

Moen, Phyllis, and Donna Dempster-McClain. 1987. "Employed Parents: Role Strain, Work Time and Preferences for Working Less." *Journal of Marriage and the Family* 49:579–90.

Mondell, Sid, and Forrest B. Tyler. 1981. "Parental Competence and Styles of Problem Solving/Play Behavior with Children." *Developmental Psychology* 17:73–78.

Moore, Kristin A., and Nancy O. Snyder. 1991. "Cognitive Attainment among Firstborn Children of Adolescent Mothers." *American Sociological Review* 56:612–24.

Mortimer, Jeylan T., Jon Lorence, and Donald S. Kumka. 1986. *Work, Family, and Personality: Transition to Adulthood.* Norwood, NJ: Ablex.

Mott, Frank L. 1991. "Developmental Effects of Infant Care: Mediating Role of Gender and Health." *Journal of Social Issues* 47:139–58.

Namboodiri, Krishnan. 1987. "The Floundering Phase of the Life Course." Pp. 59–86 in *Research in Sociology of Education and Socialization*, Vol. 7, edited by R. G. Corwin. Greenwich, CT: JAI Press.

Nock, Steven L. 1988. "The Family and Hierarchy." *Journal of Marriage and the Family* 50:957–66.

Nock, Steven L., and Paul W. Kingston. 1988. "Time with Children: The Impact of Couples' Work-Time Commitments." *Social Forces* 67:59–85.

O'Neill, June. 1985. "Role Differentiation and the Gender Gap in Wage Rates." Pp. 50–75 in *Women and Work: An Annual Review*, edited by L. Larwood, A. H. Stromberg, and Barbara A. Gutek. Beverly Hills: Sage.

Parcel, Toby L. 1989. "Comparable Worth, Occupational Labor Markets and Occupational Earnings: Results from the 1980 Census." Pp. 134–52 in *Pay Equity: Empirical Inquiries*, edited by R. Michael, H. Hartmann, and B. O'Farrell. Washington, DC: National Academy Press.

Parcel, Toby L., and Laura Geschwender. 1994. "Explaining Regional Variation in Verbal Facility Among Young Children." Unpublished manuscript.

Parcel, Toby L., and Elizabeth G. Menaghan. 1988. "Measuring Behavioral Problems in a Large Cross Sectional Survey: Reliability and Validity for Children of the NLS Youth." Unpublished manuscript.

Parcel, Toby L., and Elizabeth G. Menaghan. 1989. "Child Home Environment as a Mediating Construct between SES and Child Outcomes." Center for Human Resource Research Report, The Ohio State University, Columbus.

Parcel, Toby L., and Elizabeth G. Menaghan. 1990. "Maternal Working Conditions and Child Verbal Ability: Studying the Transmission of Intergenerational Inequality from Mothers to Young Children." *Social Psychology Quarterly* 53:132–47.

Parcel, Toby L., and Elizabeth G. Menaghan. 1993. "Family Social Capital and Children's Behavior Problems." *Social Psychology Quarterly* 56:120–35.

Parcel, Toby L., and Elizabeth G. Menaghan. 1994. "Early Parental Work, Family Social Capital, and Early Childhood Outcomes." *American Journal of Sociology* 99:972-1009.

Parcel, Toby L., and Charles W. Mueller. 1983a. *Ascription and Labor Markets.* New York: Academic Press.

Parcel, Toby L., and Charles W. Mueller. 1983b. "Occupational Differentiation, Prestige, and Socioeconomic Status." *Work and Occupations* 10:49–80.

Patterson, Gerald. 1984. "Microsocial Process: A View from the Boundary." Pp. 43–66 in *Boundary Areas in Social and Developmental Psychology*, edited by J. C. Masters and K. Yarkin-Levin. New York: Academic Press.

Patterson, Gerald, and L. Bank. 1989. "Some Amplifying Mechanisms for Pathologic Processes in Families." Pp. 167–209 in *Systems and Development*, edited by M. R. Gunnar and E. Thelen. Hillsdale, NJ: Erlbaum

Patterson, Gerald R., Barbara D. DeBaryshe, and Elizabeth Ramsey. 1989. "A Developmental Perspective on Antisocial Behavior." *American Psychologist* 44:329–35.

Pearlin, Leonard I., Morton A. Lieberman, Elizabeth G. Menaghan, and Joseph T. Mullan. 1981. "The Stress Process." *Journal of Health and Social Behavior* 22:337–56.

Pearlin, Leonard I., and Carmi Schooler. 1978. "The Structure of Coping." *Journal of Health and Social Behavior* 19:2–21.

Peterson, Gary W., and Boyd C. Rollins. 1987. "Parent- Child Socialization." Pp. 471–507 in *Handbook of Marriage and the Family*, edited by M. B. Sussman and S. K. Steinmetz. New York: Plenum.

Peterson, James, and Nicholas Zill. 1986. "Marital Disruption, Parent-Child Relationships, and Behavior Problems in Children." *Journal of Marriage and the Family* 48:295–307.

Peterson, Richard R. 1989. *Women, Work and Divorce*. Albany: State University of New York.

Phillips, Deborah, Kathleen McCartney, and Sandra Scarr. 1987. "Child-Care Quality and Children's Social Development." *Developmental Psychology* 23:537–43.

Piotrkowski, Chaya S., Robert N. Rapoport, and Rhona Rapoport. 1987. "Families and Work." Pp. 251–83 in *Handbook of Marriage and the Family*, edited by M. B. Sussman and S. K. Steinmetz. New York: Plenum.

Profiles of American Youth. 1982. *Profiles of American Youth: 1980 Nationwide Administration of the Armed Services Vocational Aptitude Battery*. Unpublished report, Office of the Assistant Secretary of Defense, Washington, DC.

Ramey, C., D. Dorval, and L. Baker-Ward. 1981. "Group Day Care and Socially Disadvantaged Families: Effects on the Child and the Family." Pp. 69–106 in *Advances in Early Education and Day Care*, Vol. 3, edited by S. Kilmer. Greenwich, CT: JAI Press.

Rao, Potluri, and Roger L. Miller. 1971. *Applied Econometrics*. Belmont, CA: Wadsworth.

Reskin, Barbara, and Patricia Roos. 1990. *Job Queues, Gender Queues: Explaining Women's Inroads into Male Occupations*. Philadelphia: Temple University Press.

Rickel, Annette U., and Thomas S. Langner. 1985. "Short-Term and Long-Term Effects of Marital Disruption on Children." *American Journal of Community Psychology* 13:599–611.

Rindfuss, Ronald R., C. Gray Swicegood, and Rachel A. Rosenfeld. 1987. "Disorder in the Life Course." *American Sociological Review* 52:785–801.

Robins, Lee N. 1966. *Deviant Children Grown Up*. Baltimore: Williams and Wilkins.

Robins, Lee N. 1979. "Follow-Up Studies." Pp. 483–513 in *Psychopathological Disorders of Childhood*, 2nd ed., edited by H. C. Quay, and J. S. Werry. New York: Wiley.

Robins, P. K., and R. G. Spiegelman. 1978. "An Econometric Model of the Demand for Child Care." *Economic Inquiry* 41:83–94.

Rogers, Stacy J., Toby L. Parcel, and Elizabeth G. Menaghan. 1991. "The Effects of Maternal Working Conditions and Mastery on Child Behavior Problems: Studying the Intergenerational Transmission of Social Control." *Journal of Health and Social Behavior* 32:145–64.

Rosenberg, Morris, and Leonard I. Pearlin. 1978. "Social Class and Self Esteem among Children and Adults." *American Journal of Sociology* 84:53–77.

Rosenberg, Morris, Carmi Schooler, and Carrie Schoenbach. 1989. "Self-Esteem and Adolescents: Modeling Reciprocal Effects." *American Sociological Review* 54:1004–18.

Rosenfield, Sarah. 1989. "The Effects of Women's Employment: Personal Control and Sex Differences in Mental Health." *Journal of Health and Social Behavior* 30:77–91.

Ross, Catherine E., John Mirowsky, and Joan Huber. 1983. "Dividing Work, Sharing Work, and In-Between: Marriage Patterns and Depression." *American Sociological Review* 48:809–23.

Rossi, Alice. 1985. "Gender and Parenthood." Pp. 161–91 in *Gender and the Life Course*, edited by A. Rossi. Hawthorne, NY: Aldine.

Rotter, Julian B. 1966. "Generalized Expectancies for Internal vs. External Control of Reinforcements." *Psychological Monographs* 80:1–28.

Rotter, Julian B. 1980. "Interpersonal Trust, Trustworthiness, and Gullibility." *American Psychologist* 35:1–7.

Ruopp, R., and J. Travers. 1982. "Janus Faces Day Care: Perspectives on Quality and Cost." Pp. 72–101 in *Day Care: Scientific and Social Policy Issues*, edited by E. F. Zigler, and E. W. Gordon. Boston: Auburn.

Rutter, Michael. 1970. "Sex Differences in Children's Responses to Family Stress." Pp. 165–96 in *The Child in His Family*, edited by E. J. Anthony and C. Koupernik. New York: Wiley.

Rutter, Michael. 1983. "Stress, Coping, and Development: Some Issues and Some Questions." Pp. 1–41 in *Stress, Coping, and Development in Children*, edited by N. Garmezy, and M. Rutter. New York: McGraw Hill.

Sattler, Jerome M. 1974. *Assessment of Children's Intelligence*. Philadelphia: W. B. Saunders.

Scarr, Sandra. 1984. *Mother Care/Other Care*. New York: Basic Books.

Scarr, Sandra, and Marlene Eisenberg. 1993. "Child Care Research: Issues, Perspectives, and Results." *Annual Review of Psychology* 44:613–44.

Scarr, Sandra, and Richard A. Weinberg. 1978. "The Influence of 'Family Background' on Intellectual Attainment." *American Sociological Review* 43:674–92.

Schachter, F. F. 1981. "Toddlers with Employed Mothers." *Child Development* 52:958–64.

Schooler, Carmi. 1987. "Psychological Effects of Complex Environments during the Life Span: A Review and Theory." Pp. 24–49 in *Cognitive Functioning and Social Structure over the Life Course*, edited by C. Schooler and K. W. Schaie. Norwood, NJ: Ablex.

Siegal, Michael. 1984. "Economic Deprivation and the Quality of Parent-Child Relations: A Trickle-Down Framework." *Journal of Applied Developmental Psychology* 5:127–44.

Simons, Ronald L., Les B. Whitbeck, Rand D. Conger, and Janet N. Melby. 1990. "Husband and Wife Differences in Determinants of Parenting: A Social Learning and Exchange Model of Parental Behavior." *Journal of Marriage and the Family* 52:375–92.

Solon, Gary. 1992. "Intergenerational Income Mobility in the United States." *American Economic Review* 82:393–408.

Starr, Mark, and Jerry Buckley. 1985. "Moynihan: 'I Told You So.'" *Newsweek* 105 (April 22):30.

Steelman, Lala Carr, and Brian Powell. 1991. "Sponsoring the Next Generation: Parental Willingness to Pay for Higher Education." *American Journal of Sociology* 96:1505–29.

Sternberg, R. J. 1985. *Beyond I.Q.* Cambridge: Cambridge University Press.

Stevenson, Harold W., and Richard S. Newman. 1986. "Long- Term Prediction of Achievement and Attitudes in Mathematics and Reading." *Child Development* 57:646–59.

Stolzenberg, R. M., and L. J. Waite. 1984. "Local Labor Markets, Children and Labor Force Participation of Wives." *Demography* 21:157–70.

Sweet, James A., Larry L. Bumpass, and Vaughn Call. 1988. "The Design and Content of the National Survey of Families and Households." Working Paper NSFH-1, Center for Demography and Ecology, University of Wisconsin, Madison.

Thomas, Duncan. 1992. "Gender Differences in Household Resource Allocations." Paper presented at the RAND Conference on Economic and Demographic Aspects of Intergenerational Relations, Santa Monica, March.

Thompson, Linda, and Alexis J. Walker. 1989. "Gender in Families: Women and Men in Marriage, Work, and Parenthood." *Journal of Marriage and the Family* 51:845–71.

Thomson, Elizabeth, Sara S. McLanahan, and Roberta Braun Curtin. 1992. "Family Structure, Gender, and Parental Socialization." *Journal of Marriage and the Family* 54:368–78.

Turner, R. Jay, and Samuel Noh. 1983. "Class and Psychological Vulnerability among Women: The Significance of Social Support and Personal Control." *Journal of Health and Social Behavior* 24:2–15.

U.S. Bureau of the Census. 1987a. *Statistical Abstract of the United States: 1986*, 107th ed. Washington, DC: U.S. Government Printing Office.

U.S. Bureau of the Census. 1987b. *Current Population Reports*, Series P-70, no. 10, *Male-Female Differences in Work Experiences, Occupation, and Earnings: 1984*. Washington, DC: U.S. Government Printing Office.

U.S. Bureau of the Census. 1993. *Statistical Abstract of the United States*, 113th ed. Washington, DC: U.S. Government Printing Office.

Vandell, Deborah Lowe, and Mary Ann Corasaniti. 1991. "Child Care and the Family: Complex Contributors to Child Development." *New Directions in Child Development* 49:23–37.

Vandell, Deborah Lowe, and Janaki Ramanan. 1992. "Effects of Early and Recent Maternal Employment on Children from Low-Income Families." *Child Development* 63:938–49.

Voydanoff, Patricia. 1987. *Work and Family Life*. Beverly Hills: Sage.

Waite, Linda J., and Lee A. Lillard. 1991. "Children and Marital Disruption." *American Journal of Sociology* 96:930–53.

Wallerstein, Judith. S. 1984. "Children of Divorce: Preliminary Report of a Ten-Year Follow-up of Young Children." *American Journal of Orthopsychiatry* 54:444–58.

Wheaton, Blair. 1983. "Stress, Personal Coping Resources, and Psychiatric Symptoms: An Investigation of Interactive Models." *Journal of Health and Social Behavior* 24:208–29.

Whitbeck, Les B., Ronald L. Simons, Rand D. Conger, Frederick O. Lorenz,

Shirley Huck, and Glen H. Elder, Jr., 1991. "Family Economic Hardship, Parental Support, and Adolescent Self- Esteem." *Social Psychology Quarterly* 54:353–63.

Whitehead, Barbara Dafoe. 1993. "Dan Quayle Was Right." *Atlantic Monthly* 271:47–50.

Wilson, James Q. 1993. "The Family-Values Debate." *Commentary* 95:24–31.

Wojtkiewicz, Roger A. 1993. "Simplicity and Complexity in the Effects of Parental Structure on High School Graduation." *Demography* 30:701–17.

Wright, James D., and S. R. Wright. 1976. "Social Class and Parental Values for Children: A Partial Replication and Extension of the Kohn Thesis." *American Sociological Review* 41:527–37.

Zigler, Edward, Willa D. Abelson, and Victoria Seitz. 1973. "Motivational Factors in the Performance of Economically Disadvantaged Children on the Peabody Picture Vocabulary Test." *Child Development* 44:294–303.

Zill, Nicholas. 1988. "Behavior, Achievement, and Health Problems among Children in Stepfamilies: Findings from a National Survey of Child Health." Pp. 325–68 in *The Impact of Divorce, Single Parenting, and Stepparenting on Children*, edited by E. M. Hetherington, and J. D. Arasteh. Hillsdale, NJ: Erlbaum.

Zimmerman, David J. 1992. "Regression toward Mediocrity in Economic Stature." *American Economic Review* 82:409–29.

Zuravin, Susan J. 1988. "Effects of Fertility Patterns on Child Abuse and Neglect." *Journal of Marriage and the Family* 50:983–94.

Index

AFQT (Armed Forces Qualifications Test), 41, 72–73, 84, 85, 113, 115, 126–127

Analytical strategy of study, 43–44

Arithmetic skills (*See* Mathematics skills)

Armed Forces Qualifications Test (AFQT), 41, 72–73, 84, 85, 113, 115, 126–127

BPI 1986, 94–95

BPI 1988, 94, 96

Behavioral problems (*See* Child behavior problems)

Blue-collar work, 14

CBCL (Child Behavior Checklist), 35–36

Center for Human Resource Research (CHRR), 31, 37

Child age, 24, 93–94

Child Behavior Checklist (CBCL), 35–36

Child behavior problems

CBCL and, 35–36

changes in, 88

child characteristics and, 92–93, 97

child gender and, 23–24, 99, 118, 120

child health and, 97

child race and, 99, 118, 120

child's home environment and, 150

Coleman's view of, 87–88

concerns of, 3, 87

descriptive findings in study of, 94–99

factor analyses of, 36

family composition and, 91–92

marital histories and, 149

maternal paid employment and, 88

maternal self-concept and, 149

as measure in study, 35–36

meta-analysis of, 36

multivariate findings in study of, 102–103, 118

multivariate models modeling effects and, 118–120

overcontrolled behavior and, 15, 87

parental characteristics and, 92–93, 97

parental occupational complexity and, 14–15, 118–120, 149

parental occupational conditions and, 87, 89–91

predicting 1988, 99–103

sample and methods of study of, 93–94

statistical interactions in study of, 149–150

summary of findings in study of, 103–105

undercontrolled behavior and, 14–15, 87

Child care, 2 (*See also* Supplemental child care arrangements)

Child characteristics (*See also* specific types)

age, 24

child behavior problems and, 92–93, 97

child's home environment in 1986 and, 53

gender, 23–24

health, 23

mathematics skills predictions and, 80

as measured in study, 43